The Rule of Nobody

ALSO BY PHILIP K. HOWARD

Life Without Lawyers:
Liberating Americans from Too Much Law

The Collapse of the Common Good:
How America's Lawsuit Culture Undermines Our Freedom

The Death of Common Sense:
How Law Is Suffocating America

The Rule of Nobody

SAVING AMERICA FROM DEAD LAWS
AND BROKEN GOVERNMENT

Philip K. Howard

W. W. NORTON & COMPANY

New York • London

For information about permission to reproduce selections from this book,
write to Permissions, W. W. Norton & Company, Inc.,
500 Fifth Avenue, New York, NY 10110

For information about special discounts for bulk purchases, please contact
W. W. Norton Special Sales at specialsales@wwnorton.com or 800-233-4830

Manufacturing by Courier Westford
Book design by Chris Welch
Production manager: Louise Parasmo

Library of Congress Cataloging-in-Publication Data

Howard, Philip K., author.
The rule of nobody : saving America from dead laws
and broken government / Philip K. Howard. — First edition.
pages cm.
Includes bibliographical references and index.
ISBN 978-0-393-08282-1 (hardcover)
1. Constitutional law—United States. 2. Law reform—United States.
3. Democracy—United States. 4. Representative government
and representation—United S tates. I. Title.
KF4552.H69 2014
340'.11—dc23
2013041183

W. W. Norton & Company, Inc., 500 Fifth Avenue, New York, N.Y. 10110
www.wwnorton.com

W. W. Norton & Company Ltd., Castle House, 75/76 Wells Street, London W1T 3QT

1 2 3 4 5 6 7 8 9 0

For my friends, who unfailingly support this mission with intelligence, trust, and hope.

CONTENTS

Appendix: Bill of Responsibilities—Proposed Amendments to the Constitution   179

The Rule of Nobody

PREFACE

n February 2011, during a winter storm, a tree fell into a creek in Franklin Township, New Jersey, and caused flooding. The town was about to send a tractor in to pull the tree out when someone, probably the town lawyer, helpfully pointed out that it was a "class C-1 creek" and required formal approvals before any natural condition was altered. The flooding continued while town officials spent twelve days and $12,000 to get a permit to do what was obvious: pull the tree out of the creek.

Government's ineptitude is not news. But something else has happened in the last few decades. Government is making America inept. Other countries don't have difficulty pulling a tree out of a creek. Other countries also have modern infrastructure, and schools that generally succeed, and better health care at little more than half the cost. The US is now ranked below a dozen or more countries in terms of ease of doing business and effective governance. These are our competitors in global markets.

Reforms, often embodied in hundreds of pages of new regulations, are tried constantly. But they only seem to make the problems worse. Political debate is so predictable that it's barely worth listening to, offering ideology without practicality—as if our only choice, as comedian Jon Stewart put it, is that "government must go away completely—or we must be run by an incompetent bureaucracy."

The missing element in American government could hardly be more basic: No official has authority to make a decision. Law has crowded out the ability to be practical or fair. Mindless rigidity has descended upon the land, from the school house to the White House to, sometimes, your house. Nothing much works, because no one is free to make things work.

It's a progressive disease: As law grows to fill the vacuum, the wheels of government go slower every year. The 2009 economic stimulus package promoted by President Obama included $5 billion to weatherize some 607,000 homes—with the goals of both spurring the economy and increasing energy efficiency. But the project was required to comply with a statute called the Davis-Bacon Act (signed into law by President Hoover in 1931), which provides that construction projects with federal funding must pay workers the "prevailing wage"—basically a union perk that costs taxpayers about 20 percent more than actual labor rates. This requirement comes with a mass of red tape; bureaucrats in the Labor Department must set wages, as a matter of law, for each category of construction worker in each of three thousand counties in America. There was no schedule for "weatherproofers." So the Labor Department began a slow trudge of determining how much weatherproofers should be paid in Merced County, California; Monmouth County, New Jersey; and several thousand other counties. The stimulus plan had projected that California would weatherproof twenty-five hundred homes per month. At the end of 2009, the actual total was twelve.

It's not hard to imagine a different way of organizing government. Pulling a tree out of a flooded creek is an obvious choice. Does our society really need the Labor Department to set wages in federal construction projects? Today, these idiocies are dictated by law. American government is run by millions of words of legal dictates, not by the leaders we elect or the officials who work for them.

Nothing will get fixed until we give back to officials the authority that goes along with their responsibility. This requires more than reform. It requires remaking our structure of government—toward radically simplified structures with room for humans in charge to accomplish public goals. That's what other countries are doing—replacing thick rule books with a few dozen goals and principles, liberating citizens and regulators alike to use their judgment and better accomplish public goals without getting paralyzed by red tape.

America must embrace again its founding values of individual responsibility and accountability. This requires abandoning the utopian dream of automatic government and giving responsible officials—real people—the authority to make practical choices.

America is at a dangerous place. Big change will happen, whether you want it or not, because the current structure is not sustainable. The impetus for overhaul will not be a miraculous moment of political harmony, but a crisis. But what should the change look like? That's the question I address in this book.

PART I

The Rule of Nobody

THE RULE OF NOBODY

The Bayonne Bridge spans the Kill Van Kull, a narrow channel that connects New York Harbor to the largest port on the East Coast, the port of Newark. The bridge, opened in 1931, has a single sweeping arch that is the fourth longest in the world and considered by architectural historians to be a masterpiece. Within this arch hangs a four-lane roadway, 151 feet above the water. That's the challenge: The new generation of large container ships built to take advantage of the widened Panama Canal, so-called post-Panamax ships, require clearance of 215 feet. For the port of Newark to remain competitive, it must be able to accommodate the new ships, which are much more efficient than smaller ships.

The government agency with responsibility for solving this problem, the Port Authority of New York and New Jersey, put its engineers to work, and in 2008 they presented two plausible solutions: either build a new bridge or dig a tunnel. Both solutions would require rerouting the roadways and condemning local residential neighborhoods. Each would cost more than $4 billion. Once the new construction was completed, the historic Bayonne Bridge and its roadway would be demolished.

The solutions seemed too formulaic to the project manager, Joann Papageorgis, a twenty-eight-year veteran of the Port Authority: "The urge to build the newest and best is not always the practical solution." She asked the engineers if perhaps the historic bridge could be retrofitted. There were obvious complications with this idea, including the structural integrity of the eighty-year-old bridge and the conundrum of keeping the roadway open while raising it. The engineers went back to the drawing board to see what they could come up with.

A few months later they presented a report. Yes, they concluded, a new roadway could be built higher within the historic arch. There would be no need to build new foundations, or a new right-of-way for the approach roads. The bridge could even stay open by raising first half the road, then the other. The total cost would be about $1 billion—a savings of $3 billion over a new bridge or tunnel. The resolution, the brainchild of lifetime Port Authority employees, was like a miracle.

That was 2009. At the beginning of 2013, the Port still lacked approval to start construction. Who, you might reasonably ask, has authority to approve a project like this? The answer is basically no one, at least not in a deliberate or timely way.

Building anything important in America requires layers of approvals from multiple levels of government—in this project, forty-seven permits from nineteen different governmental entities. Environmental review has evolved into an academic exercise, like a game of who can find the most complications. Balkanization of authority among different agencies and levels of government creates a dynamic of buck-passing. "The process is aimed not at trying to solve problems," Ms. Papageorgis observed, "but trying to find problems. You can't get in trouble by saying no." With any large project, *something might go wrong*. More studies are done.

Many public choices involve tough trade-offs, but not this one. The bridge is already there. The foundations and right-of-way are the same. The goal—to permit larger ships—is not only vital to the regional economy, but also environmentally important: The new generation of ships are cleaner and move goods more efficiently. Sooner or later, approval is a foregone conclusion. Timing is important, however, since the expanded Panama Canal will open by 2015.

But without someone to make decisions, the process goes round and round. Environmental laws allow for a shortened "environmental assessment," conducted by a lead agency. At the end of this process the lead agency can either issue a "finding of no significant impact" (known as a "FONSI") or require a full environmental impact statement. In theory, the environmental assessment is a short initial review, with a forty-five-day public comment period, followed by a decision. But any process, like a plant in rainy season, can grow beyond reason if no one can cuts it back. Here are some of the hoops Joann Papageorgis and her team had to jump through.

Getting a federal department to be a "lead agency" was the first step. Whom do you call? No official has the job of designating a "lead agency" to do the environmental assessment, so Ms. Papageorgis sent formal request letters to the Army Corps of Engineers, the Coast Guard, and other possible candidates. Months passed as agencies slowly came up with reasons why they should not have this responsibility. Eventually, only the Coast Guard was left standing. Finding a lead agency took almost one year.

An environmental assessment here could be simple; indeed, no review at all would be required for these minor alterations if the bridge spanned a railroad line or a non-navigable body of water. However, once review is triggered (here, because of a federal permit for navigable waterways), even a preliminary review has a long checklist for an initial assessment. But how much review on each item? No one has the authority to decide that. Months are consumed by public "scoping meetings."

Then the studies must be done. Here, for example, the Port Authority was required to conduct a historical survey of every building within a two-mile radius of the bridge. No environmental official has authority to waive this requirement, even where, as here, the project will not touch any buildings. Doing the historic buildings survey, like any government project, is never as simple as just doing the work. The procurement process to hire the expert requires an elaborate bureaucratic dance, often taking longer than the work. Overall, this historic buildings survey, costing about $200,000 for the expert, took the better part of a year from beginning to end.

Federal and state laws are piled high with similar requirements, mandated to make sure no issue is ever overlooked. Native American tribes, for example, must be given the opportunity to join the environmental review committees and, if they wish, to demand soil borings and excavations to try to find artifacts. Here, although no new ground is being disturbed, no official could waive this requirement. The Port Authority sent out letters inviting tribe representatives to join the environmental review project, including the Shawnee Tribe of Oklahoma and the Sand Hills Nation of Nebraska. One tribe, based in New Jersey, decided to join the review process.

A purpose of environmental review is to give decision makers the benefit of public reaction. You might think local environmental activists would be grateful that raising the roadway avoids the environmental havoc of building a new bridge or tunnel. But objecting to public choices is pretty much what they do. Even before the draft environmental assessment was published, a group called the Eastern Environmental Law Center started objecting to the project. Their main objection was not to the minimal impact of constructing a higher roadway, but to possible second-level effects: More efficient ships might make the port of Newark more successful, which might in turn increase truck traffic, which might in turn affect the quality of life of residents of Newark who live in the area through which arterial roads run. By their logic, the Port Authority should stop the project in order to guarantee that the port remains less efficient.

The EPA regional office, embracing this logic, began sending letters to the Coast Guard in mid-2012 demanding that it study whether a vigorous Newark port was in the public interest. A full-blown environmental impact statement, studying possible effects on each block in Newark, could add years to the process and, by default, drive the new generation of post-Panamax ships to other ports.

Only divine intervention seemed capable of moving this supposedly simple environmental assessment toward a decision. On July 19, 2012, the earthly equivalent of divinity intervened: President Obama listed the Bayonne Bridge as one of seven essential port infrastructure projects and "committed to completing all federal permit and review decisions for the Bayonne Bridge by April of 2013, shaving months from the schedule." "Today's commitment to move these port projects forward faster," the President stated, "will help drive job growth and strengthen the economy."

But who gave the President the authority to decide about the right balance between jobs and environmental issues? The local environmental groups acted as if nothing had changed. Local activists complained about "shoddy review" and threatened to sue to stop the project. The EPA supposedly works for the President, but it, too, was unimpressed by his statement of national priorities. Even after the Port Authority completed a macroeconomic study showing no adverse effects of more efficient ships—with the environmental assessment now over five thousand pages including exhibits—the regional office of EPA did not retract its position that "a basic impasse still exists" on the need for more review.

Eventually, on May 23, 2013, over three years after the approval process began, the Coast Guard issued a "finding of no significant impact." Now, Ms. Papageorgis observed, we "are awaiting the lawsuit."

Compared to other infrastructure projects, the Bayonne Bridge approval is greased lightning. The average length of environmental review for highway projects, according to a study by the Regional Plan Association, is over eight years. A project to replace the Goethals Bridge one mile south has taken about ten years to approve.

The Bayonne Bridge episode reveals serious problems with America's ability to rebuild its fraying infrastructure. But this is how modern government works. Public decisions grind through bureaucracy for years.

Americans don't need to be told that our government doesn't work well, but almost no one talks about how public choices are made. Debate focuses on what government does, not how government does it.

Most of what government does is noncontroversial, however. Even industrialists now support the need for environmental review. Everyone wants safe and effective drugs. No one has proposed eliminating health care for the elderly.

The problem is that government does these things so badly.

These failures of implementation become failures of policy. Rebuilding America's decaying infrastructure, for example, is supposedly a priority of both parties. America's electrical grid is out of date—transformers, on average, are about forty years old, and not digitized. The old wires and transfer stations waste about 7 percent of power. The decrepit system operates at capacity in critical regions, and its congested wires cannot transfer electricity from one region to another. That makes it impossible, for example, to transfer excess hydropower from northern states and Canada to help with peak periods in the South. The absence of transmission capacity also limits the ability to develop alternative energy sources from, say, remote wind farms. This power grid equivalent of a sand castle is leveled by any disastrous weather event, as occurred in 2012 in the Northeast with Hurricane Sandy.

Building a new electrical grid would be an obvious benefit to the environment, a boost to the economy, and a safeguard for national security. It could be financed in large part by private capital, aided by government guarantees. It would be our generation's contribution to the future, as the interstate highway system was for us.

But there's no active plan to rebuild America's electrical grid. The main reason is that government cannot make the decisions needed to approve it. New transmission lines would go through forests and across deserts. Some people will object. Multiply the Bayonne Bridge bureaucratic hurdles a hundredfold. Rebuilding the power grid—a national priority—remains on the back burner.

Government's inability to make critical choices should be a national scandal. Instead, this self-inflicted ineptitude is accepted as a state of nature, as if spending an average of eight years on environmental reviews were an unavoidable mountain range.

In this book I will assert a series of propositions, which, if you accept them, require a radical shift in our approach to governing. Here is the first.

Proposition 1: America has lost the ability to make public choices.

America has created what philosopher Hannah Arendt called the "rule by Nobody": a bureaucratic state that has taken a life of its own, without the ability to make vital choices to respond to current needs. Government, out of anyone's control, is increasingly disconnected from the society it supposedly serves.

The Bayonne Bridge process could have been shortened by years if someone had authority to draw lines of what review was really needed. "Oh, there's no need to survey historic buildings, since the project isn't touching them." That person doesn't exist.

Modern government is designed to be a kind of legal machine. But it is badly designed. Indeed, it may be one of the worst machines ever invented. Its core flaw is that it aspires to make choices without human judgment at the moment of action.

Decisions are made instead by a legal process. Legislatures and officials in the executive branch periodically introduce new goals, programs, and projects, which then get thrown into the legal hopper. From then on, public employees do what accumulated laws and regulations tell them to do. Things generally happen (or not) because that's what the legal rules say must happen.

Think of government as a giant machine of legal gears and presses. It gets ever larger as legislatures create new regulations and programs. But day to day, modern government isn't actually run by people supposedly in charge. They're more like mechanics, scurrying here and there to attend to the legal gears and machinery. With legal skill and artifice, they can coax a decision out of the machinery, as Joann Papageorgis did with the Bayonne Bridge, achieving obvious goals with herculean effort. But they're not really in charge. Government goes where the machinery takes it, creeping slowly forward on legal autopilot.

Grinding public decisions through a legal apparatus is not the handiwork of a demented management theorist. It's a philosophical mandate. Government decisions, we believe, must comply with what is known as the "Rule of Law." This hallowed concept is universally regarded as the foundation of a free society.

The Rule of Law aims at making sure government uses its powers properly, in an orderly fashion, and not by the whim of some official. By drawing boundaries of prohibited conduct, law limits the scope of state power and assures citizens of a protected zone of their freedoms.

But there's a difference between mandating a legal goal—say, "practicable" environmental review under the National Environmental Policy Act—and actually doing the review. Current legal orthodoxy, however, does not make that distinction. Law not only sets public goals, but strives to prescribe every nuance of how law is implemented. Pure legal uniformity, the theory goes, will avoid bad decisions by officials and ensure fair treatment of citizens. All government choices, even ministerial ones, must be preset with "clear law"—the more detailed the regulations, the better. As Friedrich Hayek famously stated:

> Government in all its actions . . . [should be] bound by rules announced and fixed beforehand—rules which make it possible to foresee with fair certainty how the authority will use its coercive powers in given circumstances.

This approach to public decisions is treated with almost theological reverence. It comes straight out of the Enlightenment—a rationalistic system of clear laws that will mechanize public choices. "Let all the laws be clear, uniform and precise," Voltaire advised, suggesting that otherwise judges and officials will mess things up: "To interpret laws is almost always to corrupt them."

Almost no one, not even reformers, questions this precept of how government choices get made. Political leaders devote their lives to blaming the other side for government's failures and profligacy, but this is the one place they agree. The behemoth of state may be about to lurch over a cliff, but we go to sleep comfortable that officials within it are tightly constrained by the Rule of Law.

Getting things done in government, under this legal model, is supposed to be a rote exercise of compliance. But that's not how anything in real life works. Take any problem facing our society today and ask yourself, Who has authority to fix it? The answer is nobody.

Automatic law causes public failure. A system of detailed dictates is supposed to make government work better. Instead it causes failure.

The simplest tasks often turn into bureaucratic ordeals, as with the New Jersey officials laboring through twelve days of process to pull the tree out of the flooding creek. A teacher in Chicago who called the custodian to report a broken water fountain was chewed out because he didn't follow "broken water fountain reporting procedures." On the first day of school he was required to read to his students a list of disciplinary rules, including this one, just to start things off on the right foot: "You may be expelled for homicide."

Budgets are out of control because government executives lack flexibility to shave here and there to make ends meet. Soon after his election, New York governor Andrew Cuomo thought he had found an easy way to save $50 million when he learned that a large juvenile detention center was empty, with no prospects of use anytime soon. There it was, sitting upstate, with several dozen employees—doing nothing but costing taxpayers millions of dollars. But no one had the authority to close it down, not even the governor. There's a New York law that prohibits closing down any facility with union employees without at least one year's notice. So $50 million of taxpayer revenue—that's ten thousand families each paying $5,000 in state taxes—was wasted for no public purpose.

Government programs, like most choices in life, have unanticipated consequences. In 1966, the year after Medicare became law, the architects of the program for elderly health care went into the field to see how it was working. They found that doctors and hospitals had changed their practice guidelines to maximize revenues under the program, which had been structured on a fee-for-service reimbursement model. The more tests and procedures they provided, the more doctors and hospitals would get paid, largely without charge to the patients. The architects of the law saw immediately the makings of a budgetary beast. No one had a financial incentive to be prudent when government was footing the bill.

The original cost assumptions were turned upside down. Providers developed "energetic gaming strategies" to maximize reimbursement. Doctors organized "gang visits" to old-age homes, collecting a fee for each short consultation. Frequent visits to doctors became a form of medical entertainment in retirement communities, with friends meeting in waiting rooms and trying out the latest technologies to track the progress of their ailments. Officials saw public funds pouring out the faucet and tried to stem the flow by reducing the amounts being reimbursed. Providers countered by charging more for other categories. Medicare became a form of bureaucratic mud wrestling between providers and government. It would be far more efficient, many experts observed, to abandon the fee-for-service framework and align incentives of doctors, patients, and the public. But that's not how the law was enacted.

Almost fifty years later, Medicare, with its companion program Medicaid, has morphed into the world's largest entitlement program, consuming about 20 percent of the total federal budget. Dr. Don Berwick, the acting head of Medicare under President Obama, estimated that Medicare wastes about $200 billion annually, largely because of skewed incentives in the fee-for-service structure. With majority vote, of course, Congress has the power to change law, but the politics make this almost impossible; the Affordable Care Act (known as Obamacare) takes only baby steps in this direction. Who wants to take the lead on altering what is known as a "legal entitlement"?

Government on legal autopilot doesn't have a chance of achieving solvency. In 2010, 70 percent of federal tax revenue was consumed by three entitlement programs (Medicare, Medicaid, and Social Security) that don't even come up for annual congressional authorization.

There's a tendency to attribute ulterior purpose to the failures of government. Sleazy deals are certainly easy to find. But pay a visit to the innards of the giant machine, and mainly what you find is not calculating people trying to get something for someone, but a comedy of rules without reason.

You would be shocked, I bet, to hang out in a government

office. Asking a New York City employee to chip in to help a coworker, for example, would violate rigid civil service classifications that detail exactly what an employee can and cannot do. Promoting a public employee for good performance would be unlawful; jobs must be filled by written examination, not actual performance. Reassigning a worker is dictated by rigid seniority rules. Responsibility is an alien concept: When a virus disabled two computers in a shared federal office in Washington, DC, the IT technician fixed one but said he was unable to fix the other because it wasn't listed on his form. Accountability is virtually nonexistent. "I've never seen anyone terminated for incompetence," said the New York City official in charge of personnel accountability.

How inefficient is this system? Ten percent? Thirty percent? Pause on the math here. Over 20 million people work for federal, state, and local government—or one in seven workers in America. Their salaries and benefits total over $1.5 trillion of taxpayer funds each year (about 10 percent of GDP). They spend, at all levels of government, almost $2 trillion in various contracts and programs (not including entitlements). If government could be run more efficiently by 30 percent, the result would be an annual savings of $1 trillion. But managing public employees is basically against the law.

Public policy comes to life in the daily activities of real people. America's impractical policy of making public choices can be summarized as follows:

Credo of modern American government: *Public choices must be preset by specific legal dictates wherever possible. Officials are not allowed to make practical choices, and must act in ways that are nonsensical and often counterproductive to public goals. Legal*

*rigidity should in all cases trump efficiency, innovation, accom-
modation, and free choice. Individual responsibility should be
avoided and replaced with legal dictates or processes, as set forth
in the first sentence, above.*

The failures of government run by this policy are hardly surprising. Instead of alleviating the rigidities, however, our reaction is to double down on them. The worse government works,
the more we seek to control it with legal dictates. Schools are
subjected to regulatory carpet bombing, for example, with constant revisions of testing metrics to try to force teachers to be
more effective.

What's amazing is that anything gets done in government.
This is a tribute to countless public employees like Joann Papageorgis who render public service, against all odds, by their
personal pride and willpower, despite having to wrestle daily
choices through endless bureaucracy.

Automatic law corrodes our freedom A public philosophy of controlling public choices by detailed laws is supposed to guarantee
our freedom. Who knows what mischief might result if, perish
the thought, an official had flexibility to use his judgment.

Powerlessness of officials to act sensibly quickly ripples out in
society, however, diminishing everyone's freedom. Every day, in
countless encounters with and within government, people are
prevented from acting sensibly by seemingly random legal dictates banning activities that don't fit the bureaucratic mold.

In 2011, the Community Soup Kitchen in Morristown, New Jersey, was told that it must shut down its meal service. No official
actually decided there was anything wrong with the kitchen. For
twenty-six years, it had served upwards of three hundred meals

per day to the elderly and needy, without incident. Members of various church congregations made food in their homes and provided countless grateful people with a potluck meal. That was the problem: New Jersey law requires that all food-serving establishments must have their kitchens inspected, and doesn't have a provision exempting potluck meals. The health department couldn't inspect the kitchens of all the contributors, including parishioners from three dozen churches, so officials felt they had no choice but to order the pantry to shut down. The legal logic, à la Voltaire, was irrefutable. But the practical effect was absurd. The soup kitchen, undaunted, picked itself up and was last seen raising $150,000 to build a kitchen on premises.

Regulation by rote always ends badly. In the summer of 2011, county officials closed down a children's lemonade stand near the US Open golf championship in Bethesda, Maryland—because the children didn't have a vendor's license. Officials decided not to order the children to court, and issued a summons instead to their parents. Local television crews were soon on the crime scene, interviewing the kids, who had organized the enterprise as a way to raise money for pediatric cancer. The incident was too ridiculous not to garner national attention, and the bureaucracy soon backed down. But the retreat was tactical, not a sincere acknowledgment of bureaucratic overkill. The regulations, after all, have no exception for young vendors. Indeed, the incident prompted a wave of lemonade shutdowns over the summer by diligent officials in Georgia, Massachusetts, and several other states.

Trying to get a permit in this system is an exercise in frustration, mainly because it's impossible to find anyone with authority to say yes. Opening a new restaurant in New York City, Mayor Bloomberg discovered, can require permits from eleven different agencies. The civic virtues for which Americans are justly famous are impossible to act upon without scaling giant bureaucratic obstacles. Retired scientists can't teach, because they lack teaching credentials. Local churches and civic groups find themselves discouraged from providing volunteer social services by the regulatory maze. The inexorable growth of bureaucratic requirements, each striving to prevent by rule some possible abuse—being alone with a child is prohibited by many churches and schools—smothers the spirit of community involvement.

People who work within bureaucracies, such as teachers, police, and social workers, constantly confront the mismatch between regulations and the needs of live people. The only way to do the job sensibly, studies repeatedly show, is to ignore what's legally required—for example, submitting less-than-accurate forms to get approval for adequate medical services.

The system wears people down, however. Not being able to act on their natural instincts affects their physical and mental health. Even with impregnable job security, public employees have a higher incidence of stress-related diseases. Just as Pavlov's dogs went crazy when given inconsistent signals and rewards, bright young teachers are driven out of promising careers by nonsensical bureaucracy. Here is what one California teacher said when he quit in 2012:

> I quit teaching because I was tired of feeling powerless. Tired of watching would-be professionals treated as children, infantilized into silence. Tired of the machine that turns art into artifice for the sake of test scores . . . It's a structure that consumes everyone in it, from the top to

the bottom. I didn't quit because of a single school—I quit because of the pattern of inanity that is replicated throughout the whole country.

Proposition 2: Doing anything well requires human energy and judgment.

Think of everything you have accomplished. You didn't do it by mindlessly following rules. Whether making a sale, curing a patient, raising the children, inspiring a team, or cleaning the closet, you made it happen by perceiving the challenges and making choices. Each one of those tasks requires numerous decisions on the spot. Organizational tools and processes can be important, but they never take you all the way there. "The guy standing there looking at the hole in the ground," former Georgia Commissioner Joe Tanner observed, "is best able to tell if there's a problem and how to fill it up." Management theorist Chester Barnard thought that "at least nine-tenths of all organization activity" is figured out by the people who actually execute the task.

Freedom to do things in your own way happens to be practical, because it allows people to adapt to the infinite complexity of life's circumstances. Succeeding at most projects requires originality and trade-offs. It requires human understanding; people are unique, and groups even more so. It requires give and take; collaborative teams will create solutions that none could have accomplished on their own. No endeavor can succeed, management expert Peter Drucker noted, without "a principle of management that will give full scope to individual strength and responsibility."

Freedom to do things in your own way offers something more than practical accomplishment, however. It gives life meaning. What's fun about life is making things happen—rolling up your sleeves and meeting challenges in your own way. This is the genius of American culture. It unleashes all of us to try to figure things out, adapt when they don't work, and move forward. Each new day is an opportunity for a new accomplishment by you.

The energy of a free society comes from your ownership of daily choices. This ownership of life's decisions is what freedom is supposed to offer. Freedom is not just a dutiful right to cast a ballot, or a defensive shield against abuse. Freedom is action by you. Freedom is the ability to make a difference, in your own work and projects, and also together with others in the community and broader society. Freedom to do what you think is right and sensible is what freedom is.

Now think of things that turn you off. Filling out forms that no one will read, and then filling them out again the next time. Being talked at with no ability to talk back—whether by a burned-out teacher, a robo-consumer service center, or a bureaucrat with no interest or ability in helping to solve your problem. The worst is being required to do stupid things just because a rule requires it. This is what is so profoundly discouraging to teachers.

People lose their energy when they're forced to trudge through life just doing what they're told. Centralized legal dictates make people go brain-dead. People not only don't have fun, but don't get much done. That's what's happened to government employees.

It all comes down to how government is organized. Nothing much can make sense today because no one in government is free to make it make sense. That powerlessness then ripples out into society in every area where government provides services and regulatory oversight.

Democracy is not designed to make public policy efficiently, of course. The goals and priorities of our society emerge out of a democratic process that is deliberately messy and time-consuming. Whether those goals are achieved, however, requires giving officials authority to carry them out.

American government is missing the critical component of accomplishment: human choice on the spot. America is suffering from a vacuum of authority. Public officials have lots of power, but it's largely negative. Officials can say no (and many seem to relish doing so), but they can't say yes. American government is failing not because officials who deal with the public have too much power, but because they have too little.

Giving officials authority doesn't mean they can do whatever they want, as I will discuss. Nor does it require trusting any particular person. Providing checks and balances is prudent for important public choices. But restoring judgment to official decisions does require trusting *a system of government rooted in human responsibility*. It also requires accepting, within reasonable parameters, a lack of perfect uniformity among public choices. Different people will meet public goals in somewhat different ways. These differences are inherent in the idea of each human taking responsibility. Implementation is not everything, but, given the rut America finds itself in, it's almost everything. "A government ill-executed, whatever may be the theory," Alexander Hamilton observed, "must be in practice, a bad government."

To thrive long term, America needs a government that can get things done. Here we are, still in the early years of a new century, buffeted by global forces that, virtually overnight, blow away the economic frameworks of entire communities and industries. Government must be able to adapt to unforeseeable events. It must rebuild our infrastructure. It must promote free markets and social interaction, while also overseeing joint activities to guard against abuse. It must support, not condemn, the virtues for which America is famous: a practical frame of mind and a willingness to innovate and take risks.

America needs a new way of making public choices. "Policy problems are multiplying faster than our efforts to build a rule of law around them," political scientist Donald Kettl observes. Today government can't balance a budget or pull a tree out of a creek. To thrive tomorrow, America needs a government that can implement our common goals. This requires a new approach to the Rule of Law.

RETHINKING THE RULE OF LAW

The Rule of Law is one of those pillars of society that we take for granted without pondering how it's supposed to work. We know it's the framework of a free society, and that's pretty much where the thinking stops.

My focus here is on how law provides a platform for public choices. Law's focus historically has been on prohibiting bad conduct, to protect people from criminals, cheats, and lawless officials. Today, with government overseeing the hustle and bustle of daily life, the relationship between law and freedom is more complex.

Leaving aside many nuances, the Rule of Law embodies two core values: *protection against arbitrary state action* and *predictability of legal norms*. Regularizing the use of state power with judicial oversight—for example, barring the taking of property without due process—is what achieves our founders' aspiration of "a government of laws, not of men." Defining predictable bound-aries of unacceptable conduct—for example, prohibiting theft and fraud—allows people and markets to interact freely without undue fear. Law's success as a framework for a free society can be judged in part by how people react to it: Do people feel free in their daily interactions?

Law in a democracy also provides the organizing framework for government, setting public goals and priorities. This role has been transformed by the rise of global markets and institu-tions, requiring government to ramp up its oversight respon-sibilities—setting minimum standards for virtually all social activities, in the workplace, schools, markets, factories, hospi-tals, and playgrounds. Government also provides a wide variety of services to a crowded society, from infrastructure to social safety nets. The role of law is still protective—both to safe-guard against abuses by anonymous institutions and to protect against unreasonable officials. The test of law's effectiveness in organizing modern government also comes down to how peo-ple feel about it: How's our government doing?

Law is failing miserably as a platform for public choices, as I have already begun to discuss with episodes like the Bayonne Bridge and the Morristown soup kitchen. Up and down the chain of social responsibility, responsible people do not feel free to make sensible decisions. Everything is too complicated: rules in the workplace, rights in the classroom, and machinations in government. We're bogged down in bureaucracy, pushed around by lawsuits, and unable to steer out of economic and cultural storms. But what's the alternative?

Political debate provides heat but no light. Liberals self-righteously cling to the status quo, using a victim orientation to argue against altering social programs. Conservatives call for deregulation, arrogantly dismissing government while mumbling about "starving the beast." Both are half right. Conservatives correctly point to grotesque inefficiencies and abuses. But liberals are also correct that we need government. Like it or not, regulatory oversight is essential for us to feel free. Practically everything we do is dependent on people we don't know. People we love are entrusted to the care of strangers in schools, day care centers, and nursing homes. For the same reason we want cops patrolling the streets, people need the assurance that a regulatory cop is on the beat to safeguard against abuses.

Our options for governing, however, are not limited to (1) central planning or (2) anything goes. There are better models. All, however, require human judgment.

Under current orthodoxy, the ideal government runs like a software program: Input the facts and out comes a decision. This technocratic model of the Rule of Law has many plausible virtues. Government can't act arbitrarily, the theory has it, if it is shackled to clear rules. Precision will offer predictability needed for citizens to plan their affairs. Best of all, law is pure, unadulterated by human judgment. There'll be no room for favoritism or venality when law is precise, telling officials and citizens alike how to do things properly. Law becomes a type of scientific management, laying out public choices on a legal assembly line.

Common sense might suggest that there is a continuum of public choices, some requiring more legal care than others. Shuttering a business is different from, say, telling a nursing home to be more attentive to a resident's needs, which is different from the Port Authority's decision to rebuild a bridge. Sooner or later, however, the hierarchy of state authority generally ends up at the possibility of court review—if for no other reason than to safeguard against the worst abuses. As a result, most Rule of Law scholars throw all government choices into the same philosophical vat requiring the formal trappings of "due process" and, even with ministerial decisions, strive to avoid official discretion by laying rules out in advance.

Precise regulation is an article of faith among most legal experts. "It is on the whole wise legal policy to use rules as much as possible for regulating human behavior," legal philosopher Joseph Raz asserted, because they "lend themselves more easily to uniform and predictable application." Conservative scholar Tom Campbell states as accepted wisdom that "peace of mind is promoted, particularly in complex societies, by widespread conformity to clear and precise rules." Even pragmatists, such as Professor Cass Sunstein, who understand that it is "unrealistic" to make "every decision according to judgments fully specified in advance," nonetheless believe that precise rules "narrow or even eliminate the . . . uncertainty faced by people attempting to follow . . . the law. This step has enormous virtues in terms of promoting predictability and planning."

This philosophy of regulation aspires to "rationalized completeness." Regulation will not only bar bad behavior, but will provide an instruction manual for proper behavior.

The oppression of rationalized completeness. Let's look at a social service, nursing homes, where most people would probably agree on the need for government oversight. Elderly residents can hardly take care of themselves—the average age is over eighty, and more than half suffer from Alzheimer's disease or some other form of dementia. There are about sixteen thousand nursing homes in America, caring for 1.5 million people. Making sure nursing homes provide a responsible, safe, and caring residence is an important societal goal.

Trying to accomplish that goal with precise regulations, however, leads to requirements such as these, taken from the Kansas code:

- Per facility, there shall be a weekly average of 2.0 hours of direct care staff time per resident and a daily average of not fewer than 1.85 hours during any 24 hour period.
- The nursing facility shall employ activities personnel at a minimum weekly average of .09 hours per resident per day.
- There shall be no more than 14 hours time between a substantial evening meal and breakfast the following day, except when a nourishing snack is provided at bedtime, in which instance 16 hours may elapse. A nourishing snack shall provide items from at least 2 food groups.
- Before serving, the facility shall hold hot foods at 140 degrees F or above . . . Hot foods, when served to the resident, shall not be below 115 degrees F.
- The facility shall store each prepared food, dry or staple food, single service ware, sanitized equipment, or utensil at least six inches or 15 centimeters above the floor on clean surfaces.
- The facility shall provide living, dining, activity, and recreational areas in the special care section at the rate of 27 square feet per resident, except when residents are able to access living, dining, activity, and recreational areas in another section of the facility.
- Windowsill height shall not exceed three feet above the floor for at least ½ of the total window area.
- Wastebaskets shall be located at all lavatories.
- All eggs shall be cooked.

None of these regulations, and hundreds more like them in the Kansas nursing home code, seem stupid—at least not obviously so. Eggs should certainly be cooked. There's nothing odd about having wastebaskets in the bathrooms. But is all this regulatory detail necessary? Requiring nutritious meals, sanitary conditions, comfortable rooms, and medical checkups could be stated in just a few paragraphs if regulation were written at a more general level. That's how other countries regulate nursing homes, as I will discuss shortly.

Pick up almost any set of American regulations, however, and you will see detail that instructs people exactly how to do things. There are thousands of federal worker safety regulations, for example, including seven pages dealing with wooden ladders. Many of these rules mandate features that are self-evident, such as the rule that "aisles, stairs, ramps, runways, corridors . . . shall be lighted with either natural or artificial illumination." How else can they be lit? Couldn't the requirement of light be subsumed within a general legal requirement to provide "safe working conditions"? I can also imagine exceptions to the rule— a lab where the experiments require darkness, or a mushroom farm, or a commercial photographic darkroom. Don't they have "aisles" and "corridors"?

Writing every permutation of public choice into a regulatory code naturally results in a proliferation of legal growth. Medicare will soon increase the number of reimbursement categories from 18,000 to around 140,000, including twenty-one separate categories for "spacecraft accidents," twenty-one more for injuries occurring in a bathtub, and an additional twelve for bee stings. I'm sure, with the help of comedians over a drunken weekend, we could expand the list of possible human accidents toward infinity. Perhaps this: *Reimbursement category 140,001:*

Crushed toes caused by dropping a keg of beer. How is this useful for public policy?

We could also come up with ten thousand more rules for Kansas nursing homes, each clarifying some existing requirement. If there needs to be a rule on cooking eggs, why is there no rule on whether soft-boiled eggs are permissible? Nor is there a requirement that the windows have clear glass or, indeed, face the outside. How big must the wastebasket be?

In 2011 the Colorado Department of Human Services proposed new rules for day care centers. Government oversight of day care seems like a good idea; you wouldn't want children cooped up in an airless basement. But the new rules would dictate exactly how to do just about everything: how many block sets ("at least two (2) sets of blocks with a minimum of ten (10) blocks per set"), requirements for the area of block building ("space with a flat building surface shall be available . . . not in the main traffic area"), and exactly when caregivers must wash their hands (before "eating food," "after wiping a child's nose," and seven other categories).

Let's think for a second about how humans are supposed to deal with these rules. Do regulators really expect day care workers to count the blocks each morning? Or be on constant alert for whether a toddler has meandered into a room's "main traffic area," however that is defined? After public outcry, the rules were put on the back burner for further consideration and have not yet been added to the thirty-seven pages of regulatory fine print that already exist, including that "cots or pads must be spaced at least 2 feet apart on all sides during rest time" and that "the light must be dim at nap time to promote an atmosphere conducive to sleep."

Many regulatory codes, if subjected to any systems analysis, don't resemble anything that could be called a "code." They have the trappings of official precision, but they're just spouting lots of requirements, often self-evident, without differentiating those that require special attention. A new trend is to ban entire categories of activities rather than letting responsible adults draw the line on what's appropriate. A school district in Maryland in 2013 instituted rules that banned hugging, homemade food, pushing kids on swings, ad hoc parent-teacher conferences, and distribution of birthday invitations on school grounds.

It's easy to imagine the dynamics here: Government regulators feel under pressure for more rules—from politicians to "do something," from the public to avoid last year's scandal, from special interests to accommodate all kinds of hidden agendas, and from fellow bureaucrats to outdo each other. So regulators try to imagine everything that might happen, write a regulation for just that situation, and then toss it onto the pile. The more, the better. Any activity in society that might affect other people needs a rule.

Law that aspires to completeness doesn't leave room for questions of priority and practicality. For the legal mandarins who write laws and regulations, the litmus test is, as one critic described it, whether law has successfully "eliminate[d] the human element in decision making." This, they believe, is what it means to have a "government of laws, not of men."

Federal officials and their predecessors have succeeded in writing over 100 million words of binding federal law and regulation. State and local regulators have built up a legal edifice of about 2 billion words. At this moment in our discussion, their brains are flooded with all the reasons why the Rule of Law must supplant choices by mere mortals: *Clear rules guarantee predictability in law. Clear rules protect against arbitrary enforcement. Comprehensive codes, covering every eventuality any regulator can think of, will make sure society works properly. Clear rules are vital for freedom.*

Only in the darkness of their bureaucratic caves, however, can these rationales be asserted. Out in the sunlight of the real world, these justifications look more like a hoax. Instead of legal regularity, the thick codes are a jungle of legal peril.

Proposition 3: Regulating with precise dictates undermines the goals of law in most social activities.

In *Federalist* No. 62, James Madison explicitly warned against trying to make law too dense: "It will be of little avail to the people, that the laws are made by men of their own choice, if the laws be so voluminous that they cannot be read, or so incoherent that they cannot be understood."

Modern law is too detailed to be knowable. If nursing homes were an automated assembly line, it might be possible to enter the formulas in a computer and let the microprocessor do all the work. But nursing homes are run by real people trying to care for real people. A real human can't absorb hundreds or thousands of rules. Instead of "helping people plan their affairs," detailed rules make it impossible. Even the inspectors in charge of a body of rules are "incapable of coping" with all the rules, Australian professor John Braithwaite found in studying US nursing homes: "Some of the standards are completely forgotten, not suppressed by any malevolent or captured political motive, just plain forgotten."

Schools are microcosms of how detailed law undermines the stated goals of the Rule of Law. Predictability is the first casualty. Life situations never quite fit the rules. This leads to a perception of legal risk in almost any choice. A New Jersey school superintendent described how "I run a lot of decisions by legal counsel . . . It seems like we are challenged more by everyone today—from students to parents to staff. Everyone has a lawyer." But the legal questions "often do not have yes or no answers." As a result, schools are imbued with a "culture of can't." When California allowed schools to apply for waivers of regulations, it found that "the vast majority of all requests for waivers were unnecessary"; the schools just assumed they couldn't do what was sensible.

Laws designed to ensure fairness in school discipline set off a downward spiral of law, disorder, and more law, resulting in a penal culture in many schools that no one considers fair. Fearful of getting dragged into a "due process" hearing, educators became tentative. Students so inclined soon learned they could get away with almost anything. In response to rising disorder, schools instituted more rules to try to curb the behavior— including "zero tolerance rules" that penalized students who did nothing wrong. For example, a seventh-grade girl in Indiana was suspended for a week in 2010, even though she immediately gave back a pill (for attention deficit disorder) that a friend had put in her hand. The principal said he had no choice, since she technically had "possession" for a few seconds. This legalistic rigidity reinforces the sense that right and wrong are irrelevant, and further erodes authority. After a while, police started patrolling the halls in some schools. By contrast, parochial and charter schools in the same neighborhoods, with almost none of the rules, have almost none of these problems. Instead of following rules and formal rituals, educators just do what they think is fair.

From a Rule of Law standpoint, detailed laws give us the worst of both worlds: undermining law's predictability while also, as I discuss now, leaving citizens open to arbitrary state power.

Detailed rules foster arbitrary enforcement. By replacing official discretion with detailed rules, the theory goes, no abuse of state power is possible. The reality, paradoxically, is that detailed laws create an open season for arbitrary officials.

Inspectors sometimes appear like faceless villains from a Kafka story, writing up tickets and levying fines for immaterial infractions. One restaurant owner in New York was fined because the cheese patties next to the griddle were 45 degrees, not the required 41 degrees. When removed from the refrigerator for cooking, the cheese always warms up a little. There were zero health implications for putting pasteurized cheese next to the griddle during lunch hour—the cheese slice is about to get a lot hotter when it goes on top of the sizzling burger. But the regulatory standard could hardly be more precise.

If people cannot know hundreds or thousands of rules, neither can they comply with them. Even companies with large legal staffs can't keep it all straight. When given advance notice of an environmental inspection, a company still could not achieve compliance with the myriad regulations.

Legal complexity puts people in a position of involuntary noncompliance, where government sanctions are largely up to the discretion of the particular inspector. In *Street-Level Bureaucracy*, Michael Lipsky noted that rules can be "so voluminous and contradictory that they can only be enforced or invoked selectively."

Most inspectors probably aren't mean-spirited. But they each have different ideas about which rules to focus on. Studies of nursing homes show that each inspector will focus on ten or twenty requirements—but it's a different set for each inspector, depending on their background: "If you've got a nurse, it will be nursing deficiencies in the survey report; if a pharmacist, you'll get pharmacy deficiencies; a sanitarian, sanitary deficiencies; a lawyer, patient rights, etc." As one Illinois nursing home inspector said, "We use 10 per cent of them repeatedly. You get into the habit of citing the same ones."

By striving to be crystal clear, precise rules disempower everyone from focusing on the merits. There's no room for discussion, or to push back against the unreasonable inspector. A warm cheese patty won't land you on death row. But you're still at the mercy of any official assigned to you, breeding fear and cynicism of law instead of trust.

The catastrophic mismatch between the ideology and the reality of automatic government was a central theme of Hannah Arendt and many other wise observers of the twentieth-century state. Management expert Peter Drucker concluded that government "has outgrown the structure, the policies and the rules designed for it," with the result that it is "bankrupt, morally as well as financially." Czech President Vaclav Havel called for modern societies to "abandon the arrogant belief that the world is merely a puzzle to be solved, a machine with instructions for use waiting to be discovered, a body of information to be fed into a computer in the hope that sooner or later it will spit out a universal solution."

But the ideology of automatic government remains irresistibly attractive, even as everyone condemns government for its growing failures. There is a muddled perception that detailed rules are the only way to deal with the regulatory needs of a crowded society, such as safeguarding clear air and water. Any criticism of the system is thought to be a rejection of its vital goals. As I am sometimes asked after speaking, "Are you in favor of pollution?" So let's be clear: Ineffective regulation is, indeed, sometimes better than no regulation; just the fact of government oversight will protect against the worst abuses, although at great cost to freedom and competitiveness. What society needs is not no government, or even small government, but, in Drucker's terms, "effective government."

The design flaw in modern government need not be cast in philosophical abstractions, or as failing merely to satisfy the aspirations of the Rule of Law. There are practical reasons why a structure aspiring to rationalized completeness must fail in almost every encounter with real life. The only exceptions are when a human decides to ignore the rules. A precast system is basically a bad form of central planning—less effective because it values compliance over results. Its rigidity causes almost certain failure, for two reasons. The first is that, in the hands of humans, detailed rules supplant public goals.

Bureaucratic metrics cause people to act like idiot savants. Specific rules supposedly provide clear metrics for enforcement. That's the theory, and that's why just about everyone insists on them— regulators, lobbyists, and politicians. Sometimes the metrics— as with fuel efficiency or environmental discharge limits—are the ultimate goals. But the legal details more often cause people to act in ways that undermine the public purpose.

Metrics in human activities—say, requiring no more than fourteen hours between the evening meal and morning meal at a nursing home—are usually just plausible guidelines. They're useful as a tool of organization but, by themselves, rarely align with ultimate success of an organization. Give them the force of law, and pretty soon people forget about the public purpose.

What might be called "intermediate goals"—the rules and metrics intended to make sure people do their jobs—become themselves the final goals. Observers tell horror stories of residents who went to sleep early only to be awakened rudely at 5:00 a.m. and forced to eat in order to comply with the rule.

In the No Child Left Behind law (NCLB), Congress thought it could whip schools into shape by penalizing those that did not show improvement in testing metrics. Pretty soon, teachers spent all their time "teaching to the test." Schools became drilling sheds, discouraging students instead of inspiring them. Teachers union leader Randi Weingarten joined with many education experts, including prominent conservatives, in calling out this fatal flaw of the law: "NCLB's fixation on testing has sabotaged the law's noble intention. Schools have become focused on compliance rather than on innovation and achievement."

Focusing on compliance actually impairs mental functioning, for reasons explained by philosopher and scientist Michael Polanyi in his seminal study of human accomplishment, *Personal Knowledge*. Humans have cognitive limitations. They can focus on only one thing at a time. If required to focus on complying with numerous rules, they cannot at the same time think about the regulatory goal. Focus on A, and you cannot see B. Getting things done usually draws on what Polanyi called "tacit knowledge," the vast store of know-how and instincts that reside in our subconscious. Because most rules tend to be technical and are unable to be internalized, the conscious mental effort required for compliance shuts the mental door to subconscious know-how. People with their noses in rule books do not have the mental capability to do more.

Investigating the Three Mile Island nuclear power plant partial meltdown, the Kemeny Commission concluded that the detail of the safety regulations displaced the understanding by operators of how the plant actually worked. As a result, they couldn't "respond to combinations of small equipment failures" that had caused the accident. Too many rules, the commission found, can be dangerous: "Once regulations become as voluminous and complex as those regulations now in place, they can serve as a negative factor in nuclear safety."

Making metrics the goal also encourages deliberate evasion of public purpose. In a 2012 essay, *New York Times* columnist Nicholas Kristof wrote about how parents in Appalachia, in order to maintain payments under a supplemental disability program, actively prevented children from learning to read. As long as the children could not read, the parents would continue to get a government check. A program designed to break the cycle of dependency ended up perpetuating it.

Government is filled with similar stories of distortion of public goals to satisfy bureaucratic metrics—for example, the end-of-year practice of agencies to go on a spending spree on unnecessary projects so that Congress doesn't cut their budget the next year.

Intermediate goals are an intrinsic danger in all large organizations, private as well as public—such as corporate officers who "manage" earnings to meet preset targets or who take imprudent long-term risks to achieve short-term profits. Sooner or later, when metrics replace purpose, the organization loses its way.

The aspect of detailed rules that is most destructive both of freedom and of regulatory purpose—worse even than unpredictability, arbitrariness, and distortion of goals—is that rigid dictates prevent people from dealing with the infinitely complex circumstances of real life.

Legal complexity compels bad choices. Precise rules do not permit adaptation. Their aim is to avoid variability. Everyone is bound equally. That's the attraction: Law truly rules. But bureaucratic conformity comes at a high price: No one can deal with the problem at hand. They are "frozen decisions," as organizational theorist Herbert Simon called them. What they freeze is freedom, including the freedom of officials on the spot to respond to new situations.

Environmental review is so frozen that political leaders no longer have an incentive to promote public works. When killing a plan to build a much-needed train tunnel under the Hudson River, New Jersey governor Chris Christie reportedly quipped that the project had been announced by his predecessor and would be christened by a successor.

The flaw of rigid rules is vastly amplified by legal complexity, which creates a web of interconnections, most not consciously intended. Like an overly complex machine, the failure of a small part brings things to a halt.

Rules designed for safety often introduce, as Tim Harford explains in *Adapt*, "a new 'failure mode'—a new way for things to go wrong." The *Deepwater Horizon* oil spill in 2010 was exacerbated by safety mechanisms that didn't fit the crisis. When the well started spewing mud and gas, the crew redirected it into a safety device called the "mud-gas separator." But the device "was quickly overwhelmed, enveloping much of the rig in explosive gas. Without this device, the crew would have directed the flow over the side of the rig, and the worst of the accident might have been prevented." Survivors in a life raft almost died because it was tied to the burning rig by a lifeline, and safety protocols had banned the crew from carrying knives.

Laws that restrict human communication, say, for privacy, are so complex, and so divorced from common sense notions of right and wrong, that tragedy is the predictable result. People with serious mental illness don't get needed intervention because, when brought to a hospital, they refuse to give doctors consent to tell family members and then are released without the ability to take care of themselves. A common result, as one mental health expert put it, is that they "die with their rights on."

The financial crisis in 2008 "had its origins precisely in overcomplex regulation," as historian Niall Ferguson and others have described. One government agency offered credit support for mortgages without requiring that the borrowers be creditworthy. Another agency guaranteed deposits in banks that were making bad loans. The profits of mortgage brokers and Wall Street underwriters were not tied to actual risks in their transactions. No one was taking responsibility to look at the big picture. Voilà! A worldwide recession was caused by incentive structures that were disconnected from basic principles of prudent lending.

The 9/11 Commission found numerous examples of intelligence that might have stopped the attacks that was not shared. In the summer of 2001, an FBI agent was hot on the trail of a suspected terrorist, Kalid al-Mihdhar, who was known to have entered the US in July 2001. The agent learned that another FBI agent had clues as to al-Mihdhar's whereabouts. But the FBI has rules against sharing "intelligence information" with agents in other departments and, after much back and forth, with advice from FBI lawyers, the FBI refused to share information about al-Mihdhar's movements with its own agent trying to track him down. (!) The agent searching for al-Mihdhar sent a blistering e-mail up the chain on August 29 warning that these rules were protecting only Osama bin Laden, not the American people, and that "someday someone will die." Two weeks later, Mihdhar piloted the plane that flew into the Pentagon, killing 125 people on the ground and 59 on the plane. "Everyone involved" in this incident, the 9/11 Commission concluded, "was confused about the rules governing sharing of information gathered in intelligence channels."

The sum of detailed regulation is far worse than any of its parts. None of the rules in the *Deepwater Horizon* story, or maybe even in the FBI, look idiotic in the abstract. Certainly no rule writer intended the safety rules to cause death, or confidentiality rules to shield terrorists. The regulation writers were trying to prevent harms that occurred to them when thinking of the many ways humans can mess things up. But their rules got in the way of real-life needs. The more complicated the regulatory vehicle, the sooner it will crash in real life.

Complexity and unknowable feedback explain why it's misguided to focus regulatory reform on pruning regulations that are "just plain dumb," as President Obama proposed in 2011. To be sure, there are many candidates for dumb rules—such as an environmental rule that treated a milk spill the same as an oil spill. But regulatory failure is not caused mainly by stupid rules, but by the cumulative complexity of a system based on "rationalized completeness."

American regulation is designed to fail. Circumstances are unique, but the rules are rigid. Over time, the failures mount, as the original logic progressively loses its connection to a social problem. The only "thing red tape is good for," Peter Drucker observed, is "to bundle up yesterday in neat packages."

Proposition 4: Compulsive distrust of human choice is anti-democratic.

Democracy is supposed to be a system that authorizes officials to use their judgment, not bars them from using it. The idea of a "republic" was grounded in the precept that elected representatives would serve the public by acting on their best judgment. Officials in the executive branch were to have a similar responsibility. As Madison put it:

> It is one of the most prominent features of the constitution, a principle that pervades the whole system, that there should be the highest possible degree of responsibility in all the Executive officers thereof; anything, therefore, which tends to lessen this responsibility is contrary to its spirit and intention.

Sitting in front of us, in plain view, is an assumption that guarantees the failure of the framer's vision for democracy: Officials no longer are allowed to act on their best judgment. Surrounded by public failure, you would think Americans might start to question this system.

Avoiding human choice in public decisions is not just a theory, as noted, but a kind of theology. It has become what we *believe* to be the proper way to organize public decisions, a core precept of our public philosophy. Human choice is considered too dangerous.

Here is the one place liberals and conservatives agree, lashed together by mutual distrust. The ship may be about to drift onto the shoals, but at least the other guy isn't at the helm. Liberals like detailed rules telling everyone what to do; the nursing home operator can't skimp on activities if the law mandates an activities coordinator who spends .09 hours per resident per day! Conservatives see red at the possibility of an official having any discretion; judges, for example, should only "apply law" in a mechanistic way. Business leaders and lobbyists pile on for legal precision. Just give us clear rules, they say, and we'll follow them.

Every choice can't be laid out in a rule, of course. Someone has to decide whether the bridge can be rebuilt. The teacher has to decide whether Johnny's misbehavior warrants sending him home. Here as well, all sorts of rituals have been devised to try to protect against human choice in government—participatory processes, forms for everything, evaluation by objective metrics, endless studies, a wide range of mandatory protocols, and legal hearings whenever someone doesn't like how these came out. The modern concept of "individual rights" is basically the power to challenge anyone with responsibility. Individual rights against what? Against decisions by people with responsibility.

Liberals and conservatives, made powerless by mutual agreement, close their eyes and pray before the altar of government purified from human choice. On this altar sits a vision of a giant legal machine that produces all public choices. Its instructions are often awkward, its language stilted, and its meaning difficult to discern. Sometimes compliance takes years, as with the Bayonne Bridge. Often the results are ridiculous: The children's lemonade stand is closed down. But at least, thanks to the Rule of Law, no official is free to use his judgment.

Columnist David Brooks was broadly lampooned in 2012 when he suggested that Americans no longer were willing to give people authority to make decisions. Commentators jumped all over Brooks for advocating "banal authoritarianism" and suggested, as a matter of accepted wisdom, that freedom is defined by protection against authority. Individual freedom, one critic explained, consisted of two components: "guarding against the corruption of power" and "preserving the right to do your own thing."

So . . . who approves the new bridge? The myopia of America's public philosophy is complete: We no longer see that our common good requires officials to actually make decisions. All the protections against individual judgment, diplomat George Kennan observed, mean that government cannot do its job: "The flight from the individual, the striving for the creation of machinery to replace individual insight and judgment, the labored diffusion of power . . . give to the governmental apparatus an inflexibility, an inertia, a sluggishness, and an incoherence."

America has succumbed to its own intermediate goal. Purging official discretion, not advancing the public good, has become the goal of the Rule of Law. Better to prevent a bad choice, even at the cost of banning all good choices.

Unquestioned assumptions are the most powerful forces in human affairs. If people assume something is right or wrong, they'll act on it even to the point of self-destruction. Just as the inhabitants of Easter Island built giant statues until there were no more resources to support life on the island, Americans seem content to pile society high with detailed regulations as long as they succeed in preventing anyone with responsibility from actually making a decision.

What's the solution? We must abandon our belief that human choice denigrates the Rule of Law. We must instead embrace human responsibility as the organizing principle of public choices. The protection against bad judgment is not mindless bureaucracy but good judgment—creating checks and balances that give other people oversight responsibility. America must rehumanize the structure of government.

The failure of modern government should not surprise anyone. Public choices require judgment and common sense, just like every other life activity. Real people, not rules, make things happen.

REGULATING BY PERSONAL RESPONSIBILITY

In 1988, following several parliamentary inquiries into nursing home abuses, Australia radically overhauled its regulation of nursing homes. It abandoned hundreds of input-oriented regulations (for example, requiring floor area of "at least 80 feet per resident") and replaced them with thirty-one outcome-oriented standards (such as providing a "homelike environment" and honoring residents' "privacy and dignity").

Australia also transformed nursing home enforcement, focusing on overall quality, not hard metrics or paperwork compliance. Instead of slapping nursing homes with fines whenever something was amiss, the regulators required meetings among all interested parties, including families, consumer advocates and nurses, to discuss how to improve things. The state preserved its authority to sanction or close nursing homes, but kept it in reserve.

This radical shift in approach was viewed with skepticism by regulatory experts, including Australian professors John and Valerie Braithwaite, who doubted that thirty-one subjective "motherhood statements" could possibly replace harder inputs that "could be checked with a ruler, a thermometer or by confirming a doctor's signature." "Rather embarrassed" by Australia's naïve approach, the Braithwaite team launched an international comparative study of nursing home regulation.

What they found was a transformation, for the better, of Australia's nursing homes. Quality had improved measurably. Disagreements occurred less frequently, and had been replaced instead by ongoing conversations about how to deal with problems and situations. Supposed weaknesses of broad standards—such as vagueness and opportunity for differences in view—turned out to be strengths: All constituents, including nursing home proprietors and elderly residents, felt empowered by principles that they could understand and discuss.

In the United States, by contrast, the Braithwaite team found that nursing homes were mired in a bureaucratic rut characterized by distrust and paperwork. Compliance with rules often replaced doing what was right: Sleeping residents were wheeled into activities so that a home could count them as "participating," even though sleeping residents degraded everyone else's enjoyment of the activity. In response to a regulation that required pictures on the wall, a common practice in Illinois was to tear pictures out of magazines and slap them onto walls with tape prior to inspections. Because compliance was largely evaluated by checking the paperwork, there was "a great deal of falsification of records."

The Australian approach is called regulating *by principles*, instead of by rules. Law sets forth general goals (create a "homelike environment") and principles (honor residents' "privacy and dignity"). Law also sets forth procedures for enforcement and resolution of disputes. Sometimes there are more detailed rules, but the focus of enforcement is on bringing the organization up to snuff, not sanctioning it for noncompliance.

Regulation by principles creates a starkly different way of making public choices. Instead of a legal instruction manual, public choices on what is sensible must be made by a person on the spot. "Rules dictate results, come what may," legal philosopher Ronald Dworkin explained. "Principles do not work that way. They incline a decision one way, though not conclusively."

Principles combine a centralized goal—say, a "homelike environment"—with decentralized implementation. To meet public goals, people must roll up their sleeves and use their best judgment.

Principles have many advantages over detailed rules in complex regulation, but the first is that regulation stays tied to its goals. Nursing homes can focus their energies on making a nice place to live for the elderly, not on paperwork compliance and immaterial bureaucratic conformity. Or, returning to the Bayonne Bridge, environmental review can provide facts and perspective to a decision maker who is politically accountable, not years of overturning every pebble, followed by years of litigation, for no valid public purpose.

A second advantage of principles-based law is that it restores the indispensable ingredient of democracy and, indeed, of all accomplishment: Human responsibility, not rote compliance, becomes the activating force of regulation. Someone is in charge of fulfilling the public goal.

Proposition 5: Regulating by principles revives human responsibility.

Regulating by principles releases all stakeholders from the bureaucratic labyrinth. People not only have room to make sense of daily choices, but the responsibility to do so. Instead of accountability by checking boxes—say, wheeling sleeping residents into useless activities—the proof is in the pudding. Is the nursing home (or factory, or school) meeting its regulatory goals?

This is not a radical idea for normal people. Find anything that works sensibly, and you will find real people who are focused on a goal and take responsibility to get there.

Good public schools are all run this way. In successful schools, studies show, teachers typically feel empowered to act on their best instincts by the person in charge: We "have a great deal of freedom," one teacher observed, because the principal "protects his faculty from the arbitrary regulations." What successful schools have in common, according to many studies, is a culture of focusing on the goal, and not on the rules.

Doing what's right almost always requires trade-offs in the particular situation. Nursing homes, for example, are constantly confronted with the tension between quality of life versus safety considerations. A resident may want a steak, but that increases the chance of choking. A resident may want the dignity (and exercise) of walking unassisted, but this increases the risk of falling. Physical restraints can prevent falling out of bed, but most elderly people consider them a form of imprisonment. No hard-and-fast rule can make these choices. The best approach depends on many factors, including how strongly the resident feels about it. Avoiding risk will often make residents miserable. With principles, caregivers at the nursing home can make trade-offs and customize solutions for the particular resident. Nursing homes organized around a compliance checklist, by contrast, were rated by researchers as among the worst.

Principles-based regulation also liberates the regulator to keep his eye on the public goals. Without too much difficulty, regulators can make a qualitative judgment about the adequacy of a nursing home, or school, or factory. They can certainly make this judgment more readily than they can check on a thousand requirements. Within minutes of walking into a school, education expert John Chubb told me, you have a good idea whether it has an effective culture for learning. More granular investigations and interviews can confirm those impressions or reveal lurking problems. Human judgment by an experienced professional will almost always be more effective than plodding through a facility with a thick compliance manual.

Giving officials responsibility to use their judgment is not particularly scary or remarkable. Many high-level important public choices—including decisions on monetary policy by the Federal Reserve Bank—are given to responsible individuals without much pretense of legal control.

Officials at the FAA unilaterally decide whether a new type of airplane meets the general standard that it be "airworthy." As Professor Paul Romer observes, there are no specific rules defining what constitutes "airworthiness"—no regulations on how many rivets per square foot, or tensile strength of wings, or the like. Would you like to fly on a plane that went into operation only because a manufacturer got a legal order that it complied with a book of rules? Or would you rather entrust that decision to the best judgment of experts at the FAA?

Child welfare is a notoriously difficult area of government oversight, with tensions between trying to protect children against erratic parents or dislocating them into an unfamiliar home. A rules-based system causes constant frustration, sometimes leading to tragedy—as when social workers in New York were unable to rescue a toddler from parents who were known substance abusers, because of a mandatory waiting period; the child was electrocuted when left in a dangerous situation without supervision. Overseeing child welfare using principles allows solutions to fit circumstances. Utah child welfare law, for example, allows social workers to take responsibility to customize judgments for the particular case, often in collaboration with family and their close friends. By allowing social workers "relatively broad discretion to apply the principles," social workers can act promptly and creatively.

Nothing in life works out as planned. That's why trial and error is the key to progress. Principles enable people to get the job done by adapting to the circumstances before them.

Responsibility energizes human creativity and goodwill. The spirit of America, justly admired and envied by other cultures, arises from the sense of personal ownership of life's choices. It is this ownership that empowers people to take risks, to innovate, to fail and to pick themselves up, to never give up, and to stand for what they think is right. This spirit is the main source of American exceptionalism. "Trust thyself," Emerson exhorted. "Every heart vibrates to that iron string."

Bureaucracy kills the human spirit. "A centralized administration," as Tocqueville observed, "is fit only to enervate." Discouragement is the inevitable result of a regime of rules telling people how to do things. "These are not the conditions on which the alliance of the human will is to be obtained; it must be free in its gait and responsible for its acts."

Giving people freedom to do things their own way, like rainfall on parched earth, will immediately prompt shoots of the human spirit to sprout forth. That's what happened in Australian nursing homes. People could focus on doing what's right. A study of good nursing homes in the US also found a sense of ownership by employees, with a blossoming of the human spirit manifested in daily interactions: "We listen to each other"; "we help each other out"; "we take turns"; "we are a part of the decision making"; "we care for each other"; "no one is too good to pitch in." The study found that "core leadership values . . . promoted strong lateral decision making as opposed to the traditional top-down . . . Staff were expected to solve problems at the level they occurred as opposed to bringing them up the chain of command."

Responsibility requires more than the trappings of public processes—say, mandatory public meetings and consultations. Choices must be *owned* by people trying to solve a problem. A study showed that active parental participation could significantly improve student learning, but "only if parents are given real decision-making responsibility and are placed in a position suited to their knowledge and skill. Where these elements aren't present, parents tend to become disillusioned and distrustful." Ownership of choices is also the key ingredient of civic culture: Citizens must "take pride in their common project and regard it as their own," philosopher Michael Sandel concludes.

Enthusiasm, the secret sauce of most successful human projects, requires people to think and do for themselves. It's contagious. In studying effective teachers, Professor Philip Jackson summed up the secret of one highly effective teacher this way: "The most important thing she communicates is that [she] likes being where she is and doing what she is doing."

Unleashing human energy requires a legal structure designed with ample room for humans to make a difference. This new framework will also be far simpler and more coherent.

Responsibility allows law to be radically simplified. Most regulatory detail is aimed not at setting public goals, but at dictating how to do things. Pull any rule book off the shelf, and chances are you'll find that most regulations are self-evident ("eggs shall be cooked"), or overbearing ("windowsill height shall not exceed three feet above the floor"), or readily incorporated into a general principle.

Volumes of regulations could be readily turned into pamphlets if humans had responsibility to meet broader principles. Many of OSHA's detailed rules, for example, are either superflu-

ous ("All traffic regulations shall be observed") or already incorporated within guidelines published by the American National
Standards Institute (ANSI). Hundreds of rules could be subsumed within one general principle: "Facilities and equipment
should be reasonably suited for the use intended, in accord with
industry standards."

By trying to dictate safe behavior through detailed rules,
OSHA "tries to do the impossible: create a risk-free universe,"
Peter Drucker observed, and "achieves next to nothing." Scrap-
ing away regulatory detail would permit regulators to focus on
actual safety, not rote compliance. Companies with the best
safety records, such as Alcoa, achieve dramatically better safety
with programs that focus on a culture of safety. In Alcoa's case,
success is a direct result of its "decentralized authority" and
delegating responsibility to employees on the floor. Safety in
nuclear submarines has been achieved by empowering each
sailor to take responsibility to question any unusual event, no
matter how trivial.

Simplified law opens the cognitive door, now blocked by
countless rules, to the deep store of unconscious instinct and
creativity that resides in each person. This enables people to
engage in what Polanyi described as the "usual process of unconscious trial and error by which we feel our way to success without specifically knowing how we do it."

The more complex the area of oversight, as *Black Swan* author
Nassim Taleb explains, the simpler and more flexible the regulatory framework must be: "The simpler the better."

*Redirecting our distrust: Mindless rules, not accountable officials, are
the enemy of freedom.* Distrust of human judgment keeps us cring-
ing in the legal shadows. But this fear stems more from our ide-

ology about human fallibility than a realistic prospect of tyrants taking over our lives. Other than a few ideologues on the fringes, people don't seem to mind, for example, that officials at the FAA or the Federal Reserve are making important decisions. We may disagree sometimes, but we know who they are, and where to find them.

Accountability all around is the linchpin of any successful organization. There's usually no need for rules telling people *how* to fulfill their responsibilities if they can be accountable when they fail. The nursing home is accountable to the inspector, who is accountable to a higher official and, potentially, to a court.

Accountability is not foolproof, however, and certainly can't guarantee fairness. But a system of rules is far more dangerous. It's accountable to no one.

We've been duped by modern ideology. Whom do you blame when you can't get a permit, or are required to act nonsensically? The people who write the rules are far away—both in distance and in time—from any problem on the ground. They may have long since retired. They probably can't even be identified. They're hidden within the giant legal machinery of government. What are your options—to travel to Washington and amend the regulations?

Principles, by contrast, allocate responsibility to identifiable people to make decisions that honor public law in your particular situation. They're not distant; they're right in front of you. They can be put under a spotlight and held accountable.

Dictating decisions in advance has undeniable appeal. That's what power is—controlling decisions by other people. What we haven't focused on is that an entire culture of people in Washington and state capitals are controlling us. A rules-based system centralizes decisions even as it rigidifies them.

Control is the main mission of all those distant rule writers. They don't trust a thing you do. Think for a second about the mind-set of regulators who detail each situation when a day care worker must wash her hands. Or helpfully instruct a trucker "to obey all traffic regulations." Or require review of historic buildings in an infrastructure project that will never touch any building. These regulators view their job as controlling the minutest details of how people do things. Over the past few decades, these unknown officials in federal, state, and local government have written millions of words of regulatory dictates, bossing you around for no good reason, and with countless idiotic effects.

Special interests are also control freaks, using law to force their views on others. As one child welfare advocate put it, "People who run child welfare systems cannot be left to their own devices. They will not use reasonable standards, they do have to be told, 'first, put your left foot in front of your right foot, then put your right foot in front of your left foot, then you do it again.'"

Business lobbyists are equally controlling. The ban in the Dodd-Frank law on proprietary trading by banks, known as the Volcker Rule, seems reasonable to stop banks from acting like casinos. But "proprietary trading" is difficult to define; often trading is needed to hedge risks, or to make markets for underwriting clients. Instead of giving officials some flexibility in overseeing this new directive, however, lobbyists have demanded that the regulations specify each nuance of "proprietary trading." As of this writing, the proposed regulatory structure is up to a thousand pages, and, as a banker quoted in the *Economist* described it, is "unintelligible any way you read it." Completely predictably, it will prove to be as rigid and porous as the tax code.

Crowded together under the bubble of Washington, these regulators and lobbyists spend their lives writing detailed dictates to control choices out in society. That's how they see their job. They write the rules, and decrees, and cast them onto society like a heavy net. Then they go back and write some more.

None of them have responsibility, unfortunately, for how these dictates actually function in real life. When things don't work out, the regulatory gurus are nowhere to be found. If located, they just say, "That's what the law requires. Are you against the Rule of Law?"

This is an arrogant way to regulate, far more oppressive to a free society than principles-based regulation that focuses on public goals, and far less accountable than human responsibility. It also embodies a misguided assumption that regulation, like criminal law, should be aimed at catching miscreants rather than supporting standards in a crowded society.

Proposition 6: Regulators should focus on results, not punishment.

Regulation has a bad name, for a good reason: It often requires things that make no sense, and then punishes people for not complying. Regulation by principles puts the focus where it should be, on public goals, and also on doing something more revolutionary: turn government's focus toward helping people improve, not punishing them. The point of regulation, we seem to have forgotten, is to make sure things work in a crowded society.

Crime and punishment is not the only approach to regulation. Government could take a gentler grip and try to *work with people* to make things better. This has many advantages, including enlisting the goodwill of industries that share the goal of not letting scofflaws get away with skirting their legitimate obligations. In the 1990s, for example, the head of the OSHA office in

Maine agreed to put aside sanctions for rule noncompliance for companies that would work with employees and OSHA to come up with practical safety plans. The result was a dramatic reduction in workplace hazards.

A forward-looking approach to regulation is encompassed within a movement known as "new governance"—described by Professors Grainne de Burca and Joanne Scott as regulation that is "less rigid, less prescriptive, less committed to uniform outcomes, and less hierarchical in nature." Key elements of new governance are engaging all participants in routine "regulatory conversations" about ways to improve, eschewing sanctions except when regulated entities are acting irresponsibly. Regulators aim for results, and no longer play a game of gotcha.

Australian nursing home regulation was an early prototype of "new governance," with a focus on improvements for the future rather than penalties for the past. The effect was a loop of continuous improvement. Exemplary nursing homes in Australia got even better when people in them were allowed to channel their energy toward improvement. Their success raised expectations, pulling mediocre homes toward better performance. Rigid regulation, by contrast, casts minimum standards in stone, promoting stagnant mediocrity.

Regulating softly only works, however, as long as government has a big stick. Otherwise some businesses will just go through the motions. The trick is for regulators to work *with* business, only escalating toward sanctions when it continues to lag behind responsible peers. By keeping government's authority in the back pocket as long as possible, and encouraging businesses to come up with their own solutions, the goal is to build trust in regulatory relationships to replace defensiveness and secrecy.

To varying degrees, other countries have shown the way. Japanese cars have led innovations in auto fuel efficiency because of a government approach that, in effect, rewards the innovator instead of setting minimum standards.

In Germany, regulatory law is generally less detailed than America's. The Bavarian rest-home statute, for example, includes twelve general principles, including a requirement of an "appropriate quality of attention, nursing care and sustenance," enabling "residents . . . to enjoy appropriate life opportunities," and "performance that is at the general level of the state-of-the-art." School regulations are also principles-based. A Bavarian statute requires that the principal "work together in trust" with teachers and parents. Instead of rigid "zero tolerance" rules, the regulations at one high school state simply that "dangerous objects may not be brought to school," leaving it to the principal to decide what's dangerous.

Britain decided to move to "principles-based regulation" of the financial industry in 2000. The governing agency, the Financial Services Authority, known as FSA, enforced principles such as "treat customers fairly" and "conduct its business with integrity." FSA oversight was generally thought effective, particularly for fostering more responsible conduct by banks to consumers. It also proved that regulation by principles is not foolproof; the UK regulators didn't avoid the mortgage debt crisis in 2008 any better than US regulators did.

The financial crisis prompted soul-searching in the UK regulatory community. Parliament decided to eliminate FSA and divide financial regulation among the Bank of England and several other agencies. The head of FSA during the crisis, Hector Sants, remorsefully concluded that "a principles-based approach does not work with people who have no principles." On further reflection, however, the new regulators concluded that Sants was wrong: The crisis demonstrated the need for more regulatory agility, not less. Bank of England economist Andrew Haldane, analyzing the regulatory failures, found that "too great focus on information gathered from the past may retard decision-making about the future," and called for a "rebalancing away from prescriptive rules" to provide "greater scope for supervisory judgement."

In short order, as the 1988 Australian nursing home overhaul proved, a regulatory culture can become constructive rather than cynical. Australian nursing homes also demonstrate how a decent regulatory culture can survive, at least for a while, without effective accountability. Nursing home accountability in Australia was weakened in 1997, when new conservative leadership in Australia modified oversight to allow the industry to oversee itself. Suddenly all nursing homes were practically perfect: The industry accrediting agency concluded that 99 percent of nursing homes satisfied the regulatory principles. Braithwaite and his colleagues were highly critical of this "capture" of regulation by the industry. Even with rubber-stamp enforcement, however, they found that the principles-based regulation still resulted in superior quality compared to US regulation: "We are still impressed by . . . how a captured regulatory regime can in a variety of ways still achieve a lot of good" by "institutionalizing systems that pursue continuous improvement."

Restoring human judgment to regulation doesn't mean humans will always, or even generally, succeed. The fate of human endeavor is not typically triumph, but various forms and degrees of failure. This is all the more reason why accountability is vital, and why officials must have the flexibility to adapt to new events. The solution to regulatory failure is regulatory agility, not more legal Maginot Lines.

Rethinking law's connection to freedom. Principles also can solve a deeper philosophical flaw with modern regulation: Law in a free society should not supplant free choice.

Law today does not define and protect your free choice. Law *is* your choice. Piling up detailed rules on top of detailed rules, like a giant legal mudslide, has buried both the framework of law and our freedoms.

A core misperception keeps this legal mudslide oozing into our daily lives. We fear that letting officials use their judgment will be like letting them into our homes to second-guess all our decisions. Principles and responsibility sound good in theory, but what's to stop the bureaucrat from demanding whatever he wants? We don't want to replace a system of rigid rules with its evil twin, a government autocrat. But a system of principles doesn't just change the identity and proximity of a decision maker. It also pulls law back from daily choices, so law is far less intrusive.

The Rule of Law is not supposed to impose a "right way" of doing most things. It should draw the outer boundaries defining unacceptable choice. As I will now discuss, in any proper conception of the Rule of Law, the jurisdiction of an official kicks in when your conduct departs from a zone of reasonable norms. Pushing officials back to guarding the sidelines, instead of bossing people around on the field of play, radically restricts the scope of official decisions. Having officials enforce outer legal boundaries is a far less frightening prospect than being told exactly how to do things.

THE FRAMEWORK OF LAW, PROPERLY UNDERSTOOD

Law is vital, many would say, to tell people how to do things properly. This is our first error. Law should prohibit actions that are improper. There's a difference.

Think of law as a giant corral. Antisocial behavior and arbitrary state power are outside the corral, and not allowed by law. Within the fences, however, people are free to pursue their goals in their way. This is how law defines and protects a free society. Law sets "frontiers, not artificially drawn," philosopher Isaiah Berlin explained, "within which men should be inviolable."

Law enhances everyone's freedom by enforcing boundaries against wrongful conduct (people can't pollute or breach contracts) and against arbitrary state power (the state cannot haul you into court unless you violate a law). This boundary-setting function of law, George Kennan observed, "is essentially a negative, rather than a positive, determination." Law generally tells you where you can't go, not where you can.

Law's character as a definer of boundaries has been lost to our age. Instead of defining the edges of wrongful conduct, protecting a broad zone of individual empowerment, modern law sees its role as telling people what to do and how to do it. Part of the confusion stems from the fact that law likes to be categorical, which did not pose problems with traditional legal prohibitions against, say, theft or fraud. But categorical proscriptions don't work well for modern regulation, which deals mainly with endeavors that we want to encourage, such as factories, nursing homes, and day care centers. It's hard to use legal prohibitions to oversee a caring nursing home, or a reasonably safe factory, or adequate environmental review.

Unable to use strict proscriptions, law started using strict *pre*scriptions—telling people exactly how to do things: Nursing homes must cook the eggs, and stairwells must have "natural or artificial illumination." The Rule of Law invaded the province of freedom and became Big Brother, dictating daily choices and interceding in life disagreements.

Mushing law into freedom spoiled both. Instead of feeling free, people became tentative and risk-averse. Spontaneity, the "most elementary manifestation of human freedom" according to Arendt, disappeared. Teachers lost control of the classroom. Public choices were paralyzed. Vital infrastructure projects stayed on the back burner, with no clear path to regulatory approval.

To do its job, law must be pulled back to its proper role—not dictating daily choices, but safeguarding against people transgressing outer limits. Reconceiving regulation as a backdrop of boundaries (generally, to enforce minimum standards) opens up broad possibilities for people to satisfy regulatory goals in their own way.

Praise the Lord! conservatives will shout. Let's get regulation as far away as possible from daily choices. Pull those laws back. Let people do things their own way. Oh . . . and be sure to make those legal boundaries crystal clear. We don't want any wiggle room for those officials to decide something we don't like.

Here is our second error: Law cannot preset correct choices for officials. Law can't think. Official responsibility also requires an open legal structure.

Proposition 7: Official authority requires an open area of choice defined by legal boundaries.

Law, like any life activity, requires human judgment in application. Just as freedom is defined and protected by legal boundaries, the official choices needed to maintain these legal boundaries are themselves bounded by law. Law is not a solid wall, but an organic structure of open cells, defining goals and jurisdictional authority for judges and officials, but leaving room for them to achieve public goals.

The orthodoxy of "clear law" assumes that legal boundaries will be like concrete stanchions at the edge of the highway. But life is too complex, with too many twists and turns. Each new variation requires a new guardrail placed at an oblique angle. Pretty soon concrete roadblocks are strewn all over life's activities, like the detour from hell. This is modern government.

To a free person going through life, the open texture of law is not generally visible. Law should look more like a stand of trees at the edge of the field of freedom—clearly visible and coherent, if not precise in an engineering sense. Get up close and you will see slight variations of how law is applied in different places and situations. Get even closer, and you will see countless cells of official responsibility, each throbbing with human judgment. The policeman has authority to act using his best judgment, within legal limits that are overseen by other police supervisors and ultimately by judges. The judge has authority to do justice pursuant to legal principles, overseen by appellate courts. The inspector has authority to evaluate the care of the nursing home, overseen by a higher official who evaluates the quality of the "regulatory conversation" with residents and managers, as well as overall quality. The teacher has authority to run the classroom, within limits, accountable to the principal, who is in turn accountable up the school hierarchy.

To the modern mind, letting officials take responsibility seems inconsistent with the Rule of Law. Allowing room for official judgment, we assume, is tantamount to handing over arbitrary power. One of the old saws of legal orthodoxy is that "anything that is not explicitly prohibited is permitted." *What if* the inspector is a mad tyrant? *What if* the bureaucrat refuses to move the application forward? But the ancient platitude about law is not accurate, and never has been. Law has always rested on principles like reasonableness and good faith.

Official choices are hemmed in by principles, interpreted by social norms. No official has "unfettered discretion" to do whatever he wants. Every official is hemmed in by legal goals and principles. Authority is a conditional power, rebuttable if the official acts outside the boundaries of his charge. The citizen must certainly pay attention to the official because a presumption of authority carries legal weight. But official responsibility is not license to act arbitrarily or unfairly. Legal philosopher Ronald Dworkin described the bounds of authority this way: "Discretion, like the hole in a doughnut, does not exist except as an area left open by a surrounding belt of restriction."

Principles have meaning, just as rules do. Instead of rigid commands, principles are tethered to community norms of reasonable interpretation. As Dworkin put it, "An official's discretion means not that he is free to decide without recourse to standards of sense and fairness."

Linking law to social norms is not an abdication of the Rule of Law, but its affirmation: "The first requirement of a sound body of law," Oliver Wendell Holmes Jr. observed, "is that it should correspond with the actual feelings and demands of the community." Community norms are the lifeblood of law, bringing the oxygen of accepted values to official choices. Only when law aligns with community norms of what's fair and reasonable do people feel free; only then can they interact without undue defensiveness, confident that law aligns with their reasonable beliefs.

Social acceptance of legal norms is also what makes law effective to restrain human abuse and excess. Law will deter officials from acting arbitrarily, for example, as long as its norms on legal authority and process remain core values of the culture.

But who oversees the reasonableness of an official's choice? Human judgment isn't confined to the official on the spot. In an open legal structure—principles applied by designated humans—the judgment of everyone involved surrounds every choice. Law provides a formal accountability hierarchy—from, say, an inspector to a supervisor to a judge. Public opinion independently provides accountability for decisions that seem blatantly unfair or inappropriate—whether from affected community leaders, industry and labor associations, or the media.

Bad choices can be readily overturned, just as referees overturn calls on instant replay. Principles provide "authoritative grounds" to reverse any bad decisions. But the basis for reversal is not rigid guidelines—those usually promote mindless rituals and compliance—but the judgment of others up the hierarchy that the decision "departs from the reason of law" (quoting philosopher Timothy Endicott). There's a natural process of balancing that occurs when decisions are judged against the standard of what's right and reasonable. Social norms achieve validity, as philosopher Jürgen Habermas observed, from the people supposed to be bound by them.

It is not hard to incorporate safeguards to avoid erratic decisions. A person with responsibility can be required to explain a decision, as a judge elucidates legal reasoning, to make sure it is "infused with the glow of principle," in the words of Justice Benjamin Cardozo. Choices can also be second-guessed. Important decisions—say, approving a new power line—can require approval from more than one senior official. But as soon as the wisdom of the public choice must be objectively demonstrated by a rule or hard fact, we're back in the maw of endless law—where any disgruntled citizen can throw a monkey wrench into public choices. Responsible officials must be able to choose without winning every argument thrown at them.

The radical shift here is that public choices, within a framework of principles, are now made on the basis of what responsible officials think is sensible and fair, not by rote compliance with rules or endless legal argument. The "principle becomes fully manifest . . . in the performing act itself," as Arendt puts it.

Conservatives worry that officials will run wild. But principles tied to reasonable norms are far better at preventing abuse of power than today's regulatory minefield. Principles give the citizen the opportunity to stand his ground and argue about what's reasonable. The government inspector can't get away with sanctioning nursing homes for immaterial foot faults, like imperfect paperwork. If an inspector demands impractical changes, the operator can seek relief from a higher official or judge.

Liberals have the opposite concern—that loosening the regulatory grip will motivate business to cut corners or otherwise shirk its regulatory obligations. Principles are superior here as well. The heartless nursing home will not get away with arguments that it kept its paperwork in order. Indeed, one of the paradoxes of precise regulation is that it can act as a safe harbor for bad conduct. "The more exact and detailed a rule, the more likely it is to open up loopholes," Judge Richard Posner explains, "to permit by implication conduct that the rule was intended to avoid."

Human judgment suffers all kinds of biases, including selfishness, a tendency to instant gratification, and flaws in reasoning, such as overweighting remote risks. The frailty of human judgment is why many people prefer a system of rules. But this logic exposes a cognitive bias toward thinking in extremes. Our choice is not between rigid rules or unbound discretion. Choices in a principles-based structure are hemmed in by the prevailing norms as judged by a multitude of people who are affected. There's a wisdom in crowds.

Norms are a powerful check on unreasonable behavior. People are never free to act arbitrarily, in almost any setting. Acting unfairly, or selfishly, will have undesirable consequences in relations with customers, coworkers, family and friends. A paradox of detailed law is that, by supplanting norms, it has made social dealings far less trustworthy.

Principles, unlike bureaucratic rules, activate norms. They have meaning for people. Humans can abide by precepts of fairness and public goals, as long as they can understand and internalize them. Humanizing public choices is also the mechanism by which accountability is made real. Public choices become transparent. The official decides; then someone else decides about the quality of his decisions. No longer can officials hide behind the screen of a "clear rule." The effective authority of any official choice will hinge on its fidelity to the public purpose.

Still, officials can assert positions that are overbearing and unreasonable. They can also be "captured" by industry and come to see their role as protecting regulated industries instead of the public. Getting to responsible choices sometimes requires a struggle. Unlike the paralyzed bureaucracy today, however, elections can provide new leaders to reverse course. The vitality of democracy is dramatically enhanced by an open framework of principles. Who we elect, and who they appoint, will matter again.

An open legal structure, with gray edges, discourages irresponsible behavior. An open system based on principles does not achieve legal certainty. No one will know how close to the edges they can go. The open-and-shut clarity that all utopians dream of is simply not possible in an open framework.

But precise law does not achieve legal certainty either, at least not in complex areas of regulation. Precise law obscures predictability under all the bureaucratic detail, and supplants both coherence and regulatory relevance, while bogging down people in legal provisions that matter to no one. Who cares if "windowsill height shall not exceed three feet above the floor for at least ½ of the total window area," as required by the Kansas code? Far more important is whether the room offers a "homelike environment," including reasonable light and air.

Instead of aspiring to perfect legal certainty, regulatory law should strive to *minimize uncertainty* while accomplishing public purposes. Principles are far superior to rules on both counts.

"Standards that capture lay intuitions about right behavior," Judge Richard Posner notes, "may produce greater legal certainty than a network of precise but technical, non-intuitive rules." People will agree on what's appropriate in a given situation far more consistently than on how to apply a precise rule. A study of juvenile justice in Britain, for example, found that, given broad discretion, professionals with starkly different ideological views nonetheless treated similar situations similarly. Studies of American judges and German bank regulators also found remarkable consistency. Predictability is enhanced, not eroded, by general principles tied to social norms. Aristotle makes precisely this point in cautioning against striving for rules with "more precision than the subject matter admits," and explains that officials can predictably enforce legal boundaries far better than they can write detailed language.

Let's take a vague principle, like the Australian directive that nursing homes should provide a "homelike environment." Nursing home operators can readily internalize the goal of a "homelike environment" without going through the day with their noses in rule books. They generally know what this means because they are part of a broader industry and community.

Does a "homelike environment" sound too wishy-washy? Regulators in Illinois thought so, telling Professor Braithwaite that "there are some things that the process cannot do reliably. So you don't do them. Examples are: 'Are the staff pleasant? Is the room tastefully decorated?'" Braithwaite's reaction was that "these kinds of goals are precisely those that people in companies are asked to fulfill all day long . . . The thought occurred to us," Braithwaite goes on, "that if the Hyatt Hotel group adopted the view that décor and staff pleasantness were matters for which it could not set reliable standards (and therefore should not bother with), it would soon be bankrupt."

Blurry legal edges, paradoxically, generally expand freedom in complex activities. The marginal uncertainty of blurry legal edges is far offset by the expanded freedom of citizens to do things in their own way. Straying toward the edges will put people at legal risk, which legal philosopher Jeremy Waldron sees as an advantage, not a disadvantage, of general principles: "The citizen needs to know what the law requires of him, but that is not necessarily the same as needing to know how far he can go before his behavior becomes an infraction . . . 'How much may I mislead a business partner before it counts as fraud?' A legal profession which poses these and similar questions as crucial for the ordinary citizen's understanding of the law is already in ethical difficulty."

Vagueness has virtues. Gray edges of legal principles have the benefit of driving people toward moderation, not opportunism.

When uncertainty exists only at the gray edges of a legal principle, people have a place to go safely in their productive activities; they can go to the middle. Staying within accepted norms
will offer a kind of safe harbor for operators. This enhances public goals. Nursing homes are *nice*, as happened in Australia, not
just the bare minimum. By contrast, precise rules that strive "to
cover every case," philosopher John Dewey concluded, encourage
"shrewd and enterprising men . . . to sail close to the wind, and
to trust to ingenious lawyers to find some rule under which they
can go scot free."

It is worth pausing on the distinction between soft legal
boundaries and no boundaries. Having no legal boundaries
generally undermines freedom—causing fear and prompting
people to tiptoe through the day looking over their shoulders.
By contrast, legal imprecision at the edges of a legal principle
can enhance freedom both because it allows people to use their
judgment, and because it causes most people to move toward a
safe zone in the mainstream of accepted norms. The resulting
flight to the middle introduces a trust that is usually found only
in homogeneous cultures. Instead of sailing close to the wind,
most people try to do what's right. People become less fearful.
Commerce in this and other areas accelerates when people feel
less at risk of being taken advantage of.

Here as well, principles are not a cure-all. Particularly where
there is uncertainty about reasonable norms, regulation can
profit from *rules that are guides but not mandatory*. This idea,
sometimes known as "guided discretion," provides citizens with
a snapshot of what is appropriate while still allowing judgment
on the spot. Waivable presumptions is how federal criminal sentencing guidelines now work, enabling the judge to deviate to
account for extenuating circumstances. Allowing case workers

to depart from rules was one of the successful innovations of the Utah child welfare agency. The best approach, for many areas of government oversight, is to invert the current legal structure—where the general principles are binding but the explanatory rules are generally not.

Rules, too, have their role. While command-and-control rules are generally counterproductive for activities that hinge on human interaction, there are many areas of society where detailed rules and protocols are still a vital component of an effective Rule of Law. Here are some principles about when rules should be used.

The role of rules in a framework of principles. Rules are important to establish common protocols—say, speed limits and tax rates. Baseline rules enhance freedom in the same way that the rules of a game allow people to spend all their energy playing the game, not bickering over, say, how many players a team can have. Straightforward rules, such as drinking age, or eligibility for a driver's license, are examples of precise rules that allow people to get on with life's activities.

Whether a rule or fixed procedure is useful is not a matter of ideology but of practicality. Utilitarian considerations include the efficiency of clear guidance versus the need for flexibility, as well as limitations on human time and understanding. Law professor Colin Diver, in an article entitled "The Optimal Precision of Administrative Rules," argued sensibly that a fixed age for retirement of commercial airplane pilots was an effective rule, despite its unfairness to some pilots, because it avoided difficult litigation over the conditioning and mental acuity of each pilot as he got older.

Rules that mandate formal processes are also useful when a

tiny mistake can lead to a huge disaster. Pilots are trained always to go down a checklist before taking off. Preflight checklists avoid tragedies like the famous 1935 crash of a new B-17 bomber when the test pilot forgot to unlock the flaps. By adapting the checklist protocol to surgery, doctors at Johns Hopkins cut the number of medical errors by 70 percent. Atul Gawande, in his book *The Checklist Manifesto*, provides many examples of how checklists can safeguard against tragic human error.

But checklists are not a substitute for human judgment. Too many checklists on trivial compliance—say, wastebaskets in bathrooms—diverts people from important goals, and can turn them into brain-dead automatons, as happened in the Three Mile Island nuclear accident. Bureaucracy is the world's largest and most counterproductive checklist.

Canadian management professor Brenda Zimmerman makes the distinction between activities that are *complicated*, such as surgery or sending a rocket to the moon, and those that are *complex*, such as raising a child or running a health care system. Complicated activities often require detailed organizational mechanisms, such as blueprints and checklists. Complex activities, by contrast, have "thousands of parts and players, all of whom must act in a fluid, unpredictable environment. To run a system that's complex . . . it takes a set of simple principles to guide and shape the system."

Most government oversight we have discussed involves *complex* activities, ranging from environmental review to nursing homes to worker safety. Even simple activities, such as overseeing soup kitchens and dragging a tree out of a creek, require a judgment weighing different considerations, which cannot be effectively reduced to a rule. Some activities are both complex and complicated, such as decisions involving engineering or legal guidelines striving for both uniformity (where rules are important) and fairness to the particular person (where judgment is required). These are situations where nonbinding rules can be useful.

The organizing principle of the Rule of Law in regulating complex human activities should be this: As paper covers rock, principles should generally cover rules. A legal structure that encourages human judgment is what law is supposed to be. A broad spectrum of affirmative public choices—from balancing the budget to approving new infrastructure to running a classroom to overseeing safe products—all require human judgment in context.

The Rule of Law is not supposed to be an alien institution, unrelated to human values and practical needs. It is supposed to be a framework within which humans can strive toward private and public goals. The opportunity presented by rehumanizing law is more than satisfying regulatory goals and the regularity of the Rule of Law. The opportunity is to reclaim the moral basis of American public culture.

ENDING BUREAUCRATIC AMORALITY

The ideology of bureaucracy is that it has no ideology. All that's required is objective compliance. Values are laid out in advance by legislators, and implementation is automatic. Judges and officials are instructed to do whatever it takes to avoid acting on their views of right and wrong: Morality is just a matter for private choices, not a touchstone of public choice. "To refrain from belief," as Polanyi put it, has become "an act of intellectual probity."

The goals of law are still meant to be moral—say, a safe workplace—but everything else is on moral autopilot. Law in this conception consists of fixed guardrails on the edges of freedom, and morality is left to a free market of individual choices within those objective legal boundaries. "Each citizen will rationally pursue his own interests," as Professor Donald Black summarizes the philosophy, "with the greatest legal good presumptively arising from the selfish enterprise."

This value-free philosophy of public action hasn't worked out. Among other flaws, it has spawned an open season for bad values. The corrosion of American public culture, described by observers on all sides, is impossible to ignore. Special interests grab at government as if it's a dead carcass. Law is seen as a tool for self-interest, not a beacon of fairness.

The first flaw with this philosophy of neutral morality is that neutrality is impossible. Almost every choice, at every level of responsibility, has moral implications: in the workplace, whether a worker does his fair share, and whether credit is given where due; in regulation, whether the state can respond reasonably to the immediate predicament, or whether it is imposing unnecessary costs; in democracy, whether legislators are setting priorities to meet current needs, or just keeping the faucet open for those already at the trough.

Daily dealings are permeated with moral choices. Professor Philip Jackson's study of how teachers run classrooms exposes the many ways teachers can be fair or unfair, kind or mean. The results of the study are contained in a book called *The Moral Life of Schools*. To maintain moral authority, teachers are constantly called upon to lean here and there to maintain moral balance. These choices are often both obvious and impossibly complex to explain. Disciplinary decisions require balancing the fairness to the student who is acting out, often for understandable reasons, against the need of all the other students for an orderly learning environment. Dealings with every student have moral implications. When a student is falling behind his classmates, how should a teacher respond? With discipline and rigor, or compassion and forgiveness? The choice is rife with moral implications, and entirely dependent on specific context.

The hope of value-free government was that specific legal language would guarantee a moral result. But the words of law cannot achieve fairness by themselves, any more than they can fill a hole, build a bridge, or teach a child. "Laws on paper are meaningless," legal historian Lawrence Friedman stated. "They have to be enforced or applied." Doing what's right is never formulaic. A person on the spot must have authority to decide. "The task of making a moral decision is that of doing the right thing in a particular situation—i.e., seeing what is right within the situation and grasping it," philosopher Hans-Georg Gadamer wrote, echoing Aristotle. "Moral knowledge can never be knowable in advance."

Allowing moral choice by officials conjures up nightmares about crazies taking over government. But the moral choices needed to put society back on an even keel are not mainly big legislative choices. What's missing are values in daily work: drawing on the official's sense of practicality, balance, and fairness. These are the values needed to approve the new Bayonne Bridge roadway without years of legal water torture, and to congratulate the seventh-grade girl for immediately rejecting the contraband pill, not to suspend her under "zero tolerance" rules.

Big organizations often have difficulty locating people who will take ultimate responsibility, which is why theologian Reinhold Niebuhr believed institutions are inherently less moral than individuals. The philosophy of neutral rules pushed society another giant step toward immorality by basically abandoning any pretense of moral responsibility. Just go by the book.

How we got into this moral mess is a story of good intentions gone wrong. As I will discuss shortly, the notion of moral neutrality rose to be a preeminent public value in the 1960s, as a reaction to abuses that seared our collective consciousness. We are right to fear bad values, having in mind racism, sexism, and other forms of unfairness and abuse. But trying to create a public culture without allowing judges and officials to make moral choices left behind a vacuum, with predictable results.

I understand the instinctive resistance to giving any official, many of whom are probably unwise, the responsibility to act morally. I feel it myself. Avoiding values seems like a prudent protection against some of the lunacies we see around us. What we haven't woken up to is that government, by steadfastly refusing to assert values of fairness and balance, is nurturing the extremist values we fear. The resulting harms are not manifested merely in public inefficiency. Value-free law is like acid corroding our culture.

Proposition 8: Public choices that avoid values soon embody bad values.

The abdication of moral choices has led to moral rot in society, manifested in three pervasive pathologies—encouraging selfish conduct, barring responsible conduct, and fostering a relativistic public culture.

First moral flaw—Bureaucracy empowers jerks. Morally neutral rules are designed to replace right and wrong. Within these rules there is no reason to hold back, no reason to be fair or reasonable. All that matters are the rules. This empowers people of a certain disposition to use the rules for self-aggrandizement. Pathologies are legitimized that would not be tolerated for a second in a morally healthy culture.

The moral character of choices in a nursing home, for example, is critical to its success in caring for elderly residents. The quality of care depends on *how* workers do their jobs. The burden falls mainly upon nurse's aides, usually women who are paid at or close to the minimum wage. As described by Timothy Diamond in his study of the daily life in nursing homes, the caring by nurse's aides involves "holding someone as they gasp for breath fearing it may be their last . . . laughing with them so as to keep them alive . . . helping them hold on to memories of the past."

In the late 1980s, to study "the world of nursing aides," sociologist Nancy Foner embedded herself as a volunteer for eight months in an "above average" nonprofit nursing home in the Bronx. The atmosphere on the floor where she worked was dominated by an aide, Gloria James, who was the clear favorite among the nurses in charge. She was brilliant at complying with the myriad bureaucratic requirements: All beds were made on time, toiletries were lined up neatly on a napkin, residents ate their meals at the appointed time and went to the bathroom regularly, and the paperwork was perfectly organized. From the standpoint of complying with bureaucracy, Ms. James was a model worker, exemplary even.

But Ms. James was also "mean and verbally abusive to the patients, truly frightening at times." She "yelled at residents in a terrifyingly angry voice: 'I tell you EAT,' she yelled at one woman in the dayroom. 'You don't want to eat, you can die for all I care' . . . And she turned to another woman: 'You're such a nasty pig. You hear me, drink.'" Another time, as a joke, she left an immobile resident in a chair, in an awkward and precarious position. Only the intervention of another aide prevented a possible fall. She then taunted the woman loudly while she combed her hair: "All you do is sleeping now. You a pain in the butt." Ms. James "humiliated and verbally abused patients out in the open: in front of nurses, administrators, doctors." Yet she consistently received the best evaluations. When the supervising nurses were away, they left Ms. James in charge.

Another nurse's aide, Ana Rivera, was concerned with the feelings of each resident. As Ms. James yelled at residents during lunch, "Ana quietly fed a frail and weak resident, cradling her with one arm and gently calling her 'Mama' as she coaxed her to eat." But Ana was constantly in trouble with the nurses, because doing what the residents wanted interfered with bureaucratic schedule. One resident could not move her arms but cared about her appearance, and Ana followed her requests in applying makeup. The head nurse ordered Ana to "cut back her attentions" in order to comply with rules that set strict deadlines for when patients had to be dressed and in the dayroom. In another incident, Ana was berated for using her break to take a resident down to the main dining room, as the resident wanted. Ana was also reprimanded for ordering a protective glove that would not be painful for a resident. Ana only procured the glove herself after trying for months, without response, to get permission from the nurses in charge. When the head nurse saw the new glove, she threw it away because Ana had not gone through proper channels.

Rules change human values. The supremacy of the organizational system trumps right and wrong, putting a cloak of legitimacy around people whose conduct is antisocial or even cruel. This is what Hannah Arendt called the "banality of evil" in her study of Adolf Eichmann. His defense for organizing the Holocaust was that he was just following orders. Arendt concluded that bureaucratic acquiescence was a great danger to a culture: "Most evil is done by people who never make up their minds to be good or evil."

Sociologist Robert K. Merton, writing in the 1930s, describes the "bureaucratic virtuoso who never forgets a single rule binding his action and hence is unable to assist many of his clients." These virtuosos easily lord over other officials who, out of "over-concern with strict adherence to regulations," accept a role of timidity. We all know these people. Every organization, public and private, has people who use rules as a tool for personal aggrandizement. Bureaucratic assholes are not a new phenomenon.

What is new, perhaps, is that these destructive values are increasingly embraced by the people in charge of these institutions. Professor Foner concluded that the administrators at Crescent Nursing Home "sincerely wanted workers to be understanding . . . —to treat patients . . . as they would their own mothers and fathers." But they were "intent on passing state inspections with flying colors," so the overriding value of the home was "in enforcing regulations." The result was a "model facility," in which regulatory criteria were met nearly perfectly, and residents were subjected to consistent cruelty.

Amorality is not an unfortunate side effect of modern bureaucracy, but embraced as an affirmative virtue. Professor Steven Kelman, in his study of federal procurement practices, described an official who proudly recounted that he had awarded a contract to a vendor solely on the basis of the objective criteria in the regulations—deliberately ignoring the fact that the vendor had performed terribly in prior contracts.

An amoral mind-set has now wafted into the broader culture. A plague of legal bullies has descended like locusts upon the land, using law to advance selfish goals. The Bayonne Bridge was on the verge of finally getting its approvals in 2012. Then environmental groups decided to push their weight around. "We will not hesitate to sue," said Amy Goldsmith of the New Jersey Environmental Federation. What is motivating these opponents, you might wonder? It turns out that a main ally of this "environmental federation" is the Teamsters Union, which for years has been putting pressure on the port of Newark to become a closed union shop. The teamsters aren't worried about more trucks driving through New Jersey; they'd like nothing more. They're just using legal power in environmental review laws for an ulterior purpose, knowing that nothing can get done while the lawsuit is pending.

Most participants accept this use of environmental review laws as a legal right, as if environmental laws were designed for extortion. Every day, at every level of society, people make antisocial demands based not on what's right, but on what they claim is allowed by legal rules. They get away with this behavior because no official has authority to draw the line on unreasonable claims. This is why claims in lawsuits have escalated beyond reason. The emblematic example was the lawyer in DC who sued his dry cleaner for $54 million for losing a pair of pants.

To support our freedom, the boundaries of law must support choices that are reasonable and fair. That requires judges and officials to assert those values, not abdicate their responsibility to people who use law for self-interest or self-aggrandizement.

Second moral flaw—Bureaucracy disempowers people from acting morally. Thomas Aquinas thought that people who do evil don't think of themselves as evil. What allows evil to persist, Aquinas believed, is the "lack of good" by other people. American culture is fraying not just because law empowers certain people to be jerks, but because the rest of us are disempowered from doing anything about it. People who want to act morally, like Joann Papageorgis or Ana Rivera, find themselves marginalized by law.

Bureaucracy offers a continuous narrative of public employees prevented from doing what's right. For example, an inspector in New York, after discovering that a nursing home was not providing the services that its paperwork represented, was reprimanded by her supervisor for going behind the paperwork to uncover the derelictions. Her job, he told her, was just to make sure the paperwork was in order.

Only in bureaucracy or horror movies do people get in trouble for compelling acts of kindness. In 2012 a St. Louis school cafeteria worker, Dianne Brame, was fired for giving food to a fourth-grader who had no money. She knew he had been on a free food program, but language barriers got in the way of his parents reapplying. "They look at that as stealing," said Mrs. Brame, whose husband had recently died, but "I thought it was just taking care of a kid."

Even matters of life and death are sometimes asked to yield to the rigid imperatives of a clear rule. In 2012, Florida lifeguard Tomas Lopez was fired for leaving his designated zone on the beach to rescue a drowning man just over the line. "On radio I heard Tommy saying 'I'm going for a rescue but it's out of our zone,'" said another lifeguard, who added that the "manager told him not to go and to call 911." Lopez said he couldn't just sit back, and was prepared to get fired, adding, "It wasn't too much of an upset, because I had my morals intact." After publicity about the incident, Lopez was offered his job back. He declined.

Incidents like these are the result of deliberate design, not just the bad values of the particular supervisors. Professor William Simon described how the welfare reforms after the 1960s ended up creating a heartless bureaucracy explicitly designed "to alienate the worker from the purposes of the norms she enforces." Instead of social workers overseeing the well-being of welfare recipients, the reformed welfare system was administered by clerks mechanically applying detailed eligibility rules. The evils of oppressive paternalism from the prior system had been real—for example, midnight raids to enforce "man-in-the-house" rules (which disqualified a mother from receiving welfare if an adult male was part of the household). But reforms aimed at creating more formulaic entitlements "came at the cost of other [evils] that were . . . their mirror images: indifference, impersonality, and irresponsibility."

In one case studied by Professor Simon, the benefits to a recent Cuban refugee were terminated because she had failed to procure a letter of enrollment from the school of one of her four children. She had enrollment letters for three of her children and, three times in the prior six months, had produced enrollment letters for all of her children. She could not secure the fourth letter as required by the rules because the school was closed in August. When it reopened, she got the letter and presented it to the welfare case worker, "who responded that it was too late: 'There is nothing I can do.'" In fact, as Professor Simon discovered after interviewing the case worker, she meant only that the applicant needed to go to another department, which would have immediately reinstated her.

Mindless bureaucratic cruelty is a recurring theme of observers of the modern state. The incident in the welfare office could have come out of "the Circumlocution Office" in *Little Dorrit* by Dickens, "it being one of the principles of the Circumlocution Office never, on any account whatever, to give a straightforward answer."

Iraqis who worked with the US military as translators and in other support jobs during the Iraq war faced death threats after the pullout of American troops. Congress had authorized special visas, but the immigration bureaucracy was professionally indifferent to their imminent peril. In one case, recounted by Kirk Johnson in his book *To Be a Friend Is Fatal*, a forklift operator for the army named Omar applied for asylum in June 2011, with official letters of recommendation from his American supervisors, including phone numbers, and other proof of his bona fides: "I need a speedy solution to my situation, which is filled with persistent threats. People want to kill me because I worked for the US Army. Please help me come to America." He received a form response in October, saying that his application could not be processed without a "valid email address for a supervisor or HR officer who can identify you and verify your employment." Then ensued another nine months of correspondence, if you call it that, in which each request by him—always unfailingly polite, even as death threats against him escalated—were answered by variations of nonresponsive form letters: "Dear sir/ma'am, we have checked your case and found that it's in processing pending verifying your employment." In total there were sixty pages of correspondence, with Omar politely sending proof of his employment, and nonresponsive form letters back. As Johnson put it, "It's like asking Siri to save your life . . . You're talking to a robot that seems incapable of learning, much less giving you a visa." Omar's number finally came up with the dissident Iraqi militia one year to the day after he applied for his visa. He was called from his apartment one evening and later found beheaded. By that point, although American immigration officials had obviously been reading his letters, and he apparently met the criteria for a special visa, there had been no hint of action, or even of a genuine response to his situation. Whoever was receiving the letters had obviously been trained, as Hannah Arendt found with Eichmann, never to think for themselves.

The higher up the hierarchy one goes, as I will discuss when addressing the failure of democracy, the more officials seem willing to overlook moral implications in pursuit of legal conformity. Professor Simon describes how, at one point, the federal agency in charge of welfare threatened Massachusetts with sanctions because of "paper errors"—the files of some 6 percent of recipients lacked a Social Security number. Instead of checking the recipients' names with the Social Security Administration, state officials decided to solve the problem by terminating relief for thousands of people "unless they provided [their Social Security numbers] promptly." In this parallel moral universe, what mattered was paperwork compliance, not the personal catastrophe of cutting off benefits to people who may have been entitled to them.

Third moral flaw—Avoiding public morality unleashes moral relativism. America is missing its keel of core values. That's why the culture is wildly bobbing back and forth. These are not mainly values of right versus left, but values of proportion and balance that arise in every classroom and government inspection. These are the values of the Golden Rule.

Aspiring to value-neutral government is hopeless, but there's a "moral force to immorality," Polanyi notes, because judges and officials feel virtuous for not being "judgmental." This "enables the modern mind, tortured by moral self-doubt, to indulge its moral passions in terms which also satisfy its passion for ruthless objectivity."

Fairness is the first casualty of this neutral ideal of public choices. If people can interpret law in a self-interested way, law takes on those selfish values. The moral vacuum is now filled with opportunists of every stripe—extremist loonies who dominate American politics, trial lawyers, public unions, special interests, self-aggrandizing billionaires, disruptive adolescents . . . the list is getting long.

The natural end of moral relativism is widespread alienation and self-destructive individualism. When right and wrong no longer matter, then it's every man for himself. Theologian Stanley Hauerwas describes the downward spiral this way:

> People feel their only public duty is to follow their own interests as far as possible . . . As a result we have found it increasingly necessary to substitute procedures and competition for the absence of public virtues. The bureaucracies in our lives are not simply the result of the complexities of an industrialized society, but a requirement of a social order individualistically organized.

Without the freedom to act on moral values, there is not even a vocabulary for public virtue. We are stuck, as Hauerwas concludes, with either "a totalitarian strategy from the left or an elitist strategy from the right." It's either a rigid rule or anything goes.

Let this be our motto: Just tell me the rules. In 2013, an elderly woman collapsed at an assisted living facility in Bakersfield, California, and a nurse called 911. The operator asked the nurse to try to revive the woman with CPR, but the nurse refused, saying it was against policy at that facility. "I understand if your boss is telling you, you can't do it, but . . . as a human being . . . is there anybody that's willing to help this lady and not let her die?" "Not at this time," the nurse replied. During the seven-minute sixteen-second call, the dispatcher continued to plead with the nurse: "Is there a gardener? Any staff, anyone who doesn't work for you? Anywhere? Can we flag someone down in the street to help this lady? Can we flag a stranger down? I bet a stranger would help her." By the time the ambulance arrived, the woman had died. The executive director of the facility defended the nurse on the basis that she had followed the rules: "In the event of a health emergency . . . our practice is to immediately call emergency medical personnel for assistance . . . That is the protocol we followed."

America is losing its soul. Instead of creating legal structures that support our values, Americans are abandoning our values in deference to the bureaucratic structures.

In 2011, firefighters stood on the beach in Alameda, California, and watched a suicidal man flailing in water 150 yards offshore. None made an effort to rescue him because the municipality, dealing with budget cutbacks, hadn't "recertified its firefighters in land-based water rescues." The firefighters were told there might be unspecified "legal liability" to unspecified parties for uncertified rescues. Out of concern for doing something "illegal," they watched for an hour until the man finally succumbed in the 60-degree water and drowned. A woman passing by on the beach swam out to rescue him, but too late, and ended up bringing in his body. The Alameda fire chief, asked the next day if he would have saved a drowning child, said, "Well, if I was off duty I would know what I would do, but I think you're asking me my on-duty response and I would have to stay within our policies and procedures because that's what's required by our department to do."

The firemen are not bad people. This is a bad public culture, because it looks to law instead of basic values. We no longer believe in our beliefs.

Government is not supposed to be a morality-free zone. The point of democracy is to put people in office who will assert good values, not who promise to avoid them. The structure for values is the same as already discussed: Law sets goals and boundary principles, leaving people to try to do what's right within that framework.

A healthy public culture must aspire to being fair and sensible. Only then will most citizens embrace again norms of fairness, balance, responsibility, shared sacrifice, and other considerations that, woven together, comprise the moral tapestry of a strong culture. Good legal structures promote social trust, and freedom, by encouraging broad conformity with responsible norms. "Given the billions of transactions people engage in each day," Amitai Etzioni notes, "a social order based on laws can be maintained without massive coercion only if most people, most of the time, abide, as a result of supportive social norms, by the social tenets imbedded in law . . . Above all, laws work best and are needed least when social norms are intrinsically followed."

Chief Justice Earl Warren observed that "law floats in a sea of ethics." That sea of ethics has suffered a kind of inversion with law. Instead of the oxygen of social norms breathing life into law, norms are smothered by too much law. We gasp for practicality whenever dealing with government because no one can breathe ethics into the situation.

By what moral standard should officials make public choices? Reasserting just two core principles would do much to restore trust in public choices. The first is always to ask: What is the right thing to do here? The second, to discourage self-seekers, is this principle:

Proposition 9: No act of government is morally valid unless it can be justified as being in the common interest.

The only purpose of government is to serve the common good. No selfish cause is a valid purpose. On this point most jurists and philosophers agree. Even helping the downtrodden must meet this standard: A safety net, like other acts of fairness, reduces social fear. Protecting individual rights ensures the freedom of everyone.

The touchstone of every public choice must be the public interest: How will this decision enhance society? Just asking the question goes a long way toward defanging the relentless selfishness of modern public life. If a decision or law can't be justified as being in the broader interests of our free society, it is morally invalid.

A point of disagreement is whether moral choices can be pre-set in advance. Philosopher John Rawls fabricated an imaginary world in which the morality of choices is determined without knowing where you stand in that world; right and wrong would be determined by people sitting behind "a veil of ignorance." Maybe as a mind game this is useful. But the assumption that morality can be determined in advance is not only false, but insidious. Pursuing moral goals—say, providing universal health care or other social services—does not achieve social trust if those goals are implemented in a way that is wasteful or heartless, or allows citizens to manipulate the system, or drives the country toward insolvency.

The fear of Rawls and others is that the public officials are not trustworthy. That's why they want moral choices preset. Aside from the abject failure of their approach, this view of the Rule of Law, as Professor Brian Tamanaha argues, is also profoundly anti-majoritarian. Handcuffing official choices eviscerates the main goal of democracy—our freedom to choose representatives empowered to act on their values for the common good.

Red warning lights start blinking in our brains at the notion that some official—a fallible human—will have leeway to decide the right thing to do. But you don't have a choice. The policy choice here is not whether to embrace moral neutrality. That's an impossibility. *The choice here is to decide whose values you least distrust:* either the values of people using law for selfish ends— like local groups blocking an infrastructure project or a nurse's aide on a power trip—or the values of judges and officials with responsibility to make fair choices for the common good.

Distrust of officials can never be solved, only ameliorated. The best approach is to provide oversight that will create the conditions of trustworthiness—such as transparency, accountability, and checks and balances by other officials. No structure has ever been devised to preclude in advance a bad person from acting badly. An accountability structure will nonetheless engender public trust, to varying degrees, if people believe that it will generally dissuade rational people from acting badly.

How this works in practice is no mystery. Until a few decades ago, making choices of right and wrong was an explicit part of any official's job. Today, despite the dictates of bureaucracy, successful schools and departments are led by people, such as Joann Papageorgis, who view their job as doing what's right.

Most daily choices are easy, not hard, at least when circumstances are presented. People seem to know a right answer when they see it, often without being able to articulate the reason. Even when disputes have metastasized into litigation, judges "frequently see well enough how to decide on a given state of facts," Holmes noted, without being clear as to the legal logic.

It's been so long since officials have tried to access their sense of right and wrong that some may not know where to start. Venturing into the daylight may be blinding. But there are two practical handles to grab onto for moral choices: First, resuscitate the role of professional values, and second, when possible, push public choices down to people on the ground. Making moral choices in the concrete situation will prove far less treacherous than today's effort to legislate morality across life's infinite diversity.

Reclaiming professional responsibility. Providing social services, Professor William Simon concluded after studying child abuse and other difficult social problems, is best done by decentralized administration, managed with the values of professionalism: Instead of rote compliance with rules, professionals need to "see themselves as autonomous, responsible participants in the implementation of a public program designed to alleviate individual need."

Reviving professional values holds enormous promise for the moral credibility of public choices. The idea of a professional is someone trained to apply (to "profess") values in that area of endeavor. Regularizing values for the common good is why professions exist—so that engineers and accountants adhere to the same standards, lawyers pledge to comply with law, doctors take the Hippocratic oath, social workers adhere to codes of ethics, and public servants promise to serve the common good. Professions aren't what they used to be, but that's because they, too, have been degraded by legal orthodoxy into being self-interested guilds, advancing selfish agendas at the expense of their founding values. Most professional societies have all but given up enforcing subjective standards.

Vestigial professional values have remarkable staying power, however. Most individual professionals seem to want to do what's right. Studies repeatedly show that, given a responsibility to meet a legal goal, professionals do a remarkably consistent job. That's one reason principles-based law is more predictable than a system of detailed rules. Herbert Kaufman's classic study of forest rangers shows how professional values led to a coherent policy despite the virtual autonomy of 792 forest rangers across the country.

Professionalism can even trump politics. When a senior aide to President George W. Bush, economist Douglas Holtz-Eakin, was appointed to run the Congressional Budget Office, he wrote a report concluding that the President's proposed budget would not, in fact, stimulate the economy or increase tax revenues, and would also favor the wealthy. When asked how he could turn on his political patron, Holtz-Eakin pointed to the importance of professionalism: "The only shield one has in a job like this is your professional credibility."

Professional values do not replace legal boundaries, but they give meaning to boundaries and impose a responsibility to adhere in good faith to those bounding principles. Nor are professions a cure-all; they, too, require reality checks to prevent expertise from going to their heads. But professional judgment is vastly superior to rigid rules. Giving responsibility to public professionals, accountable to each other and the public, is an essential element of effective regulation, and far superior to lobotomizing people with mind-numbing rules.

Pushing public choices down to the ground. Restoring morality to public choices also requires giving more authority to people on the ground. Teachers should be encouraged to "pursue the unique potential of children," Michael Lipsky observes in *Street-Level Bureaucracy*, not fit them all into the same bureaucratic mold. Many social challenges can be addressed only with the active participation of the people actually involved. Reducing bullying in schools, for example, works best when the students and their families are involved in the solution.

The idea of pushing responsibility down to the lowest practical level is known as "subsidiarity." Subsidiarity originated as a religious principle because it empowers people, à la Aristotle, to make moral choices that reflect the needs of the particular situation. It is now a core tenet of the European Union, David Cameron's "Big Society" initiative in the UK, and the communitarian movement. Its underlying premise is to reconnect citizens to the public life of society.

Government should look citizens in the eye and respond to their situation—"*at least to be open to the possibility* that each client presents special circumstances and opportunities that may require fresh thinking and flexible action," as Lipsky suggests. This doesn't mean government can solve their problem. Often all an official can do is explain why the law doesn't permit a solution. People are usually satisfied with government, studies show, when their point of view has at least been considered. Conversely, frustration boils over when they are required to act stupidly for no reason other than that the rule requires it.

In most social services and regulatory oversight, there must be room for the question "Is this right or is this wrong?" Eligibility criteria can be completely objective at, say, the Department of Motor Vehicles, but the moral stature of most public choices requires the possibility of give-and-take between citizen and official.

The overt paternalism of the welfare system prior to the 1970s, much maligned by critics, was often beneficial, Professor Simon concluded. A case worker dealt directly with the recipient and could respond to unique needs—for example, increasing benefits to a diabetic who had extra food expenses. Contrary to common perception, the case worker did not have arbitrary powers. Any adjustments from standard criteria were typically reviewed by a supervisor "with extensive knowledge of the worker, the case, and the immediate context of the decision." A tragedy of the 1960s reforms, he observed, was that an entire class of professional social workers was effectively discarded, replaced by clerks.

I asked the head of the Children's Aid Society in New York City, Richard Buery, what change in government policy would foster better social services. "Just give us responsibility for helping a designated population—whether organized by neighborhood or by specific families. Give us sufficient resources, the discretion to work with them based on their needs and our expertise, and hold us accountable for results. To help people, we need to build relationships over time. We need to be there for them, whatever their problems. We need to be able to act on the knowledge we have gained as professionals. They need to trust us. Balkanizing social services into separate categories of providing meals or supplemental education or the like doesn't allow us to build relationships. Government should evaluate us by the improvement in our population, not whether we complied with the bureaucratic metrics of providing so many meals or instructional programs."

Subsidiarity should be a core value for reorganizing modern government. Pushing public choices down to the community has many virtues, including fostering citizen self-respect and understanding common interests. Local authority also has the virtue of bringing accountability down to the place where people can judge whether it has been faithfully executed. Probably the most effective check on "unrestrained authority," Professors Philippe Nonet and Philip Selznick conclude, is the "moderating effect of community involvement."

Stabilizing qualities of a moral keel. Conventional wisdom is that moral choices must be avoided because Americans are diverse and no longer share common values. Indeed, public choices will often be disputed—potentially, whenever someone doesn't get what he wants. But officials must have authority to make moral decisions, philosopher Isaiah Berlin observed, *because* people inevitably disagree. Otherwise arguments can go on forever.

Authority has a gravitational pull. Having a decision maker with responsibility to decide what's fair radically changes human behavior, bringing disparate values closer together. In a relativistic legal culture, people let their imaginations run wild with selfish rationalizations. When an official can make moral choices, by contrast, people must compete on what is fair and reasonable. Arguments must be framed in broader moral terms, including the effects on others and society as a whole. Polarization is replaced by reasoned argument: "Why is this approach good public policy?" The volume goes down. The effective tactic is to appear balanced, not to pound your chest and bellow about your rights.

Think of any group activity in your life that works well—

whether at the office, church, or Little League. In each one there will be people who do what's right and sensible in the circumstances. Their record is probably not perfect, since they're human, but they achieve credibility not only by their skill, but by their dedication to joint goals, and by the appropriate way in which they deal with others. The complexity of these types of moral traits can never be legislated, but is the glue holding together any healthy enterprise and society.

Day to day, moral choices are essential to fair law, effective government, and social trust. Government has legal power without asserting moral values, but power without morality promotes cynicism instead of allegiance, selfishness instead of the common good. A healthy society requires people to believe that public choices will be fair and reasonable, for the good of all. That's why the only effective authority is moral authority.

HISTORY OF HUMAN CHOICE IN AMERICAN LAW

The role of human choice in law has rarely been put under a light. Law is a tool to temper human excesses, so perhaps it's understandable that law doesn't like to highlight that it, too, is a human institution.

There's always been a myth that law is somehow better than mere mortals. Judges, as keepers of the legal flame, have often pretended that they are oracles of natural law—that judges "do not make law but only 'discover law.'" Looking back on those pious pronouncements, we can smile at their naïveté as we do at young children believing in Santa Claus.

We have our own myth about legal purity, however. Ours is

that precise law obviates the need for human choice. We assume that "clear law" has the capacity to purge human discretion. Like squeezing a balloon, however, legal detail just forces discretion somewhere else, often less trustworthy—starting with the arrogant dictates of the rule writers themselves.

The infatuation with specific legal rules has gone up and down in American legal history, like an oscillating sine curve. What is new in our time is not a tension between official discretion and legal controls over that discretion. What is new is a governing philosophy that strives to supplant official discretion altogether.

Current Rule of Law orthodoxy represents a clear departure from America's constitutional traditions. Our founders would be surprised indeed to see a system of government where legal detail now dictates public choices.

Constitutional debates over legal specificity. The capacity of written law to prescribe right conduct was one of the central debates over ratification of the Constitution. The two sides, known in history as the federalists and the anti-federalists, argued whether precise legal language could restrain the new national government from usurping state powers.

Anti-federalists feared that the language of the Constitution was too open-ended. Their position was perhaps best summarized by a saloon keeper who said that the Constitution "was made like a fiddle, with but a few strings, so that those in power might play any tune upon it they pleased." The leading anti-federalist spokesman, who wrote as "Brutus" (probably Robert Yates of New York), argued against general principles using worst-case scenarios: "The clause which vests the power to pass all laws which are proper and necessary . . . leaves the legislature at liberty to do every thing," including to "abolish all inferior governments."

Responding, James Madison in *Federalist* No. 41 wrote that instead of focusing "on the possible abuses which must be incident to every power or trust," the opponents should consider "how far these powers were necessary means of attaining a necessary end." Ultimately, Madison argued, some federal official must have authority to make decisions for the common good, even if that involves a risk of abuse: "The point first to be decided is whether such a power be necessary to the public good; . . . the next will be . . . to guard as effectually as possible against a perversion of the power to the public detriment."

The capacity of language to draw clear legal lines was also part of the debate. The anti-federalists wanted constitutional language that was "clear and exact," historian John Howe describes, "so that it could effectively control official power and preserve republican liberty." Precision was their goal: "The line cannot be drawn with too much precision and accuracy," anti-federalist John Dewitt declared. They were appalled by the "studied ambiguity of expression" of the Constitution. One critic doubted whether "there existed a social compact on the face of the earth so vague and indefinite."

But the "unavoidable inaccuracy" of all language, Madison explained in rebuttal, made the dream of carefully delineated powers an elusive and counterproductive goal: There is "no language so copious as to supply words and phrases for every complex idea, or so correct as not to include many, equivocally denoting different ideas."

The debate got resolved not by precise language but by broad limiting principles of the Bill of Rights. Maryland anti-federalist John Francis Mercer was one of those who eventually came around to thinking that people, not words, would make the difference:

It is a great mistake to suppose that the paper we are to propose will govern the U. States. It is The Men whom it will bring into the Govern't and interest in maintaining it that is to govern them. The paper will only mark out the mode & the form. Men are the substance and must do the business.

The fall and rise of judicial discretion. Legal specificity was also debated during the eighteenth and nineteenth centuries—first as a legislative tool to limit judicial discretion, and then as a judicial reason to constrain legislatures.

Just before the American Revolution, colonial leaders started writing detailed statutes, as historian Gordon Wood describes it, to try to limit "the much resented judicial discretion by royal courts." Their theory of controlling judges sounds familiar: "The new state legislatures [would] write down the laws in black and white . . . turn[ing] the judge into what Jefferson hoped would be 'a mere machine.'"

This enthusiasm for detailed codes soon faded, when everyone then got tangled up in statutory complexity. Every "attempt by Virginians to systemize and clarify their laws," Wood observes, was "'the parent of new perplexities.'" Instead of eliminating official favoritism, detailed statutes became a vehicle for it. Connecticut clergyman Moses Mather in 1781 complained that "when particular statutes had to be enacted for every circumstance . . . the laws proliferated and led to a confusion that wicked men could exploit for their private advantage." Nor did the statutory dictates constrain the judiciary: "Judicial discretion, far from diminishing, became more prevalent than it had been before the Revolution, as judges tried to bring some order out of the legal chaos."

By the end of the eighteenth century, the needle had started to move back toward simpler laws applied by judges: "All the legislatures really should do is enact a few plain general rules of equity and leave their interpretation to the courts," Mather concluded. "Much will depend upon the wisdom and integrity of the judge."

For much of the nineteenth century, judicial authority was preeminent in the legal pecking order. The legal philosophy of laissez-faire was based on judicial skepticism of legislative dictates. To a certain extent this skepticism was based in the impracticality of trying to dictate choices in advance. New York Chancellor James Kent, author of the most influential American legal commentaries, stated that "the great objection to all kinds of codification, when it runs into detail, is that the rules are not malleable, they cannot accommodate to circumstances, they are imperative."

But the Wild West perception of laissez-faire is probably overblown. Legislatures were passing all kinds of laws, many at the urging of business interests wanting to erect barriers to entry to potential competitors, such as this 1838 Michigan statute dictating barrel quality: "All barrels in which beef or pork shall be packed . . . shall measure seventeen and a half inches between the chimes, and be twenty-nine inches long, and hooped with twelve good hickory, white oak, or other substantial hoops."

Laissez-faire reflected a bias toward business, cloaked in a philosophy that legislatures in a free society lacked the authority to tell people how to do things. Invoking the freedom to enter into contracts, the Supreme Court declared unconstitutional statutes that interfered with the "freedom" of children to work seventy hours a week in cotton mills.

Where judges got the authority to overturn legislative judgments was a little murky. No one wanted to admit that the higher legal principles invoked by the judiciary just reflected cultural norms of a nation enthralled by the industrial revolution.

Public choices in the new administrative state. The discretion of public officials arose as a central legal debate in the early twentieth century when the progressives finally deposed laissez-faire.

With the Progressive Era, legislatures emerged from the shadow of the courts and started enacting regulatory laws aimed at rapacious industrial practices. The new social legislation generally set forth broad principles, not detailed dictates. A 1911 Wisconsin law on working conditions, for example, mandated that employers "furnish employment which shall be safe" and "furnish and use safety devices and safeguards . . . reasonably adequate to render such . . . place of employment safe." Section 2 of the Sherman Antitrust Act, which prohibits monopolization, is five lines long in its entirety.

Progressive reformers saw clearly the need for official discretion, and did not fear it. Roscoe Pound, a prominent law professor and future dean of Harvard Law School, decried "mechanical jurisprudence" and called for individualized judgments by regulators in the executive branch. What was needed, Pound said, was for executive officials and commissions to function as "traffic officers . . . to tell us when to cross."

The old guard saw red. Law was only law if it represented truth and certainty. It was bad enough that judges were no longer oracles of ultimate values. It was an invitation to tyranny to let officials of the executive branch regulate private parties. The only safeguard, Professor Ernst Freund argued, was detailed law: "No discretion as to scope of action or choice of means can be

allowed to subordinate officers . . . The legislature must . . . regulate the exercise of official powers in every particular . . . because
the officer has no one to look to for instruction and guidance
except the letter of the statute."

Freund pointed to abuses, such as a statute in New York that
allowed officials to give liquor permits based on "good moral
character"—often, to friends and campaign supporters. He
wanted more laws like the 1896 Raines law, which cured that
abuse by eliminating the authority of local excise boards. Freund
had allies among a wide group of legal scholars who were worried about "faithless administrators" and "the headless fourth
branch of government."

But the tide was against them. Government action was
needed. Northwestern Law School dean John Henry Wigmore
said Freund had it backward: "The bestowal of administrative discretion, as contrasted with the limitation of power by
a meticulous chain-work of inflexible detailed rules, is the best
hope for government efficiency."

Official discretion was the operating precept of the New
Deal. Harvard professor and future Supreme Court justice Felix
Frankfurter, in a series of lectures published as *The Public and
Its Government*, acknowledged that administrative discretion
"opened the doors to arbitrariness," but argued that the remedy
was professionalism and accountability. James Landis, an important New Dealer, was a cheerleader of administrative flexibility:
Instead of "a legalistic approach that reads a governing statute
with the hope of finding limitations upon authority," he advo-
cated "grants of power with which to act decisively . . . Modern
regulation required . . . the 'practical judgment' of 'men bred to
the facts.'"

The 1937 Brownlow report on government organization

underscored the individual nature of public accomplishment: "Government is a human institution . . . It is human throughout; it rests not only on formal arrangement, skill, and numbers, but even more on attitudes, enthusiasms, and loyalty . . . It is certainly not a machine . . . What we want is not a streamlined, chromium-trimmed government that looks well in the advertisement, but one that will actually deliver the goods in practice."

The old guard kept pushing back. What the traditionalists wanted was not legal detail, however. No one was advocating thousand-page statutes, and agency rule making hadn't even been invented. What the traditionalists wanted was more judicial control of administrative choices.

All these debates got put on the back burner during World War II. Facing the pressures of a world war, executive power operated like the New Deal on steroids.

Postwar: Bureaucratizing government decisions. After World War II, the debate over administrative discretion revived in calmer language. Former New Dealers no longer felt the imperative of crisis to go to battle to preserve official authority. Traditionalists realized that judges would never have enough bandwidth to oversee countless regulatory choices. Surely there was some way of ensuring Rule of Law regularity in public choices.

Congress went back to the drawing board and, in 1946, passed the Administrative Procedure Act. The APA, as it is known, basically squeezes into regulatory agencies all three branches of government—not only executive powers, but the power to make law by writing binding regulations and the power to adjudicate disputes with their own administrative law judges. Federal courts were still available to review executive decisions, but only after people had "exhausted administrative remedies."

The new processes proved to be exhausting indeed. Instead of asserting their authority, government officials did the opposite; they found refuge from responsibility in the endless legal argument. James Landis, in his 1960 report to JFK, noted that officials were bogged down in "procedures ill-adapted for the performance" of their functions.

Special interests soon learned that the new procedures were almost perfectly designed to preserve the status quo. Paralyzing government was easy; just ask for another hearing, and file another brief. "Nothing is impossible," as one official described Washington, "until it is sent to a committee."

In little more than a decade, the New Deal culture of executive decisiveness had evolved into bureaucratic bloat. "The tendency today is to achieve administrative arrangements geared completely to the workings of mediocrity," George Kennan observed in 1959, "arrangements which, as the saying goes, 'the least talented can operate, and the most intelligent cannot disturb.'"

But no one much cared. There was no crisis to solve. Most of society was happily focused on the good life. A storm was gathering, however.

The 1960s: Ceding public authority to individual rights. The storm violently burst in the 1960s. Civil rights, polluted rivers, Viet Nam, unsafe cars, sexist mores, disabled children locked away . . . all poured down onto the American parade. Loud thunder from assassinations, race riots, and antiwar demonstrations terrified a nation that, until recently, had aspired to cars with fins and ranch houses. Everyone sought shelter. One place they fled to was law.

Law completely rebuilt itself. It changed its goals, many long overdue—such as civil rights laws and environmental laws. Social norms changed for the better.

A country that took pride in its fairness now faced up to its complicity. Just as the progressives gave the lie to laissez-faire, so too the 1960s reformers punctured the illusion that America was fair.

Law did more than adopt new values. Americans never wanted to go through this again. How could we guarantee that future officials would never make unfair choices? Yale professor Charles Reich had an answer: make government decisions the "new property" of people who were affected. In a decade drowning in distrust, the Supreme Court grabbed onto this theory of "new property" like a life preserver. The constitutional protection of due process—putting government to the proof before it can take away someone's "life, liberty, or property"—now applied to almost every government action, even a decision to remove a disruptive student from a classroom.

Officials were put in the penalty box. No official could decide anything without proving why it was fair to whoever complained. This "new property" extended beyond acts of governing to basic management choices, such as personnel decisions. Any aggrieved employee could sue if he lost his job, or even if he didn't get a promotion.

The New Deal's governing philosophy was turned on its head. Governing was too important to be left to officials. Make everything a matter of legal proof. If someone didn't like the government decision—say, where the highway was planned—just bring a lawsuit and make government prove its case. "Sixties civics celebrates voicing but not listening," Hugh Heclo describes. "It carries a righteous insistence on opening the public square for all the previously excluded to be heard, without a serious effort to really hear and weigh other views. By its nature, it is an inclusiveness that divides."

Initially it appeared that judges, as in the age of laissez-faire, were again simply asserting supremacy over the executive branch. The radical expansion of due process gave judges enormous authority, a modernized version of the conception of judges as ultimate arbiters of government choices. Now, however, instead of drawing lines on the permissible boundaries of government regulation, judges started making administrative choices themselves—whether to build a highway, provide public benefits, or fire an employee.

It was like laissez-faire in reverse. Government started being run by courts. Some judges, given broad powers to second-guess government decisions, went overboard and made legislative judgments—for example, taking over the school system in Kansas City and ordering several billion dollars to be spent on new facilities and teachers. In Boston, Judge Arthur Garrity ordered busing of students to schools miles away from their homes. Children who lived on the same block often went to different schools.

The backlash was severe: "Judicial activism" became an epithet for judges who transcended the boundaries of their proper responsibility. After a brief reign as substitute legislatures, judges were also felled by the plague of distrust. Just as officials could no longer assert values needed to make public choices, judges felt they should just be referees overseeing a neutral contest, and should never assert values of right and wrong. "Choosing among values is much too important a business for judges to do the choosing," federal judge Charles Wyzanski announced.

If officials and judges were distrusted, corporations were presumed guilty. Corporate irresponsibility was impossible to avoid: rivers so polluted that they caught on fire, and cars so misengineered that they rolled over on normal turns. GM sent corporate goons to trail Ralph Nader, further proof that no business could be trusted. Not only did we need regulatory oversight to guard against pollution and unsafe conditions, but we needed to put business in the blocks to make sure it didn't squirm out of its obligations. But how could business be regulated when we didn't trust the regulators?

For half a century, legal scholars had debated whether judges or the executive branch should have the upper hand. Now they had a new idea: No one would make choices.

A new school of legal philosophy, called the "legal process movement," taught that right and wrong should be replaced by a chance for everyone to make an argument. Public choices, the theory went, could be proved by objective evidence in a court that had been purged of values. This posed a practical challenge: There's rarely objective evidence to decide whether a teacher is any good, or a nursing home is suitable. How could officials justify correctness of public decisions?

Detailed rules provided the answer. The APA had specifically authorized agencies to write regulations with the force of law. Why not use regulations to replace decisions by officials? A leading expert, Professor Kenneth Davis, concluded that "administrative rulemaking is in my opinion one of the greatest inventions of modern government."

Rule making took off like a rocket. Between 1969 and 1979 the *Federal Register* nearly quadrupled in length, expanding not just the scope of regulation, but the granularity of its mandates. Forest rangers used to have guidelines in a pocket pamphlet. Now they had volumes of rules. The purpose of regulation was not to confine executive discretion but to eliminate it altogether. Legal detail replaced public choice. Law would tell you not only what to do, but how to do it. The rhetoric of both liberals and conservatives "converged on the term 'discretion,'" Professor William Simon observed, "contrast[ing] legality with discretion."

Pretty much everyone signed on to the idea of using detailed rules to minimize discretion. Liberals and conservatives like rules, as discussed, because they distrust each other. Corporations liked detailed rules because rules provide a safe harbor and, as a bonus, rules are a barrier to entry for potential competitors. Public employees like rules because rules absolve them of responsibility; by following the rules, they avoid having to justify the fairness of their decisions. Precise rules were also the sure antidote against violating someone's rights: The rule made me do it.

Lawsuits exploded in this rules-based regime. Judges told not to be "activist" let people sue for anything. Eliminating judicial authority to draw lines of reasonableness shifted legal power over to self-interested plaintiffs' lawyers, who soon learned they could sue for the moon and extort settlements even in cases (as with some asbestos claims) that were fraudulent. Legal fear progressively eroded daily freedoms. Teachers were told never to put an arm around a crying child. Diving boards and jungle gyms were ripped out. Employers stopped giving job references.

Out of the cauldron of the 1960s emerged the most amazingly impractical public philosophy ever devised: No one could take responsibility to make public choices. Legal restrictions on official choice now reached its apogee: No president, no judge, no official, no teacher, no anyone, would have authority to draw on their judgment. Public choices would be automatic, like spell-check in a word processing program, or go into the purgatory of perpetual process.

1980–present: Regulation without responsibility. The Supreme Court saw the developing paralysis of public choices, and tried to reclaim authority for all branches. In the 1984 *Chevron* decision, it held that agency decisions should be presumed correct, and not be overturned if based on "a permissible construction of the statute." Over the next two decades, the Court rendered a series of decisions limiting judicial interference over agency choices. It also noticed the explosion of litigation and handed down rulings encouraging federal judges to dispose of meritless lawsuits by motion.

But it was too late. America's public culture had changed. The new legal norm was to avoid norms. Making a "value judgment" had become an accusation, not a responsibility. Distrust of officials had become pathological. Americans had never trusted government, but "traditional American distrust is more like doubt," Hugh Heclo notes. After the 1960s that "suspicion of power" shifted "to a postmodern distrust of motive."

Any act, even an official talking with someone, became grounds for suspicion. One high-ranking New York City official lost his job—in a front-page scandal, no less—because he had the temerity to be seen chatting with a potential contractor while they were waiting for a scheduled meeting to start. Nor is distrust confined to dealings with business. When brought in by Mayor Bloomberg to help streamline operations, Deputy Mayor Stephen Goldsmith was told he couldn't walk around and ask public employees about their ideas to improve things, because that would violate a prohibition on "direct dealing." He could only talk with designated union representatives.

Laws got longer and longer. Any public choice should be preset by law. Every detail of implementation should be codified. The 2010 Affordable Care Act was twenty-seven hundred pages, including a twenty-eight-word definition of "high school" and hundreds of mandates for further rule making, including "rules for counting resident time for didactic and scholarly activities and other activities," and rules determining the payment amount "for dual-energy x-ray absorptiometry services (identified in 2006 by HCPCS codes 76075 and 76077 (and any succeeding codes)) furnished during 2010 and 2011," whatever that means.

Laying everything out in detailed law is often comfortable for people on the receiving end. No one has to take responsibility for whether things actually work. There's no need to agonize over tough choices—to balance a budget, fire a problem employee, or decide what's right or wrong—if you lack that authority. Judges, members of Congress, and public officials have become comfortable not having to make decisions of right and wrong. Officials and judges have become high-level versions of the welfare clerk described by Professor Simon: "There is nothing I can do."

Our founders sought to create a government run by wise men, accountable to the people. After the 1960s we created a government run by clerks and jerks, accountable to no one and empowered only to say no. But another storm is gathering, and threatening to break any minute. This is a storm of affordability and paralysis. Our society can't afford to keep the public faucet wide open, wasting as much as it helps, or to wallow in bureaucracy when competing globally. Humans need to take back control of public choices.

GOVERNMENT BY REAL PEOPLE, NOT THEORIES

In one of the lands in *Gulliver's Travels*, called Lagado, everyone follows a theory slavishly, with consistently disastrous results. Houses fall down because a professor at Lagado Academy believes in building the roof first and the foundation last. Crops don't grow, because of a plan about using hundreds of hogs to root the soil and fertilize it at the same time. People walk around in rags because of a theory that spiders should be able to weave silk. Lagado is a place, as Jonathan Swift describes it, that aims for utopian perfection—buildings that never need repair, and fields that need no tilling—by making everyone abide by a theory instead of doing things for themselves. "The only Inconvenience is, that none of these Projects are yet brought to Perfection, and in the mean time the whole Country lies miserably wast, the Houses in Ruins, and the People without Food or Cloths."

Modern American government is also organized to put theory above reality. Public choices, we believe, should be made pursuant to clear rules, set in advance, whatever the consequences.

The consequences, as in Lagado, are wholly predictable: Nothing much works. Government staggers toward insolvency because no one is able to adjust unaffordable programs. An official lacks the authority to pull a tree out of a "class C-1" creek.

The orthodoxy of what is known, ironically, as "clear law" permeates our culture, unquestioned at the highest intellectual levels. It's hard to believe that Hayek, of all people, could ever have believed that public choices could be mechanized with precise law—making decisions by following "rules announced and fixed beforehand." It was Hayek who preached the gospel of individual liberty, explaining why all accomplishment required the initiative of individuals. How could he not have seen that human values and initiative are required for public choices as well?

Washington is Lagado, with every gear calibrated to grind

public choices through the intricate legal mechanisms. But what can we do about it? Government will muddle through, we expect, just as it always has. One silver lining is that government provides a perpetual (if expensive) source of schadenfreude. Every week there are new idiocies that allow us, sitting up in the stands, to feel superior to the clowns who run government.

But this is a degenerative condition. American culture is corroding before our eyes. It would have been inconceivable, a few years ago, for a teacher to be scared to put an arm around a crying child, or for a fireman to stand on the beach for an hour and watch a man drown because he had not been recertified for land-based rescue. Creeping legalisms are eating away at America's social capital. Citizens have been reprogrammed by the legal culture to be takers, not participants, in democracy. As one Tea Party supporter put it, "Keep your government hands off my Medicare."

The failures of the public sector—worsening schools, decaying infrastructure, unsustainable deficits—are just symptoms of progressive democratic breakdown caused by a structure in which no one has authority to make public choices. Powerlessness then leads to polarization and anger. Political leaders barely speak to each other. The gears of the giant government machine are self-destructing even as they grind up much of what is good in our culture.

Sooner or later, something has to give. The solution is not reform of this or that area. The solution is to rebuild our governing structure, on the foundations of the Constitution, to allow humans to make public choices. "Who governs?" is obviously an important question, political scientist Samuel Huntington observed. "Even more important, however, may be the question 'Does anybody govern?'"

Proposition 10: Law must empower officials to apply social norms.

A litmus test for functioning government—indeed, for functioning anything—is whether responsible people are free to make sensible choices.

Our modern instinct is to demand proof. What's practical or fair, however, is rarely provable. Most choices are not matters of objective logic or fact, but of instinct and values. Even in courts, with a higher threshold of legality, "justice is a concept by far more subtle and indefinite," Justice Benjamin Cardozo observed, than "is yielded by mere obedience to a rule." There are a thousand ways to do anything, but they almost always require choices made in the particular situation. "No scientist has chosen a spouse or bought a house," as historian Jacques Barzun put it, "using scientific methods."

Does it make sense to pull the tree out of the creek right away? Or to suspend the seventh-grader when she immediately rejected the contraband pill? How much environmental review is sufficient? Judges and officials must "look to custom," Justice Cardozo observed, "to determine how established rules shall be applied."

Today, the law governing public choices is more like a running joke. Did you hear about the cafeteria worker fired for theft because she gave food to a hungry child? Or the lifeguard fired because he tried to save a drowning person just across the line of his stretch of beach?

People will disagree. Sometimes the legislature must change norms—as Congress did with antidiscrimination laws. But "we must not dramatize the incompatibility of values," Isaiah Berlin cautioned. Even where traditions differ, "there is a great deal of broad agreement . . . about what is right and wrong, good and evil." In any event, "we must decide as we decide; moral risk cannot be avoided."

Proposition 11: Authority, properly understood, dramatically expands freedom.

We confuse authority with power. Authority is not power for self-interest, but the opposite. Authority in a democracy, Vaclav Havel explains, is a temporary delegation to make group choices. Authority is a *job*—the job of making sensible public choices. The person is on the hot seat. Authority "is lost when a person betrays that responsibility."

Authority dramatically enlarges, not diminishes, our freedom. Hobbes focused on authority as protection against social violence. But authority is also essential in a crowded society to open up opportunities for forward movement in joint activities. Authorizing officials to act provides the hub by which others also are empowered:

- The teacher's new ideas matter—only because the principal has authority to say yes. Collectively, all these choices encourage innovation and spontaneity that make the school a success—not a mosh pit of rules and disrespect.
- Environmental decisions can be made in a year, not a decade—because an environmental official has the responsibility to balance competing considerations. Collectively, these choices allow the power grid to get rebuilt, and America to achieve a more efficient and sustainable energy footprint.
- The soup kitchen can continue to have meals prepared at the parishioners' homes—because the health officer has the freedom to take into account the facility's spotless record. Choices like these allow the community to take ownership for social services. People feel they can make a difference.

By itself, individual freedom is weak tea, a thin brew of isolated actions and selfish pleasures. That's why defining freedom by absence of authority is a formula for futility and unimportance. Community and other social enterprises are what create the opportunities for real accomplishment. But joint endeavors require authority, because unanimity is virtually impossible in any large group. The "simultaneous recession of both freedom and authority in the modern world" is no coincidence, Arendt explained, but inherent in the flawed premise that authority is evil: No authority "means to be confronted anew . . . by the elementary problem of human living-together."

Giving back authority to officials to make public choices creates a kind of marketplace for good ideas and values. Innovative ideas get currency. Effective officials earn moral authority and become role models. Today, by contrast, official decisions are perceived to be made by the grim reaper, applying a kind of penal code that is disconnected from what's fair or reasonable. Tomorrow, when officials must strive to achieve public goals sensibly, everyone will look to see what's fair and what's not, and react accordingly.

Looking for nobility may seem unimaginable in the sludge heap of modern government. But that just shows what this legalistic machine has wrought. It wasn't too long ago that Congress was led by people broadly admired and credible, such as Howard Baker and Bill Bradley. There are lots of good people who, if given the responsibility, will put government back on a sustainable course.

Nor is blind trust required, certainly not of any particular person. Think of it as hiring traffic cops. You just need to trust the necessity to have traffic cops. A crowded society requires public choices of stop and go. "Authority implies an obedience in which men retain their freedom," Hannah Arendt explained. What the citizen and the official "have in common is the hierarchy itself, whose rightness and legitimacy both recognize."

Finally, the risk of corruption is far less with an identified official than in a dark bureaucratic thicket. Corruption and venality "shun the bright light of day," the Sovern Commission concluded after investigating scandals in New York City in the 1980s. Rigid controls, designed to ensure integrity, in fact create a breeding ground for venality. The safest system, studies repeatedly conclude, is to give responsibility to identifiable officials.

Giving officials authority does not guarantee fairness. We learned this lesson in the 1960s. But taking away authority to make public choices, we now know, degenerates into gridlock and loss of freedom.

Letting go of our legal stranglehold. "The difficulty lies, not in the new ideas," John Maynard Keynes famously observed, "but in escaping from the old ones."

Our quest for legal precision is hopeless. Language itself is too uncertain, and dependent on unspoken frames of reference. A central insight of philosopher Ludwig Wittgenstein is that law takes its meaning from norms and values of the society. Law is never self-executing—no Geiger counter, as legal philosopher Jeremy Waldron puts it, that starts buzzing when people transcend the boundaries: "Words do not determine meaning, people do. No amount of staring at the words of a rule, then staring at the world, then staring at the words again, will tell us when we have a proper application."

Yes, it is possible to write rules that can be enforced by quantitative measures. But they generally put us in Gulliver's land of Lagado, where nothing works—where teachers become idiot savants, teaching to the test, and where restaurant owners get fined for a cheese patty that is 45 degrees instead of 41 degrees.

The instinct to shackle officials focuses narrowly on one goal of the Rule of Law—avoiding arbitrary power. It happens to be self-defeating: Putting legal shackles on officials also shackles you, usually just as much as it constricts the official. You're both handcuffed to thousand-page rule books.

Shackling officials also forgets the main goal of law, which is to provide the framework for a free society. Avoiding arbitrary decisions is vital, but only against the frame of reference of having already authorized officials to make public choices. "Unless government is effective," management expert Peter Drucker noted, "all other goals are useless."

Proposition 12: American government must be rebuilt on the principle of human responsibility.

American government needs to be meeting challenges all around us. This requires humans to take back control of government, and start making responsible public choices. At every level of public responsibility—the White House, the state house, the court house, the school house, even your house—people need to be given back the authority needed to fulfill their responsibilities.

Restoring responsibility requires a historic overhaul, not just reform. I will shortly discuss the major changes needed to bring human breath and values back into each branch of government. The structural changes, while radically altering how decisions are made, basically simplify the structures of each branch and make responsibility more coherent.

Law and the government it authorizes work sensibly only when rooted in human values and understanding. "The Rule of Law is, in the end . . . a human ideal for human institutions," philosopher Jeremy Waldron concludes, "not a magic that somehow absolves us of human rule."

This happens to be the founding premise of American government. The Constitution is filled with broad principles, written in the vaguest terms, that have meaning only as applied. The Fourth Amendment bans "unreasonable searches and seizures." Based on that legal principle of four words, police, prosecutors, and judges every day are called upon to draw the line of what that standard means in a particular context. The principle has been interpreted in countless legal opinions, which give it substance in different contexts. Decisions are unavoidably controversial, and experts constantly debate its controlling norms. But this vague principle is effective to make us feel free. Notwithstanding its gray edges, citizens go to bed every night comfortable that government will not barge into our homes and start rifling through our drawers. Law by principles, interpreted by judges and officials, is the main tradition of American law.

At the end of his life, Hayek recanted his earlier notions of mechanical law, saying he had reconsidered "the supposed greater certainty [when] . . . all rules of law have been laid down in written and codified form." Hayek concluded, "I am now persuaded . . . that judicial decisions may in fact be more predictable if the judge is also bound by generally held views of what is just, even when they are not supported by the letter of the law." Law's credibility, Hayek understood, hinges on its congruence with social norms: "The rule of law is effective . . . only insofar as it is part of the moral tradition of the community."

The current dysfunction of government, however, has one almost irresistible feature: It removes the need to take responsibility. Automatic government appeals to citizens who, understandably, don't trust people in Washington. Government insiders love the legal software program that runs government. All of Washington clings to this feature. And why shouldn't they? Who is responsible for the budgetary excesses and pervasive failures of government programs? Exactly. No one. Insiders are insulated from responsibility by impenetrable layers of law.

Getting lost in legal dictates is part of the culture of the new Lagado. Career bureaucrats, career lobbyists, and career politicians sit together in huge, windowless rooms—furrowing their foreheads and speaking in a language unknown to normal people—and write regulations that try to anticipate everything that might go wrong. Aspiring to clear rules by using language no one else understands is an odd convention. But in government it's an article of faith. Only then can we expunge the demon of human judgment.

My fear is that Americans are attracted to a society without responsibility. Every day we see people gaming the system in the name of so-called legal rights. Today, instead of asking what's right or wrong, we, too, have been trained to ask, "What does the law provide?"

Tocqueville, unbelievably, predicted how the instinct for legal control would lead to trained helplessness:

> It covers the surface of society with a network of small complicated rules, minute and uniform, through which the most original minds and the most energetic characters cannot penetrate . . . The will of man is not shattered, but softened, bent and guided; men are seldom forced by it to act, but they are constantly restrained from acting. Such power does not destroy, but prevents existence; it does not tyrannize, but it compresses, enervates, extinguishes, and stupefies a people, till each nation is reduced to nothing better than a flock of timid and industrious animals, of which the government is the shepherd.

Tocqueville understood the public's attraction to a system without responsibility, but didn't get all the way to Hannah Arendt's perception that there is no shepherd. Nobody is in charge. Millions of words of detailed regulation have usurped official responsibility, and severed the links of government to broader society.

Modern democracy is not designed for governance and freedom, but to do what the accumulated law tells it to do, whatever the consequences. It is, by law, out of control. Sooner or later, this giant legal edifice, designed deliberately to avoid human choice, will collapse of its own weight. It must be rebuilt.

PART II

Restoring Human Control
of Democracy

DEMOCRACY WITHOUT LEADERS

I n 1933, in the depths of the Depression, Congress enacted the Agricultural Adjustment Act to alleviate dire conditions among farmers. About 25 percent of the population lived on 6 million farms, and the collapse in global markets had left farmers without any assurance that they could feed their families. The law basically guaranteed a floor price through direct subsidies. Cotton farmers were among the recipients.

Today, eighty years later, 2 percent of Americans live on farms that are much larger and mainly owned by corporations. But the statutory subsidies have never ended. Over the last decade cotton farmers alone have received about $2.5 billion per year.

In 2002, Brazil brought a proceeding before the World Trade Organization claiming the cotton subsidy violated free-trade agreements, allowing US cotton farmers to flood global markets with cheap cotton. The WTO agreed and in 2009 authorized Brazil to impose trade sanctions against US products, including suspension of intellectual property rights that would total $800 million per year. The way this works is that innocent US businesses would, in essence, have their products expropriated; for example, Brazil customers would no longer have to pay license fees for US movies and music. Faced with outraged screams from the affected industries, Congress finally acted, but not in the way you might expect. It agreed to pay off Brazilian cotton farmers—sending them $147 million annually in hush money so that corporate cotton farmers in America could continue to receive billions in New Deal–era subsidies.

Getting rid of obsolete laws is not something Congress does often. This isn't because of lack of authority. Congress can change any law it wants, within constitutional limits. But democracy has become a one-way ratchet. Congress adds programs but almost never subtracts them. Because laws on the books are mandatory, even for Congress, the practical effect is similar to the absence of authority: The people supposedly in charge of making law end up deferring to it. In the halls of policy in Washington, as well as in daily public choices, law has replaced responsibility to do what's sensible and moral. Decade after decade, Congress has piled new laws on top of old ones.

At this point, American democracy is basically run by dead people—by past generations of legislators and regulators who wrote the laws and regulations that dictate today's public policy, allocate most of annual budgets, and micromanage public choices. It's not surprising that Washington works so badly. Imagine if you had to run a business by following every idea that any former manager ever had.

The Constitution, of course, is meant to be timeless. So are basic principles of right and wrong, such as laws prohibiting fraud and other crimes. But most laws in the regulatory state are more like management tools for a crowded society—aiming to avoid unsafe workplaces and unclean water, and providing safety nets to avoid human suffering. Whether these programs should continue, and in what form, should depend on how they actually work and stack up with other priorities. Obsolete programs have real costs—the hard-earned income of 250,000 American families, each paying $10,000 in federal taxes, is being diverted into the pockets of corporate cotton farmers. The taxes of another 14,700 families are diverted to pay off Brazilian farmers.

A philosophy of law that deliberately dictates daily choices also unintentionally dictates democratic choices. The giant legal machine has become too big for its elected masters to control. Each branch of government is mired in the accumulation of legal detail. Congress wrings its hands over the national deficit, but its leaders act as if that's a discrete problem, not a symptom of the legal accretion and the unintended costs and consequences of old laws. The President is hemmed in by so much law that he no longer effectively runs the executive branch. Even ministerial choices, such as personnel decisions, or deciding how to pick a committee of outside advisers, are rigidly controlled by law. The judiciary has stepped in to sort out constant legal disputes over public decisions, but democratic choices are not supposed to be made by unelected judges peering through the magnifying glass of the one citizen or organization that happened to bring the lawsuit.

Public law is supposed to be subordinate to democracy—the tool by which our elected leaders advance public goals. Law instead has trumped democracy. It's hardly surprising that Americans have lost faith in democracy. It doesn't much matter whom we elect. Who's in charge? The law's in charge, whether or not it makes any sense.

The abdication by Congress

Article I of the Constitution states, "All legislative Powers herein granted shall be vested in a Congress of the United States." Making sure laws serve the public good is the job of Congress. Passing a law does not satisfy the legislative responsibility, but imposes an additional duty on Congress to make sure that the law actually functions for the good of society. The test of law is how it works, not whether it was duly enacted.

You wouldn't know that from watching Congress in action, which is why the first task is to shine a light on how miserably Congress has defaulted on this responsibility. No elected leader in memory has sought to reconcile existing American law with current priorities. This is a serious flaw in our democratic structure. Without a systematic mechanism to update old laws, the US is an outlier among developed nations.

Every law has unintended consequences. Most laws, when enacted, represent somebody's vision of the public good. The public purpose of a law often evaporates, however, as circumstances change. The Depression crisis on farms, for example, had disappeared by 1941, when the onset of World War II resulted in inexhaustible demand for cotton and other subsidized crops. Generations have passed since any farmers were in danger of starving.

The need to adjust law is no different from making choices in life. To succeed, you must adapt. No law ever works out as planned, and the mismatch only grows with time.

For example, when mandating special education as an open-ended right, Congress focused on eradicating an injustice, once and for all. Now the law itself is a symbol of budgetary injustice—as one principal put it, "almost like reverse discrimination against the average kid." Some special-ed students have multiple teachers and therapy professionals devoted to them, while others demand special private schooling, sometimes costing over $100,000 per year. Special ed now consumes over 25 percent of the total K–12 budget in America, for a tiny fraction of the student population that actually needs it. By contrast, less than 1 percent of the school budget is spent on programs for gifted children, or for social services for students in disadvantaged neighborhoods. Is this the right use of scarce school resources? No one is even asking the question.

Programs that are cast in concrete will always become millstones on society. Practically every area of regulatory oversight—health care, schools, consumer safety, the environment, public personnel—is governed by obsolete legal structures. In each case, the main problems arise from unanticipated consequences of well-meaning laws—and the almost unbroken record of neglect by Congress to adapt laws to current public needs.

The trend to make statutes as specific as possible—in part due to a political urge by Congress to tell the President and his appointees what to do—only accelerates the obsolescence. "EPA is hobbled by overly prescriptive statutes that pull the agency in too many directions and permit managers too little discretion to make wise decisions. Congress should stop micro-managing EPA," concluded a 1995 report of the National Academy of Public Administration. "At the heart of the most severe federal regulatory problems is the poor quality of primary legislation," noted a 1999 report of the Organisation of Economic Co-operation and Development (OECD), a member organization of thirty-four major countries, which found that American statutes are characterized by "excessive detail, legalism, and rigidity."

Congress fails to coordinate laws. Laws do not exist in isolation, but work with other laws affecting the same conduct or activity. Laws must be coordinated with each other in order to make them coherent to the people expected to abide by them. People need to understand what "the law" requires. That's why coherence is a core value of the Rule of Law.

Congress has created no disciplined mechanism to make laws and regulations fit together. Drafting of statutes is done by whoever wants the law, often special interests; the drafts are cleaned up by a congressional Office of Legislative Counsel but not reviewed for substance. New major regulations are vetted by the White House, but it does little to clean up old regulations. The effect, predictably, is a giant disorganized pile of programs and bureaucratic requirements that goes by the noble name of the Rule of Law. There are eighty-two teacher training programs, seventy-nine renewable energy programs, and sixteen programs that teach personal finance (but none, as far as I can tell, that teach government finance).

Accumulated piles of law make getting permits and licenses in America much more complex than in other developed countries. The US ranks behind sixteen other countries in ease of getting construction permits, according to rankings by the International Finance Corporation (IFC). Raising the roadway of the Bayonne Bridge, as noted earlier, required forty-seven approvals from nineteen different government entities—including multiple environmental agencies, fire departments, and a host of municipal agencies. Big companies have large legal staffs to deal with the hydra-headed monster guarding the portals of progress, but small businesses and individuals find themselves whipsawed by the uncoordinated and overlapping requirements. Following Hurricane Sandy in 2012, the difficulty of getting permission to rebuild led one frustrated homeowner to wrap her home in red tape.

Liberal blogger Matthew Yglesias recounted his frustrations spending weeks trying to get a permit in the District of Columbia to rent out his apartment. Most of the "red tape, long lines, inconvenient office hours, and other logistical hassles," he found, had "nothing to do with . . . the main purpose of landlord regulation." All this unnecessary bureaucracy, Yglesias concluded, is "a large and needless deterrent to the formation of the humble workaday firms that for many people are a path to autonomy and prosperity."

America's federal system, with parallel lawmaking at the state and local levels, contributes to regulatory confusion. "I don't think there's another country in the world that has anything like our system," observed Amy Friend, the chief counsel to the Senate Banking Committee, about financial regulation: "We've got fifty state regulators, and we have four federal banking regulators, and we have a credit union regulator, and on top of that we have market regulators, the SEC and the CFTC."

But many other countries also have lower levels of lawmaking. Part of what the national government does in those countries is coordinate the different levels with one lead agency: A principle of "one-stop shopping" is considered a key component of good government. The Netherlands has pioneered this approach, creating one-stop shops in areas ranging from construction to welfare. In Germany, the administrative code explicitly provides that "planning approval . . . [encompasses] all public interests affected thereby. No other . . . permissions, authorisations, agreements or planning approvals are required."

America's regulatory disorganization is starting to resemble third-world countries. India, for example, requires "a daunting array of permits" for relatively simple activities, allowing corruption to flourish as exasperated businesses and individuals pay "speed money" to fixers to help grease their paperwork along. In America, still blessed with law-abiding citizens, the effect is to discourage people from taking initiative at all.

Law has made government ungovernable. Government tortures itself as well as citizens with these byzantine regulatory structures. One study "found a federal agency that needed an 18-foot chart, with 373 boxes, to explain its rulemaking process, and 'this process was not unusually complex.'"

A few years ago, Common Good did an inventory of all the laws affecting a school in New York City. Literally thousands of rules, emanating from every level of government, dictate actions by people who are supposedly spending their time educating America's youth. Disciplining a student potentially requires sixty-six separate steps, including several layers of potential appeals. Organizing an athletic event could require almost a hundred steps. Bureaucratic forms and requirements are everywhere. Firing a teacher who is inept, or mean-spirited, or burned out, is basically impossible. All these legal requirements, weighing heavily upon principals and teachers, could fill a law library: due process, special education, zero tolerance, No Child Left Behind, tenure, work rules, student rights, privacy rules, to name a few.

Disjointed legal accumulation has reached its paralytic nadir in the rules surrounding public employees. Like an industrial-age nightmare, civil service laws in many states remove human judgment from every important personnel decision—whom to hire, promote, reassign, and lay off, and who does what work, in what way, and in what hours. New York City has over a thousand job classifications—each with its own bureaucratic requirements. It would be illegal, for example, to ask the clerk inputting numbers to then calculate the sum. That requires someone in a different job classification. Union contracts are layered on top of these. "Micromanagement" is too flexible a term: How to use a new photocopy machine, in one New York union agreement, must be determined through a process of collective bargaining.

Public unions made it to the headlines in 2010, when sweetheart pensions negotiated over the years effectively bankrupted a number of states and municipalities. Political deals with public unions resulted in laws that allowed public safety workers to retire in their forties, with pensions "spiked" by overtime in their final year so that they could retire with nearly full pay. In some cases public workers were rehired by government the next day, so they were paid double. There is no rhyme or reason to all the laws and contracts for public employment. These benefits and requirements just piled up over the years, as successive union leaders used their political clout to "do something" for union members.

Other countries have succeeded in building an honorable public service with a culture of professionalism. But they don't have rules that dictate how to use a copying machine. Even France doesn't allow people to retire in their forties. American government is an awful place to work. Who wants to clank around in heavy legal armor, unable to use your own judgment? The suffocating legal culture repels good people from public service— "expulsion of the fittest," as former New York City Commissioner Sam Schwartz put it.

Managing government sensibly is impossible. "Think of city government as a big bus," Los Angeles Deputy Mayor Michael Keeley explained. "The bus is divided into different sections with different constituencies: labor, the city council, the mayor, interest groups and contractors. Every seat is equipped with a brake, so lots of people can stop the bus anytime. The problem is that this makes the bus almost undriveable."

Management expert Peter Drucker suggested that all agencies and programs be periodically reviewed by asking these questions: "What is your mission? Is it still the right mission? Is it still worth doing? If we were not already doing this, would we go into it now?" I would add a final question: Is this a sensible way of achieving the public goal?

I doubt that 10 percent of federal, state, and local statutes would emerge unscathed from this analysis. Environmental review was never intended to delay projects for a decade. Special education was not intended to dominate school budgets. Civil servants were supposed to be honored professionals in a "merit system," not a caste of untouchables.

The challenge, at this point, is that every public goal is weighed down by all this law. Incremental change will do nothing. Reforming this or that stupidity doesn't fix all the others. Nor is blanket deregulation the answer. Most laws embody goals that the majority of Americans, including me, consider vital: worker safety, environmental protection, and social services for the needy. But the complete lack of discipline—an "almost lawless passion for lawmaking," as historian Henry Steele Commager described it—drags down productive activity throughout society. The OECD has concluded that America's haphazard legal structure "will increasingly penalise the United States as the pace of globalisation and innovation steps up."

American society is drowning in law, and Congress is standing on the beach, watching. Why won't it act? Because Congress, like the firemen in California, feels powerless to break free of all these laws.

Democracy for the status quo

Congress doesn't seem to be aware that it is responsible for how law actually works. It treats existing law and programs with the reverence of the Ten Commandments—except that they're more like the 10 million commandments.

"Members of Congress don't 'do' law," Congressman Jim Cooper told me. "They raise money, give speeches, and do favors." They don't even try to understand law, much less change it. "Many of them have probably never cracked open a copy of the US Code," Cooper noted. "The level of ignorance of what law requires is astounding." Cooper recalled a fellow member on the House Armed Services Committee who didn't know the difference between the War College and West Point. In *Act of Congress*, Robert Kaiser quotes a Democratic staffer describing how members on the House Financial Services Committee "are like deer in the headlights . . . They don't really understand the issues or what to do."

Nor do members of Congress read the texts of new laws they're asked to vote on. As House Speaker Nancy Pelosi famously said about the twenty-seven-hundred-page Affordable Care Act, "We have to pass the bill so that you can find out what is in it." This is yet another unintended effect of the inhuman complexity of modern law: It not only crushes citizens, but is beyond the understanding of our democratically elected representatives. Who understands the new laws? Staff, perhaps. In his memoir, Senator Ted Kennedy commented on "an enormous shift in responsibility over the last forty or fifty years" from elected members to professional staff, who, he observed, end up shouldering "over 95 percent" of the legislative responsibility.

This abdication of responsibility by Congress would shock our founders. Who else has authority and accountability for whether law works? On the other hand, put yourself in their shoes. Where would you start? Public law has become too big, and too complex, for any elected leader to take on. If nursing home inspectors can't keep all the rules straight, how can members of Congress understand an exponentially larger body of law?

Democracy supposedly brings fresh breezes of public opinion to government. But that obviously isn't working. Washington is buffeted by public anger but goes nowhere. Elected officials come and go, but instead of steering us toward responsible solutions, the ship of state only gets heavier in the water.

There's a tendency to attribute evil purpose to the failures of Washington. Partisanship and hypocrisy are certainly front and center in daily news. But there are also plenty of good people there. Why can't they triumph over the forces of darkness and, at least sometimes, fix something?

One reason is that the game is rigged for powerful people and groups—aided by a system of campaign finance and electoral rules that gives the advantage to incumbent officials who promise to protect programs that benefit their supporters. The internal rules of Congress are designed brilliantly to avoid action. Filibusters, holds on legislation and appointments, committees that strangle sensible bills for purely partisan effect, and extensive debates on insignificant issues are among the tools available to accomplish doing nothing.

Campaign finance rules act as mortar for the status quo, giving a kind of blocking power to special interests. Organized political funders like trial lawyers or the NRA essentially have one or the other political party in their pockets. It's hard to do anything in Washington without feeling their power. Nearly nine out of ten Americans in 2013 said they wanted background checks for firearm purchases, but the Senate wasn't able to assemble enough votes to get it done. On litigation reform, a senior Democratic congressman agreed with me that restoring reliability to justice would be useful in containing health care costs, but he said he would never support any reform, even one supported by patient groups, as long as trial lawyers opposed it. As he put it, "That's where we get the money."

But there's more to the story than being bought. Special-education advocates are not, as far as I can tell, big financial supporters. But no politician wants to cross them, because they may chain themselves to your door. The power of a small group that vociferously cares about an issue will always trump the greater good. The auto industry avoided stricter fuel efficiency guidelines in the 1990s by mobilizing thousands of disability advocates to protest discrimination against large cars. This phenomenon is not solved by campaign finance reform.

But the power of interest groups is overwhelmingly a blocking power, not a power to get new benefits. Vested interests can prevent old law from changing, but it's rare for any interest group to get a new law that looks like a special-interest giveaway. If a prosperous group of cotton farmers showed up for the first time and asked for $2 billion in new subsidies, they would be laughed out of the Capitol. If special-ed advocates showed up at Congress and demanded 25 percent of the total K–12 budget, they would be told, politely, that there are many other priorities as well. But cotton farmers and special-ed advocates get those benefits because of the historical happenstance that the benefits are already embodied in law. It's easy politics to let people keep what they have. It's risky to try to take it away.

Democracy is not so much in the control of powerful interests as it is anchored in the status quo. One of those anchors is law, or, more accurately, a multiplicity of laws that prevent government from resetting priorities.

A critical constitutional flaw. The Constitution has a design flaw, not visible until the last half century, but of critical significance in the current state of paralysis. It is almost impossible to amend or repeal old laws. Our founders were concerned about *preventing too many laws* but never debated *how to undo laws that didn't work out.* The same checks that deter making new laws also prevent changing old laws, except with far greater force. Once enacted, each law develops its own constituencies. Those interest groups surround the law with armies of lobbyists, contributors, and voters whose goal is never to lose what they have.

This constitutional presumption against change is what gives special interests almost invincible powers to keep things the way they are. A proposed statutory amendment must first successfully negotiate the legal labyrinth of legislative committees and political gatekeepers. Changing one word of a statute then requires a majority of Congress to run a gauntlet of special interests, desperate to avoid losing what they view as an entitlement, hitting them over the head with money and other blandishments.

As law piles up, year after year, Washington is overwhelmed by legal Lilliputians—lawyers, lobbyists, litigants, and lifetime bureaucrats, all wielding the incomprehensible yet invincible sword of Law. "You can't take away my rights!" Everywhere in the halls of power, no political leader can turn a corner without running into the sharp point of some law. No one, not even the President, can stand up to its power. Every year, Congress creates new laws, hoping to direct it to more productive ends, but in fact only increasing its inertial force.

At this point, government is permeated with a sense of futility. You can prevent bad things from happening with great effort, but you can't actually fix what's wrong with government. As columnist Gerald Seib observed, "America and its political leaders, after two decades of failing to come together to solve big problems, seem to have lost faith in their ability to do so. A political system that expects failure doesn't try hard to produce anything else."

The sense of powerlessness has become self-fulfilling and offers the most plausible explanation for why Washington has degenerated into a culture of perpetual partisanship.

Washington as a deviant subculture. Without any realistic opportunity to change things, a kind of mold has grown over the structures of democracy. Senators wake up in the morning thinking not about how to meet America's challenges, but how to make the other side look bad. At a lunch with business leaders, two Democratic senators crowed about having the other side "on the ropes." When a business leader asked how that would help resolve the nation's problems, they looked at him as if he were speaking a different language.

There's no shame in acting solely for partisan reasons. When Senator Chris Dodd was trying to get votes for Dodd-Frank, Senator Harry Reid and other senior Democrats called and told him not to compromise with any Republicans because, as Robert Kaiser tells the story, they didn't care much "about the fate of the bill—they wanted to score political points." Senator Dodd, at that point a lame duck, ignored them.

Governing has been replaced by posturing. Politicians propose "message" bills and amendments that they have no chance of enacting. As of this writing, the Republican House has voted forty-seven times to repeal Obamacare. Sometimes they propose laws they don't even believe in, just to make the other side look bad. The White House under George W. Bush pushed a litigation reform bill both inadequate to solve the problem and particularly noxious to Democrats. That was the point, as a White House staffer explained to me: to propose a bill that the Democrats would never enact. Then the White House could blame Democrats for not solving the problem.

Potential agreement is itself reason enough for disagreement—you wouldn't want the other side to have any accomplishments. Both parties agree that EPA should be a cabinet-level department, but neither will support it while the other occupies the White House and might get the credit. When Republican Senator Lamar Alexander proposed a school bill that reflected, exactly, the policy platform of Democratic senators, the Democratic chiefs of staff reflexively decided to oppose it. When another staffer pointed out that the bill contained what they wanted, the response was immediate and definitive: "We can't support a Republican bill. We need to keep the issue for our side."

Humans in a bad culture lose all connection to right and wrong. Psychologist Philip Zimbardo's experiment with students at Stanford playing jailers and prisoners showed how normal people—knowing they are play-acting—nonetheless become monsters. The shocking humiliations imposed by army jailers at Abu Ghraib, Zimbardo explained, were a predictable response to the isolated hothouse in which they spent their days.

Washington, too, has evolved into its own culture. It has become inbred on many levels. The policy of both parties on budget deficits seems to be maximum irresponsibility. Reacting to the Simpson-Bowles deficit reduction plan, Democratic leader Nancy Pelosi said, "This proposal is simply unacceptable," while Republican leader Paul Ryan, a budget hawk, refused to vote for it. "It's not true that bipartisanship in Washington is dead," observed Will Marshall of the Progressive Policy Institute. "There's a perfect bipartisan conspiracy to bankrupt the country."

The partisanship might as well be prearranged, like professional wrestling: When liberals demand gun control, more money flows into conservative coffers from supporters of the right to bear arms, and vice versa. The same mutually advantageous polarization can be seen in abortion, tax policy, and environmental issues. Pounding the table in congressional hearings is also like professional wrestling, just theater for its own sake: Politicians' public display of "anger is usually not a means to an end," Kaiser found, "but an end in itself."

Political leaders trumpet hot-button issues with fervor while in office but somehow become less ideological when a better job comes up. When the $1.6 million job of running a notorious pork barrel trade association came up in late 2012, dozens of members of Congress from both parties reportedly expressed interest in applying for it.

Because political agendas often bear no relation to the merits, meetings in Washington have an other-worldly quality. You meet with supposedly important people, who, instead of engaging in candid discussion, take notes and then say something vapid like, "Thank you for explaining this to me." You know there are wheels turning inside them, but you have no idea in what direction. Everything is calculated, all artifice and posturing. It's creepy, like dealing with drones or robots. Almost nothing is spontaneous, or heartfelt. This happens even with people you know; it's how they're trained. In public meetings, they make statements for the record. Everything has an unspoken subtext. Then, just when something is about to happen, some operative makes a deal to sabotage it. After a few hours on Capitol Hill, I need a shower to wash it all off.

A group that no longer shares basic values with the society

is categorized by sociologists as a "deviant subculture." Washington has become a deviant subculture. So have Albany, Sacramento, Springfield, and many other state capitals. The values of government are not congruent with, and are often opposed to, the values of the society it supposedly serves. Washington has abandoned core responsibilities. Self-interest is its stock in trade, not a cause for shame. Its cynicism is often 100 percent pure: Political leaders dream up tactics to *avoid* fixing problems. The simplest decisions—raising the debt ceiling to avoid default on the national debt, or confirming judicial nominees with exemplary records—become opportunities for political brinksmanship. Congress has become a "vetocracy," Francis Fukuyama observes, using obscure congressional rules as a way to extort favors. Obama's nominee for ambassador to Russia, Michael McFaul, was put on permanent hold "due to a senator wanting the federal government to build a facility in his state."

Instead of fixing bad laws, members of Congress have learned that it's far better to get credit, and some contributions, by promising never to touch them. Hidden within the twenty-seven hundred pages of the Affordable Care Act are numerous giveaways to politically influential interests. For example, a provision authorizing pilot projects for better medical malpractice justice—aimed at avoiding the waste of $100 billion or so of "defensive medicine"—got changed at the last minute to *bar* any pilot project of expert health courts without juries. This last-minute sop to the trial lawyers eviscerates the whole idea of trying other approaches. There's no artifice in it: Instead of a Trojan horse hiding a troop of trial lawyers, the statutory pilot program became more like a Trojan stick pony mounted by trial lawyers gleefully waving their swords.

Everyone plays his part in this subculture of self-interested government. Public employees justify their own importance by being sticklers for the rules, often at a cost to society. Their union leaders make backroom deals that make government unmanageable and, in some states, insolvent. Lobbyists don't even pretend to be anything other than self-interested. Just give them some money. Government is incredibly cheap to influence, especially when all you want is to block action. Political media takes all this at face value because political theater is entertaining.

Washington is not filled with powerful people. It is filled with people who have no authority to do much of anything other than to prevent change, and maybe pay a favor here or there. Everyone scurries around the baseboards, playing the game and grabbing for scraps.

People who have power don't act this way. When they have authority to fix a problem, most will try to get the credit for doing so. Even tyrants try to please the people—Mussolini made the trains run on time. "This notion that members of Congress are power-hungry—absolutely the opposite," Congressman Barney Frank observed. "Most members like to duck tough issues."

People with self-respect also don't act this way. The transparent bluster of politicians and officials reveals a deep sense of personal insignificance. Most self-respecting people wouldn't want to spend most of the day begging for campaign money, or go on camera pointing fingers at the other side instead of actually accomplishing something.

New leadership would be useful but is not sufficient. Just put a virtuous person in charge, we hoped when electing in 2008 the freshest new face in generations: "Change we can believe in." Or, two years later, just elect Tea Party ideologues committed to reducing the size of government. That hasn't worked either.

Fixing American democracy requires a new vision for how government can work. Today it is unable to make vital choices. There's not even a serious discussion about first principles of democratic governance—for example, how Congress can take responsibility for whether laws serve the public good.

Democratic values exist in rhetoric only. Government is not responsive to the needs of its citizens. It is not responsible fiscally. It has evolved to protect the people who work within it. The constitutional branches, instead of balancing each other's weaknesses, have settled onto a sofa together, playing a fantasy version of dystopic democracy instead of the real thing. No one can correct government's direction, even in daily choices, because the law doesn't let them. The electoral system is rigged toward the status quo. The public is kept at bay by an open spigot.

Democracy must be built anew. The goal is a new government culture in which officials see their job as making vital choices for the public good, not tending to the status quo. But changing a culture is hard. Anthropologists say that bad cultures generally must first collapse. Fixing the worst symptoms, such as campaign finance, rigged primaries, or the arcane rules of Congress, is unlikely to suffice. The scope of the required overhaul requires taking government down to its constitutional foundations, and rebuilding simplified programs and structures that allow officials to focus on the common good. It will also require constitutional amendments to correct and rebalance the responsibilities of each branch.

A NEW CHARTER FOR PUBLIC LEADERSHIP

The organizing principle for rebuilding American government must be the same as for any effective organization: human responsibility.

The summary of needed changes is this: First, clean out the current mess so that officials have space to make necessary

choices. Next, clarify authority and accountability so that officials can no longer hide behind rules—including adding five
amendments to the Constitution that I am calling a Bill of
Responsibilities (set forth in the Appendix). Finally, reengage
citizens by creating new mechanisms for citizen oversight to get
fresh breezes blowing through the closed chambers of government. I will discuss each of these in turn.

None of this can happen except through massive, organized
pressure by the public. The first and highest hurdle, therefore, is
for the public to embrace the need for big change. The American
public has to accept the fact that government is broken, and cannot be fixed on its current terms.

Ask yourself: How can our country move forward when environmental review takes a decade? How can government balance
public budgets, or adapt to new challenges, when legislatures are
unable to change old laws? How can America remain competitive when simple business ventures require dozens of approvals? How can government do anything sensibly if no official can
make a decision? The need to change how government makes
choices seems unavoidable.

Replacing automatic government with human responsibility will disrupt the habits of those within it. Many will scream
bloody murder. Changing democracy is inconceivable to them.
Once in place, however, the new structure will seem entirely
ordinary—just a common sense way to make public choices. Law
will be coherent. Public debate over law will focus on what's right
and practical, not consist of a cacophony of people demanding
legal rights. The President will have authority to manage the
executive branch. OSHA will focus on worker safety, not sanctions for immaterial noncompliance. Whether to approve a new
power line will be decided by a politically accountable person—
after adequate review, but not a decade. Social services will be

delivered locally, by responsible people using their own judgment. Teachers can be themselves, accountable for their overall
effectiveness, not isolated metrics. Political hypocrisy and self-
interest will be given the lie by trusted civic watchdogs, reporting on what's actually going on.

But how can this possibly happen? The defining characteristic
of modern democracy is that it can't change anything. Nothing
today is politically feasible. Nothing. Government is on autopilot, its legal flaps locked in an unsustainable position, headed
toward a stall and then a frightening plummet toward insolvency and political chaos. This is the situation, political scientists say, when dramatic change is likely.

Big change around the corner. Institutions tend to take a life of
their own. For private companies, pressures from the marketplace often require radical adaptation or corporate death.
Governments usually take longer to feel pressures, often long
after they have lost support of its society. The situation must
degenerate to a point where people go to the trouble and risk
of overthrowing the current government. As the Declaration
of Independence states, "All experience hath shewn, that mankind are more disposed to suffer, while evils are sufferable, than
to right themselves by abolishing the forms to which they are
accustomed."

This is why governments rarely reform themselves through
incremental changes. What happens instead, political scientists
Frank Baumgartner and Bryan Jones explain, is that pressures of
dysfunction and distrust grow until, like the stick-slip phenomenon of earthquakes, some unforeseen event causes a tectonic
shift that will cause collapse of the current orthodoxy. Usually
the trigger is widespread fear or anger. Who would have thought

that the self-immolation of a street vendor in Tunisia would touch off the "Arab Spring"?

Most significant public policy shifts in American history have occurred in just the way Professors Baumgartner and Jones describe, generally in a cycle of every thirty or forty years. Pressures build for decades, until it seems like nothing will ever change, and then the old order collapses. The last time was the 1960s. That shift was toward individual rights. Before that was the New Deal (providing social safety nets), the Progressive Era (ending laissez-faire with the regulatory state), and so on back through history until the American Revolution.

Each of the historic shifts in America's history were led by people with a coherent vision of how society should change. The founders had a radical vision, enunciated in the Declaration of Independence, that "all men are created equal" and should each have a voice in government. Progressive reformers had a vision that government should regulate rapacious corporate combines. They finally succeeded in dislodging laissez-faire when the revelations in Upton Sinclair's *The Jungle* caused wide public revulsion. Martin Luther King Jr. had a vision: "I have a dream . . . where [my children] will not be judged by the color of their skin but by the content of their character."

America is overdue for a shift in values—away from automatic government and toward a structure that allows humans to make choices needed to adapt to local needs and global challenges. My vision is this: Overthrow the bureaucracy, and return to a system based on human responsibility.

The current system is a form of tyranny. The fact that the tyrant is a bureaucratic blob instead of Birmingham police chief Bull Connor mainly means that our freedom is smothered instead of subjugated at the point of a weapon. The solution is to walk away from it, and replace the massive legal mess with a radically simplified structure focused on public goals. Make officials take responsibility to meet those goals.

Practical people resist talking about major shifts because it seems too big. Just get one thing done, they say, and then do another. But small ball doesn't work for fixing broken government. Incremental change isn't the path of history. Incremental change doesn't capture public enthusiasm, and is easily blocked by some special interest. Swinging for the fences only works in time of crisis, but small ball never fixes ingrained habits.

Not creating a new vision for governing is risky. Change coming out of a crisis is not always good. The difficulty of democracies to adapt to scarcity or entrenched interests often causes the needle to swing to the opposite extreme, putting a strong man in charge. This is what ancient historian Polybius famously predicted was always the next social stage after democracy. The shift from democracy toward dictatorship usually came, Polybius observed, when "people had grown accustomed to eating off others' tables and expected their daily needs to be met," and preferred a "monarchic master" who promised to redistribute property.

It is impossible to say when the forces will conspire to make change happen. But the stars of social unrest are unavoidably aligning. America no longer offers a government *for the people*. Look at every area of public law. Program by program, the tangle of old legislation is paralyzing society—from New Deal subsidies to endless environmental review to layers of bureaucracy for simple activities.

Nor is it a government *by the people*. Centralized legal dictates disempower citizens at every level of society. Community is an empty concept, rendered powerless by centralized bureaucracy that blocks citizens from taking ownership for local services or even from pitching in. School bureaucracy is a fortress against citizen involvement. Mandatory staffing and other regulatory requirements makes it too expensive to operate small nursing homes, which, studies show, are often much better than large ones.

Big change is inevitable. The important question is what it should look like. A new vision, particularly if it can galvanize public support, can help guide what the change will be. It should be driven not by wonky ideas of new systems, but by moral imperatives of what is a fair and practical way of making choices in our democracy. Here is an overhaul plan, including constitutional amendments to dislodge the status quo, that is informed by successful legal transformations in history.

Proposition 13: Clean house: Congress should appoint independent commissions to propose simplified codes in each area.
Simplifying legal codes, history shows, has transformational effects on the functioning of society—like replacing a muddy road with a paved expressway.

No infrastructure is more important than legal infrastructure. America's competitive advantage in world markets after World War II was attributable in part to the reliability of commercial law, which was recodified in a "Uniform Commercial Code" written after the war and widely adopted by the states. The UCC, as it is known, was drafted by a group of commercial law experts led by Professor Karl Llewellyn, who was inspired by codifications in Germany at the turn of the twentieth century.

Throughout history, legal overhauls have taken the form of "recodifications" to clarify and simplify law. Recodifications almost always happen the same way—by delegating the job to a small commission. Area by area, small committees of experts should be charged with proposing simplified codes to replace the mass of accumulated laws and regulations. These proposals can then be debated, modified, and approved.

In the sixth century, the Roman emperor Justinian commissioned three jurists to organize the law into the *Corpus Juris Civilis* to replace the "vast mass of juristic writings" that had become "a kind of cancer" on society. Their legal compilation is credited with stimulating a burst of commercial activity across the ancient world.

The new codes commissioned by Napoleon in the early nineteenth century influenced law around the world. The jurist appointed by Napoleon to lead the effort, Jean-Etienne Portalis, was confronted with what he described as a "confused and shapeless mass of foreign and French laws . . . of contradictory regulations and conflicting decisions; one encountered nothing but a mysterious labyrinth, and at every moment the guiding thread escaped us." His committee of four judges presented a simplified draft code after five months, which was then reworked by the French Council of State over the course of a hundred sessions, almost half of which were presided over by Napoleon himself.

The Napoleonic codification aspired to clarity and simplification. The civil code portion, known as the "Code Napoleon," accomplished this by making sure the new code rarely strayed from the level of general principles. As Portalis put it, "The role of the legislation is . . . to establish principles . . . and not get down to the details of questions which may arise in particular instances. It is for the judge and the jurist, imbued with the general spirit of the laws, to direct their application."

The American legal establishment in the nineteenth century resisted efforts at codification. To a society that believed in laissez-faire, legislated codes seemed like an opportunity for mischief, and also inconsistent with the prevailing belief that common law judges, not legislatures, should be the ultimate arbiters of law. Nor was there a felt need to modernize law, since the common law tradition allowed judges to adapt principles to the industrial age. With the dawn of the Progressive Era, legislatures started passing regulatory laws, but without any tradition of maintaining them in coherent codes. Perhaps this is another reason why American lawmaking is a one-way process, with sound and fury at the time of enactment and total disregard thereafter. In its approach to legislation, American democracy is like a crazy person who hoards all his possessions.

The potential benefits of a recodification in America are as great as the current clutter is inexcusable. Dumpsters can be filled with obsolete laws. Inflexible dictates can be replaced by open frameworks that permit officials to act sensibly.

A special commission on school law, for example, could recommend a radically simplified structure—built around local control, attracting better teachers, and giving full scope to individual responsibility. Legal and union micromanaging would be replaced by a few common protocols and distant oversight. School leaders could be creative; communities could get involved; bureaucratic forms would be purged; special education would be balanced against other needs; standardized testing would be only one criterion for evaluation, not a rigid metric that makes teachers act like idiot savants.

A special commission on infrastructure approvals could streamline environmental review with one main innovation: Give a federal agency the job of deciding when there's been sufficient review. Today no one has the job of deciding how much review is enough. The regulations are replete with directions that the "lead agency" must study this and that, but that agency is usually the project proponent, and so is constantly second-guessed by the courts. Round and round the process goes. More detail gets added. Years go by. Environmental review is a ship without a captain. The solution is to give authority to an agency, perhaps the Council on Environmental Quality, known as CEQ, to decide when review is sufficient for major projects. That decision should then be given deference by courts unless clearly arbitrary. That's how other countries do it, including countries that are far "greener." It is rare for overall review of an infrastructure project in Germany, for example, to last more than three years.

Remaking legal structures also allows the US to rationalize overlapping federal and local laws. Multiple approvals at different levels of government should be consolidated into what other countries call a "whole of Government" approach. From the standpoint of the citizen, it matters not where the paralysis comes from. Paralysis is paralysis. Federalism concerns are valid, and require Washington to pull back from overbearing micro-management of schools and other local services, but interstate projects such as power lines require national choices.

Congress will have the final say over new codes, but it cannot do the work of coming up with coherent proposals. Enacting a new law is difficult enough. Ending benefits violates the laws of legislative physics. Hundreds of legislators would spend years trying to throw bones to this or that favored constituency. Special commissions can present Congress with complete new codes—with shared pain and common benefits—while providing legislators the plausible deniability of not themselves coming up with the plan.

Initiating an ambitious project of spring cleaning commissions to rationalize and recodify America's public law may seem like the legal equivalent of sending a man to the moon. But it's hard to see an alternative. How else can we "slough off from government all the many activities which are obsolete [and] which have outlived their usefulness," as management expert Peter Drucker recommended?

In almost every area of society, outmoded law impedes Americans from accomplishing public and private goals. The embedded flaws are far too interwoven, too rooted in self-interest, and too grounded in a defective philosophy of public choice to accomplish piecemeal. The jungle is too thick to be pruned. Far more effective to walk away from it, and, as with other recodifications through history, to replace it with new, simplified codes.

Proposition 14: All laws with budgetary impact should sunset periodically.

Going forward, laws will still need periodic review and revision. But we now know that the iron law of unintended consequences—a reason why laws must be reconsidered regularly—also subverted the goals of the Constitution: The constitutional protection against passing too many laws became a bulwark protecting obsolete laws. This requires a constitutional solution: an amendment mandating that all laws with budgetary impact must expire after a period of time—say, after fifteen years. (See proposed Twenty-Eighth Amendment in the Appendix.)

The problem of obsolete law was familiar to our founders. Thomas Jefferson famously suggested there should be a revolution every twenty years: "A little rebellion now and then . . . is a medicine necessary for the sound health of government . . . as necessary in the political world as storms are in the physical." Madison felt that "the infirmities most besetting Popular Governments . . . are found to be defective laws which do mischief before they can be mended, and laws passed under transient impulses, of which time & reflection call for a change." But the overriding debate at the constitutional convention was about preventing federal intrusions into state sovereignty, and the framers focused on checks against new law, not getting rid of old law. If the framers were here today, there's little doubt but that they would be appalled by the disorganized piles of legal accretion.

Aligning an old law with current needs often requires starting with a blank slate. Politically, this is almost impossible. That's why sunsets should be made a constitutional obligation. Congress can be challenged if it tries to shirk its duty to rethink programs. Otherwise it can readily circumvent a sunset provision merely by passing a one-sentence law reauthorizing old laws. This has been the experience of many states with sunset laws.

Because thinking outside the box is difficult for people inside it, an independent commission should be charged with recommending what to do with an expired law. Texas, for example, has a body, the Texas Sunset Advisory Commission, that periodically conducts a review of state agencies to determine which have outlived their usefulness—for example, abolishing the Texas Board of Tuberculosis Nurse Examiners, which by the time it was eliminated certified only four nurses in the state.

Sunsets will compel Congress to take responsibility to oversee how laws actually work. Probably the greatest fear is that good programs will be abandoned. On balance, the certainty of ossification seems a far greater peril than the remote possibility that Congress would turn its back on a worthwhile public goal.

Congress's oversight of regulations. Congress today not only enacts laws and forgets about them, but also delegates to agencies the power to write regulations with the force of law. A spring cleaning will sweep out the accumulated obsolescence here as well. But there's still an open question: How can Congress exercise continuing oversight over the regulatory rule writers?

Conservatives have long objected that Congress delegates too much lawmaking authority by passing laws with vague goals, and then leaving it to an agency to act as a mini-legislator. In reaction, Congress in recent years has taken to drafting statutes with granular specificity. Rigid statutes are then enforced through rigid regulations—a phenomenon of rigidity squared. The twenty-seven-hundred-page Affordable Care Act is now being implemented with regulations that, so far, are 7 feet high, with more to come.

The White House oversees major new rules with cost-benefit scrutiny, and every rule gets litigated to the hilt by the interest groups that dislike it. But this way of making regulations bears no resemblance to the constitutional scheme. Congress, the lawmaking branch, is basically left out of the process.

Far better for Congress to write simpler statutes, and develop an effective way of overseeing agency rule making. One proposal on the table is to require advance consent by Congress for each major rule. But this is a formula for paralysis, given Congress's record of doing almost nothing. Proposals will just stack up and go nowhere, and liberals, in response, will insist on making original statutes as detailed as possible.

A solution is for Congress to reserve the power, at any point, to overturn regulations *without* presidential consent. The constitutional logic is that a delegation of lawmaking power should always be subject to withdrawal of consent by either branch that approved that delegation. The President effectively already has that power, since he controls the agencies. There's a constitutional wrinkle, requiring a sentence in a constitutional amendment to make clear that Congress too can veto a regulation, without "presentment" to the President for his signature. Letting Congress withdraw delegation for a particular rule will put lawmaking responsibility back where the framers put it.

Proposition 15: The President must have effective executive powers restored.

Article II of the Constitution states, "The executive Power shall be vested in a President." What this power means depends on who is talking. The outer boundaries of presidential power are often debated, such as the position by George W. Bush that the President could incarcerate terrorist suspects in Guantánamo without judicial oversight. There is a comparable controversy over whether President Obama can refuse to enforce certain immigration laws he doesn't like.

Little attention is paid, however, to whether the President has executive power to do the rudimentary tasks of running government. Modern presidents, according to common wisdom, wield great power. That's accurate in matters of foreign policy and national defense. But this common belief about presidential power is inaccurate for most domestic decisions. The President lacks the ability even to manage the executive branch.

Think of the core responsibilities of a President, and then ask whether he has the power to achieve them. For example:

- Bureaucracies always fall into ruts. Does the President have the ability to reorganize agencies to shake things up a little—

say, to avoid wasteful duplication and unnecessary bureaucratic layers?

- Implementing legal goals, as discussed, always hinges on
choices by responsible people. So shouldn't the President of
the United States have authority to actually make decisions
within the statutory framework—such as expediting important public works? George Washington's view was that the
President had the right to make all public choices, and that
other public officials existed only because of "the impossibility that one man should be able to perform all the great business of the state."

- Sometimes public employees drag their feet and refuse to
respond to presidential priorities, as with the EPA regional
officials who essentially ignored the President's order to expe-
dite the Bayonne Bridge. Can the President manage the public workforce and terminate employees who are slothful or
insubordinate? Madison thought the President's power over
public employees was an essential prerequisite to the post:
"If any power whatsoever is in its nature executive, it is the
power of appointing, overseeing, and controlling those who
execute the laws."

- The White House can develop its own bunker mentality and
get trapped in its own bubble. Can the President seek confi-
dential advice from outside advisers, or appoint small groups
to deliver an independent perspective?

- Often circumstances change after Congress creates a program, or there are unintended consequences, or there are new
ideas or technologies that can improve a program. Does the
President have flexibility to adapt or innovate, or to refuse to
spend allocated funds when circumstances have changed and
the expenditure would be wasteful?

No is the answer to all these questions: The President lacks the authority to make basic executive judgments. Slowly but surely, presidential powers have eroded to the point where the President cannot do the job.

Running any large organization, not to mention the world's largest government, is fraught with the difficulty of nonresponsiveness. It's too big to direct from the center. When Eisenhower was about to take office, President Truman famously contrasted running government with the army: "He'll sit here, and he'll say, 'Do this! Do that!' *And nothing will happen.* Poor Ike—it won't be a bit like the Army. He'll find it very frustrating."

Every president has confronted difficulties in governing. Even Truman, however, could not have imagined the legal tangle that has overgrown the White House. The President often has to get judicial permission—whether related to firing personnel, or letting contracts, or approving vital infrastructure. In domestic policy, the President is little more than a worker tending to Congress's massive legal machine. The fact that much of this legal machinery was imposed by legislators long gone, reflecting past priorities, only rubs salt in the constitutional wound.

The decline of presidential authority since the New Deal has been dramatic. For example, two months after the Civil Works Administration became operational in 1933, the person FDR had put in charge, Harry Hopkins, had employed 2.6 million people in thousands of rebuilding projects. By contrast, when Congress authorized an $800 billion stimulus package in 2009, the President had no authority to build anything, and most of the funds got diverted to a temporary bailout of insolvent states. The money was basically wasted.

Congress today sees its role as constraining executive decisions rather than empowering them. Its first salvo after the New Deal was to subject most agency decisions to judicial review (the 1946 Administrative Procedure Act). Abuses of power by Presidents Johnson and Nixon provided fresh impetus to rein in what Arthur Schlesinger Jr., capturing the mood of the 1960s, called "the imperial presidency." One by one Congress removed presidential management prerogatives: putting tight controls on advisory committees (the 1972 Federal Advisory Committee Act, known as FACA); removing any flexibility not to spend allocated funds to avoid waste (the Impoundment Control Act of 1974); and not renewing presidential authority to reorganize executive agencies in 1984.

These limits on presidential authority had predictable effects. For example, in 2010 almost $500 million was spent on the Ares I rocket program after it had been canceled, but the President had no authority to impound the money. The President's powerlessness to reorganize executive departments is one reason the President cannot consolidate the eighty-two separate teacher training programs.

Courts too got into the act of constraining presidential power, adopting the philosophical mind-set of Rule of Law theorists, who objected to the New Deal: The more judicial control, the better. The President's inability to streamline environmental review, as I will shortly discuss, was the effect of an appellate court ruling in 1971.

There have been efforts since the 1980s to restore some presidential authority. Congress in 1996 authorized the President to exercise a "line-item veto" over specific projects in an omnibus budget bill. In 1997, President Clinton exercised the veto eighty-two times, saving taxpayers $2 billion in avoided pork barrel projects. In 1998, however, the Supreme Court held the line-item veto unconstitutional (over three dissents) on the basis that the "presentment clause" requires the President to either veto the entire legislation or accept it completely.

Restoring the "executive power" of the President at this point is a practical imperative. An agile executive branch is essential in a fast-changing world, given the ponderous decision making of Congress and the courts.

The first principle for restoring the President's executive power is that Congress should not interfere with internal administration, aside from setting basic parameters. When the original civil service law was enacted in 1883, for example, its constitutionality was questioned as an interference with the President's prerogative to hire whom he wanted. The Attorney General agreed to give a clean opinion only after the law was changed to give the President authority to pick among the top three candidates based on test scores. By that logic, today's legal shackles on personnel decisions clearly overreach constitutional boundaries. Similarly, Congress's dictating how the President can organize advisory committees goes way past the constitutional line—why can't the President take advice in whatever form he wants?

How Congress writes laws also implicates separation of powers. The hyper detail of modern statutes reflects an assumption, largely unquestioned, that Congress should hardwire executive decisions in the future by prescribing minute details of implementation.

Nothing could be further from the constitutional conception of separation of powers than Congress telling the President how to get the job done. "It is one thing to be subordinate to the laws and another to be dependent on the legislative body," as Hamilton put it in *Federalist* No. 71: "The first comports with, the last violates, the fundamental principles of good government; and whatever may be the forms of the Constitution, unites all power in the same hands." Congressional micromanagement of the executive suggests the need for a constitutional rebalancing.

The controlling principle for executive authority should be similar to that of law generally: Congress should set goals and a framework for achieving them, but leave ample room for the executive to make choices within that framework. John Locke, no fan of consolidated authority, concluded that "many things . . . must necessarily be left to the discretion of him that has executive power in his hands." Madison also believed that Congress lacked authority to remove such executive powers: "If the constitution has invested all executive power in the president, I venture to assert that the Legislature has no right to diminish or modify his executive authority."

This doesn't mean the President can do whatever he wants. The idea of checks and balances assumes an overlap of responsibilities—what Hamilton in *Federalist* No. 66 referred to as a "partial intermixture . . . necessary to the mutual defense of the several members of the government against each other." Congress has ample tools, such as the budgetary constraints, to push back at presidential activities it believes are inconsistent with public priorities. Today, the separation of powers has become a muddle, with Congress dictating executive choices while delegating much of its lawmaking responsibility.

Because Congress and the courts have trespassed over the line of executive authority so egregiously, constitutional amendments within the new Bill of Responsibilities should make clear that the President has authority over personnel, presidential advisers, and management of the executive branch.

Proposition 16: Judges must act as gatekeepers, dismissing invalid claims.

There may have been a time, in decades past, when lawsuits were relevant mainly to the litigants. Judges then could reasonably see their responsibility merely as doing justice between the parties. The interests of broader society were not relevant in most cases. Today, however, lawsuits are instruments of social paralysis.

As I and others have discussed elsewhere, fear of possible law-suits has injected defensiveness into daily dealings throughout society—escalating health care costs; causing removal of see-saws, diving boards, and other fun implements of childhood; and, in the land of the First Amendment, spawning a culture of gag orders in personnel reviews and recommendations. (Never, ever, give an employee honest feedback. You might get sued.) Instead of protecting an open field of freedom, letting anyone sue for almost anything has created a legal minefield.

Fear of lawsuits has also corroded the ability to govern. Experts estimate that 90 percent of the time expended in propos-ing a new environmental regulation is work to build the record for possible litigation. This is another reason rationalizing old regulations can never be accomplished one by one, because the White House would find itself in a litigation maelstrom lasting, oh, perhaps a century.

Fear of litigation is like a sword of Damocles poised above every public choice, driving public employees to go by the book instead of doing what's right. The inspector doesn't make an exception that seems fair—say, allowing the meals at the com-munity pantry to be cooked at private homes—because it might be later thrown back at him in a different situation. The prin-cipal feels compelled to suspend a student under rigid rules despite obvious unfairness.

Leaning over backward to permit claims, judges tell themselves, amounts to better justice. But courts instead have become enablers of people to use law for selfish ends. Lawsuits are incredibly easy to abuse. Letting any self-interested party throw a monkey wrench into a project undermines the freedom of all. Why should a self-interested corporation be able to delay implementation of a safety regulation just by filing a claim?

The history of environmental review shows how it got hijacked by courts and descended into a spiral of endless process. The National Environmental Policy Act of 1969 nowhere suggests a judicial role in enforcing its provisions. The drafters expected that the newly formed Council on Environmental Quality would provide the needed oversight. What happened is that, in the heyday of judicial activism in 1971, a federal appeals court couldn't contain its enthusiasm and declared that courts would become an active regulating partner. Here are the opening words of the opinion by Judge J. Skelly Wright in the *Calvert Cliffs* case:

These cases are only the beginning of what promises to become a flood of new litigation—litigation seeking judicial assistance in protecting our natural environment. Several recently enacted statutes attest to the commitment of the Government to control, at long last, the destructive engine of material "progress." But it remains to be seen whether the promise of this legislation will become a reality. Therein lies the judicial role. . . . Our duty, in short, is to see that important legislative purposes, heralded in the halls of Congress, are not lost or misdirected in the vast hallways of the federal bureaucracy.

The drafters of NEPA were shocked. They didn't intend courts to be the arbiters of environmental review. But environmental supporters were not going to look a gift horse in the mouth. The statute was turned into a weapon for any group to stop or delay any project. Instead of a tool for balancing the common good, environmental review became a weapon against democratic choice. Just by filing a claim, a fringe environmental group, backed by the teamsters with an ulterior motive, can delay an important infrastructure project like the Bayonne Bridge.

Governing is not supposed to happen in a courtroom. Courts are there to make sure government doesn't transcend the boundaries of law, and to protect liberty and property from government abuse. Courts are not supposed to decide, for example, whether to approve a power line, or to approve a new regulation. They can oversee those choices to make sure the fix isn't in, or to guard against violations of a statute. But the judicial job isn't to pull out a magnifying glass to analyze each speck of thousand-page reports, or second-guess a public judgment about economic progress versus environmental impact. Public choices should generally be accountable at the polling house, not the court house.

The triumph of environmental review is manifested in the fact that 160 countries have since mandated environmental review. But there are few countries, even ones with robust environmental records, that have review processes that go on for more than a couple of years. The difference is that other countries have someone authorized to decide how much review is enough. In Germany, for example, there's a report, then public and agency review and comment, and then some official has authority to make a decision. Courts get into the act only to make sure the decision was within official bounds and does not violate someone's personal rights.

Judges should radically change their approach in dealing with public claims. Judges must act as gatekeepers—distinguishing between claims over a private right or a legal duty and those that seek to second-guess policy choices. Unless arbitrary, policy choices should generally be considered as being within the pre-rogative of politically accountable officials. The courthouse door must always be open, but whether an official acted unlawfully needs to be determined by the judge as soon as possible. Otherwise the overhang of an invalid claim paralyzes government.

But how does a judge decide where to draw that line? There's no formulaic way to distinguish between a lawsuit that protects against government abuse, and a lawsuit that is itself an abuse of process. Today that tension is resolved by letting anyone sue for almost anything. Judges today are reluctant to interfere with what is called "the right to sue." That attitude is basically backward: Lawsuits are not an act of freedom, to which courts should give deference, but are themselves an act of state power. The claimant is invoking the power of the court to compel the defendant to do something—often, to enjoin an official from fulfilling a public responsibility. That presumption should be flipped, except in situations where government is taking some-one's private property or liberty. Public choices should not be subjected to months or years of legal scrutiny unless a litigant makes an affirmative showing of illegality or abuse of discretion.

Drawing on a precedent in criminal law, Professor E. Donald Elliott has proposed that all civil claims should undergo judi-cial scrutiny before someone is required to expend resources and be at risk to a lawsuit—just as judges must approve a search warrant as a safeguard against government abuse of power. By this preliminary judicial review, bogus claims will get stopped before they start, and lawyers will learn to exercise more care and be more reasonable in their claims.

In general, judges in America have made a hash of their responsibility to maintain boundaries of who can sue for what. "An equal right to oppress or interfere," Isaiah Berlin observed, "is not the equivalent to liberty." By letting anyone sue for almost anything, judges have dramatically undermined our freedoms: Citizens go through the day looking over their shoulders, and officials find themselves accountable to courts, not the electorate, at the complaint of any self-appointed zealot. Getting judges to refocus on their proper role requires a constitutional amendment as part of the Bill of Responsibilities (see Appendix).

CITIZEN SUPERVISION OF GOVERNMENT

Government today exists in a giant bubble, occupying its own dedicated office buildings, even its own city, and is largely segregated from citizens who deal with the real-life effects of law and regulation. To most people within it, how things work out in society (or the world) is remote and not relevant. American government is self-referential. The existing culture of government is all they know. This is not a formula for a healthy democracy. There's no fresh air from the public to purge the toxins of political gamesmanship and bureaucratic inertia.

The framers understood the need for active citizen involvement; Ben Franklin described the constitutional structure to a bystander as "a republic, if you can keep it." But how exactly does engaged citizenship happen? The framers hoped that the House of Representatives, with its frequent elections, would provide citizen input to align government's values with the citizens' values. Madison described the House as "an assembly of men called for the most part from pursuits of a private nature, continued in appointment for a short time, and led by no permanent motive." This plan hasn't exactly worked out. People get elected to the House of Representatives, and then they stay in Washington to run a trade association. Instead of a body of independent citizens, it is better described as a house of hacks.

Government can't be left alone. As in all human affairs, self-awareness requires the help of others. Much of what happens in government would shock the public if they knew about it. Periodic eruptions of outrage occur when some inside deal floats to the surface—such as the $400 million "bridge to nowhere" in Alaska, which got killed only because of the happenstance of publicity.

Even enlightened leaders can fall prey to the internal logic of some lousy idea. It happens repeatedly. My adopted city, New York, has been blessed with several excellent mayors since the early 1980s, but I could compile a thick catalogue of their awful initiatives that, if implemented, would have materially diminished the value of the city—for example, tearing down Grand Central Terminal, or replacing the lights in Times Square with dark office towers, or, earlier, Robert Moses's plan to build a freeway across lower Manhattan. Most major cities have established civic groups, led by volunteers, which have acquired a reputation for speaking out for the public good. Mayors ignore them at their peril—losing support of citizen leaders, getting bad press, and looking like fools when the idea flops.

The influence of civic groups comes from public credibility. What they say carries weight because they are believed to be speaking for the greater good, not their self-interest. They have moral authority. The civic group that saved Grand Central had a long history of prominent citizens taking bold stands based on what they believed was right, led, in that case, by the writer Brendan Gill and Jacqueline Onassis. In ancient Rome, authority was a completely different concept from power—denoting a person or group who earned public respect. Moral authority cannot be self-appointed or created by some procedure; moral authority is bestowed by those who are observing the situation. "The sovereign may confer power," Edward Gibbon observed, but the "esteem of the people can alone bestow authority."

Moral authority is underestimated as a tool to facilitate collective action. If a trusted group stands behind a proposal, it is harder for a self-interested lobby to derail it. The power of independent commissions, such as the "base-closing commissions" appointed to get past the political problem of deciding which military bases would be closed, is that they usually have no axe to grind. Their moral authority then takes on the power of accepted wisdom, manifesting itself in media coverage, public opinion, and respect by those in power.

Moral authority is influential, but whom would you trust in Washington to give a balanced view of the right thing to do? There are plenty of interest groups. Indeed the city is overrun by groups with something to protect—over fourteen thousand by one count. Common wisdom is that these interest groups are the vehicle by which citizens interact with government and hold it accountable. Collectively, these groups probably represent most of America—from industries to professions to do-gooders to hobbyists.

But interest groups lack moral authority because they operate on the basis of promoting their narrow interests. AARP lobbies to get as much as it can for the elderly—whatever the cost to its members' grandchildren. The Sierra Club lobbies as hard as it can for a pristine environment—whatever the cost to jobs. The Chamber of Commerce lobbies as hard as it can to preserve corporate subsidies and tax breaks—whatever the effect on public deficits. Political accountability is thus balkanized into countless intermediate goals.

We all want clean air and water, affordable health care, and a vibrant economy. But each of these goals, if pushed too far, conflicts with another goal. In Washington the heart is competing with the lungs, and trying to deny blood to the hands and feet. Pretty soon, in a real person, the body would die, the heart along with it. That's more or less what interest groups are doing to government—no group is willing to relinquish even a fraction of its benefits.

Washington is organized to avoid moral authority. The defect is not the character of individuals (mostly), but the blinders they wear. On the rare occasions when moral authority emerges, as with the deficit reduction plan of Al Simpson and Erskine Bowles, it has the power to change the debate. It may not force action, but it has staying power and eventually does force the players to start taking real positions.

Good government requires the moral oversight of active citizens. But you don't wake up in the morning and become an active citizen. Civic activism generally requires an organizing group where people can come together—even better if the group is led by citizens with a reputation for candor and credibility. One organizing approach is outside commissions and advisory groups that are politically independent. Other countries have created permanent independent advisory groups, such as the National Regulatory Control Council in Germany, which is charged with evaluating legislative proposals. They have found that advisory committees are a way of introducing fresh thinking into the effectiveness of regulation. America should create them as well.

Proposition 17: America needs a Council of Citizens to oversee government.

Diplomat George Kennan suggested creating a new branch of government, which he called a Council of State, whose job would be to represent the greater good. Composed of nine citizens, it would be picked by the President from a larger pool of a hundred people "of high distinction" (half nominated by the governors and half by an independent committee). It would have no power, but would issue reports and opinions focusing on long-term implications of current policy. Its unique virtue would be the absence of any political ambition or obligation by its members. Its members would speak from their hearts, not their personal interests or ambitions.

Creating this independent authority (I would call it a Council of Citizens, with five-year renewable terms, chosen as in a papal conclave rather than by the President) potentially could provide the moral keel for public choices. Its credibility would enable it to slice through political artifice without much resistance, increasing the risks to bad leaders who take irresponsible positions—say, to saddle society with long-term costs for short-term political gain. It could embolden good leaders to do the right thing. This Council, as conceived by George Kennan, could provide adult supervision needed to refocus democracy on the common good. "To meet the unprecedented challenges of the modern age," Kennan wrote in 1994, "I confess I am unable to see any way . . . other than by the creation of some sort of an advisory body in which deeper forms of judgment about our national

problems, and ones more clearly detached from political involvement . . . can be evoked and given consideration."

Citizen oversight has been a goal of democratic thinkers since
ancient Athens, which required officials to stand before citizens
annually and give an account of their actions (this citizen audit
was called the *euthyna,* or "action of setting straight"). Benjamin Franklin presided at the 1776 Pennsylvania Constitutional
Convention, which created a "Council of Censors" that could
call a constitutional convention and "recommend to the legislature the repealing of such laws as appear to them to have been
enacted contrary to the principles of the constitution." The 1937
Brownlow Committee recommended "a citizen board to act as a
watchdog of the merit system." Because government inevitably
sinks "into indolent routine," John Stuart Mill wrote, "the only
stimulus which can keep the ability of the body itself up to a
high standard, is liability to the watchful criticism of equal ability outside the body." Plato's utopian community, called Magne-
sia, would be advised by a "nocturnal council" of elder statesmen
who would be the ultimate repository of good values.

Credibility is built into the structure of most advisory committees—not just from their independence, but also because an
advisory committee generally has influence only if most of its
members come together behind a cogent point of view. When
its members can't agree, Professor E. Donald Elliott explains, its
influence vanishes.

Countries such as Canada and Germany have found that independent oversight committees can endow good ideas with a
seal of approval. The public is less likely to be suspicious when
actions are vetted by an independent body. Advisory committees can thus help society break free of the paralyzing distrust to
empower responsible political leadership.

Today there is no counterbalancing force to the incessant demands of self-interest on every government act. Politicians get worn down by the constant clawing, and suffer little cost when they give in. It is a reality, of course, that stakeholders will organize and do whatever they can to avoid losing some preferred legal status. You and I would do the same thing. But the job of democratic leaders is to resist selfish entreaties.

Effective social norms, as Hobbes explained, hinge in part on fear: "What manner of life there would be, where there were no common Power to feare." Congress must fear the failures of existing laws. Officials must fear dragging their feet. Special interests must fear loss of credibility. Today, they fear nothing, insulated by the irresponsibility of all around them. One of the main roles of a Council of Citizens will be to evaluate the moral basis of policy choices. As a truth teller, the Council of Citizens can introduce shame into a political culture that today accepts cynicism as standard operating procedure and public failure as the norm.

I would also give the Council of Citizens one official responsibility: to appoint the members of independent commissions, including the spring cleaning commissions charged with recommending simplified codes in each area. In the current political stalemate, the appointment process for these panels could guarantee failure; each side would appoint partisans who would agree on nothing. That's what happens in the ill-conceived Federal Advisory Committee Act, which basically requires that commissions be composed of "stakeholders" from every conceivable interest group. Stakeholders exemplify the problem, not the solution, for accountability in modern democracy. What America needs are people who think not like stakeholders, but as representatives of the public good.

The Council's absence of power is not a detriment, but a

virtue. There is enormous power, paradoxically, in not having power. Citizens coming together for the public good have outsized influence precisely because they are seeking to do what's right, and not seeking power or benefits for themselves.

Proposition 18: Fixing democracy is a moral imperative for citizens, not just public officials.

Our mature democracy is bent over with the heavy weight of entitlements, sinecures, and bureaucracy. It can't keep going this way. It needs to make new choices. But do you think either political party will lead the needed changes? The odds are about zero that the Democratic Party will abandon, say, the perquisites of public employee unions. The odds are also low that the Republican Party will accept the need for a more flexible government.

The only way is to change it from the outside. This is an advantage of democracy: Citizens can come together to demand change. The new vision for government, as I've tried to persuade you, should be the old vision of human responsibility. We must scrape away decades of encrusted law—radically simplify public programs and mandates, and put people in charge again.

This seems ambitious, even to me. The reason to break out in this new direction is not because the path is clear, or the odds look good, but because it's the right thing to do. Government is broken. It will only get worse. The harm is not just wasteful government. Pervasive law is a cancer in our culture, eating away at the spirit that made America great. Over the past half century, many respected thinkers have tried to warn us: Arendt, Barzun, Berlin, Drucker, Havel, Hayek, Huxley, Polanyi, among many others. Aleksandr Solzhenitsyn, in a 1978 Harvard commencement address, saw growing legalisms leading Americans away from core values of self-determination to a dispiriting paralysis:

A society based on the letter of the law and never reaching any higher fails to take advantage of the full range of human possibilities. The letter of the law is too cold and formal to have a beneficial influence on society. Whenever the tissue of life is woven of legalistic relationships, this creates an atmosphere of spiritual mediocrity that paralyzes man's noblest impulses . . . After a certain level of the problem has been reached, legalistic thinking induces paralysis; it prevents one from seeing the scale and the meaning of events.

Think of all the opportunities we're losing. Every morning, Americans of good will wake up with potential of forward action in every aspect of life—to be spontaneous, to try this or that, to come up with a new program at a school or church or workplace, to start a new business, to help the kids set up a lemonade stand, to find meaning in their own efforts, and to have fun. Now imagine how much red tape might tangle you up, or unknowable legal risk will cast a pall over your dreams. The bureaucratic constraints facing officials and executives are nothing compared with the practical difficulties of a real person grabbing hold of his own idea and running with it.

Now think of your connection to democratic government. Bureaucracy has smothered the essential ingredient of democracy, citizen ownership. We don't own our government. We acquiesce in it. Most Americans seem to be in a trance—sleepwalking alongside this huge government, seemingly made safe by its size and legalistic processes. It's what we thought we needed. We lost trust in the establishment, and we lost trust in ourselves. Law would tell everyone how to do things properly. We didn't trust the dynamic of free people judging each other. Law would tell everyone how to do things properly. Now we lack the imagination to remember how a free society is supposed to work, including how officials can make necessary public choices. Worse, the system has sapped our spirit to do anything about it.

Americans need an intervention. The key to fixing democracy is motivating ourselves to make it happen. The first step, as with other bad habits, is to acknowledge the need to change: I know that government is broken and will not fix itself. The next step is to confront our own fears: I understand that a crowded society requires common choices, and that I can delegate authority to make public choices without the sky falling. The next step is personal commitment to the rehab plan: I know I must take responsibility, joining with others, to force democracy to rebuild itself.

Fixing democracy requires organizing a popular movement. There's no other responsible way: The system won't change itself, and reactive changes during a panic will be ugly. The new movement should have a platform of core principles of democratic governance, including a plan for a spring cleaning. Most important, it should be led by people who are not seeking power for themselves.

Leaders with moral authority, such as Gandhi and Martin Luther King, can aim far higher than any active politician. Political leaders can embrace change after the movement has galvanized public support—as Lincoln, for example, eventually embraced abolition. But political parties rarely lead real change, because they have trouble seizing high ground. Professor Anthony Appiah in *The Honor Code* shows the force of movements grounded in moral arguments and led by people who seek nothing for themselves. That's how William Wilberforce and others were able to ban the slave trade in England in 1807. The Chinese practice of binding the feet of young girls, considered a symbol of beauty and sexual attraction for centuries, virtually disappeared as a result of moral arguments by missionaries that it was barbaric.

The movement here must also be framed in moral terms. The American practice of binding every public choice in a legal tourniquet is immoral: It chokes off choices that are based on right and wrong, and stifles the human spirit needed to make anything work.

Modern government is permeated with moral rot, not just practical failures. Congress's abdication of responsibility to fix old law raises a host of moral issues, including draining the public fisc in obsolete programs. The fact that the laws were enacted by legislators long gone does not absolve the current members of responsibility for letting them stay on the books. "If any action carries moral significance," philosopher Joseph Raz observes, "so does its omission."

Many programs, even the most virtuous of them, are immoral as applied. It is immoral to waste $200 billion in Medicare merely because a statute written in 1965 misaligns incentives by doctors and patients. Forget the politics: That amount of waste could be rechanneled to save the oceans, or rebuild America's infrastructure, or pay off debt for the benefit of our children. The inconvenience of changing how participants get free health care is a moral drop in an immoral tsunami. Standing by to watch $200 billion pour down the drain is immoral. Anyone who defends the current program is acting immorally.

Every public program should be scrutinized in moral terms. It is immoral to spend over 25 percent of the K–12 budget on special ed. It is immoral not to terminate public employees who shirk their responsibilities. It is immoral that millions of jobs lie wasting because no one has authority to approve new infrastructure projects.

"The ultimate question for the responsible man," theologian Dietrich Bonhoeffer concluded, is "how the coming generation is to live." Our parents left us with, if not a perfect society, a modern infrastructure and little debt. We are leaving our children antiquated infrastructure, dysfunctional government, and crushing public debt. Are we acting morally?

Does this argument seem too harsh? Yes, I am throwing a bucket of cold water over you. Like mindless government, we're in a kind of democratic stupor, not really understanding how the public sector, after decades of stasis, could start degenerating so rapidly. It's hard to come to grips with the fact that our vaunted system of democratic government—this is America, for goodness' sake—could work so badly. Tocqueville understood that a centralized government could survive for generations on blind allegiance and absence of crisis: "Centralization . . . maintains society in a status quo alike secure from improvement or decline," which "we come at last to love for its own sake . . . like those devotees who worship the statue and forget the deity it represents."

Your skepticism is healthy. If our system of government has become so self-destructive, why haven't people done anything about it? For the same reason you haven't: We're all busy doing other things. We have been living off the cultural capital provided by past generations.

Ask yourself again: How would you fix any of these areas of government? Wherever you think America needs to go, we can't get there from here. Fixing American democracy is not possible without starting with a clean slate.

The forces aligned against change look powerful. Public unions, business lobbies, and other groups all claim to have armies guarding the status quo. But their power depends on you. They're just agents, not participants in productive society. Who are they really representing? Public allegiance to these groups is an inch deep. Do grandparents really want to bankrupt their grandchildren? Do business leaders really want government to fall over a fiscal cliff?

Do good teachers want a system that protects bad teachers while smothering schools in dense bureaucracy? "Men wonder to see into how small a number of weak and worthless hands a great people may fall," Tocqueville explained. Insiders "regulate everything by their own caprice," but that's only because they "speak in the name of an absent or inattentive crowd."

Washington is a house of cards. Any popular movement that stands up to it with an accurate indictment and a credible plan can push it over, particularly in a time of crisis. Its ideology about centralizing public choices in what it calls the Rule of Law is empty rhetoric, given the lie by its pervasive failure. When crisis hits a government organized by centralized choices, and "society is to be profoundly moved," Tocqueville predicted, "its force deserts it" and "the secret of its impotence is disclosed."

Government insiders will rise in unison to shout down this indictment of their rule. But they have no moral authority. They fail us, day after day. Their argument will be entirely predictable. What about a "government of laws, not of men"? What would our founding fathers think of a radically simplified government, where implementation of broad principles was left to the judgment of officials and judges?

Our founders, of course, gave us precisely the system they decry: "Just powers," as Thomas Jefferson wrote in the Declaration of Independence, "derived from the consent of the governed."

Automatic government is a false philosophy. Freedom diminishes as government loudly grinds toward paralysis. America can be saved only by liberating the force that built it. Are humans free to do what's right? That's what's missing. That's why, daunting as the prospect may be, we must rebuild modern government.

APPENDIX:
BILL OF RESPONSIBILITIES
Proposed Amendments to the Constitution

There have been twenty-seven amendments to the Constitution. The most recent, the Twenty-Seventh Amendment, proposed in 1789 and ratified in 1992, prohibits changing congressional pay raises from taking effect until "an election of representatives shall have intervened." One has been repealed (the Eighteenth Amendment, which prohibited the sale of alcoholic beverages, was repealed by the Twenty-First Amendment).

Under Article V of the Constitution, the process for amending the Constitution basically requires two steps: First, the amendment must be proposed either by a two-thirds vote of each house of Congress, or by a constitutional convention called by legislatures of two-thirds of the states. Second, the amendment must be ratified either, at the choice of Congress, by legislatures of three-fourths of the states or by constitutional conventions in three-fourths of the states.

To the existing twenty-seven amendments, I propose adding five new amendments that would become the Bill of Responsibilities. These amendments could be acted upon together or separately.

1. The Twenty-Eighth Amendment would impose a mandatory sunset so that all laws and programs with budgetary impact

would automatically expire every fifteen years, and could not be reenacted without new findings and a report from an independent commission. This amendment would not generally apply to criminal laws, for example, but would encompass most regulatory and social welfare programs. This amendment also would give Congress the authority to invalidate regulations that were promulgated pursuant to a legislative mandate—in effect, putting Congress on an equal footing with the executive branch, which currently has unilateral authority, subject to judicial review, to repeal regulations:

> **Amendment XXVIII:** No statute or regulation requiring expenditure of public or private resources (other than to oversee legal compliance or enforcement), shall be in force for longer than fifteen years. Congress may reenact such a law only after finding that it continues to serve the public interest and does not unnecessarily conflict or interfere with other priorities. Before making its determinations, Congress shall consider recommendations by an independent commission on whether and how to amend any such statute or program. At any time, Congress by majority vote of each house shall have the power to invalidate any regulation promulgated under a statutory delegation, without presentment to the President.

2. The Twenty-Ninth Amendment would restore to the President authority to manage the executive branch more actively by issuing executive orders, subject to congressional override, to reorganize agencies, veto specific items in proposed budgets, and impound money to avoid waste. Today the executive branch is mired in obsolete congressional mandates, maintained by congressional inertia rather than deliberate choices. This amendment would give the President authority

to push back while still leaving the ultimate judgment with Congress:

> **Amendment XXIX:** By executive order, subject to being overridden by majority vote in each house, the President may: reorganize executive agencies and departments; veto line items in proposed budgets; refuse to spend budgeted funds for any program in order to avoid waste or inefficiency; and undertake to accomplish statutory goals, consistent with statutory principles, by means other than those set forth in the statute or implementing regulations.

3. The Thirtieth Amendment would restore to the President authority to manage and terminate government personnel, subject only to budgetary guidelines and a neutral hiring protocol to avoid handing out jobs as "spoils." This amendment is intended to return civil service to its roots as a "merit system," not a sinecure of permanent employment. It is not possible to restore responsibility to government, giving officials flexibility to act sensibly and morally, unless they can be accountable. Historians of public service believe that modern civil service is neither effective nor responsive—an unrecognizable mutation of the original progressive vision for good government. Ossified civil service has become a symbol of bad government, and must be abandoned:

> **Amendment XXX:** The President shall have authority over personnel decisions in the executive branch, including authority to terminate public employees, within budgetary guidelines and neutral hiring protocols established by Congress.

4. The Thirty-First Amendment would restore reliability to American civil justice by requiring judges to safeguard rea-

sonable boundaries of who can sue for what. Lawsuits today are a tool for extortion and delay, with corrosive effects on free interaction throughout society. The first principle of fair justice is that like cases should be decided alike. That core precept requires judges to assert values of reasonableness, as a matter of law, to bring consistency to what has become a legal casino:

> **Amendment XXXI:** Notwithstanding the provisions of the Seventh Amendment and any state law or constitution, in lawsuits that may impede the conduct of government, or that may diminish general freedoms of persons in society, judges shall make rulings of law drawing boundaries of reasonable claims and defenses, and dismiss claims and defenses falling outside those boundaries. No person shall be required to respond to any lawsuit unless a judge shall determine that the claims are reasonable and there are reasonable allegations to support them against each person.

5. The Thirty-Second Amendment would create an independent Council of Citizens to evaluate and issue reports on the workings of government. Government has acquired a life of its own, disconnected from the needs of society, but there is little focused objection because government maintains a monopoly on public discourse. This advisory council would be a locus of moral authority, untarnished by political ambition or monetary self-interest. Democracy needs citizen supervision:

> **Amendment XXXII:** A Council of Citizens shall be established as an advisory oversight body on the workings of government. The council shall consist of nine members,

chosen by and from a Nominating Council composed of two nominees by each governor of a state. The members shall each have a term of five years, and may be renominated and chosen to serve additional terms. The council shall have no mandatory duties other than to nominate independent commissions to advise Congress on the rewriting of laws. Congress shall provide funding adequate to support staff and shall provide an honorarium to each member of the council in an amount equal to the salary of a member of Congress.

ACKNOWLEDGMENTS

This project benefited from the generous support and feedback of a number of scholars. Yale Law professor E. Donald Elliott is an extraordinary thinker, as well as an encyclopedic source of learning about administrative and constitutional law. I am pleased that he is now also a colleague at Covington & Burling. Comparative law expert James Maxeiner opened the door to a treasure trove of information about foreign law, and was also a close reader of numerous drafts. Columbia Law professor William Simon not only paved the way, but pointed me toward other useful sources. Professor Mary Ann Glendon read the manuscript and made thoughtful comments. I profited also from discussions with Professors Richard Arum, Philip Bobbitt, William Damon, Mitch Daniels, Stephen Goldsmith, Jonathan Haidt, Marshall Kapp, Paul Light, Alan Morrison, David Schoenbrod, Richard Stewart, and John Yoo. The dean at Duke Divinity School, Richard Hays, pointed me to sources I never would have found. Daniel Kahneman and Lord Leonard Hoffmann pushed me to question my own assumptions.

Research help was vital. Matt Brown and Andy Park at Common Good were consistently thoughtful and resourceful. Alex Keller spent two years exploring the nooks and crannies of American and intellectual history, to great effect. Other researchers included Evan Joiner, Ben Miller, Gordon Siu, Jonathan Waisnor, and Betselot Zeleke.

Access to the inner workings of government was indispens-able. Patrick Foye opened doors at the Port Authority, including to the inspirational Joann Papageorgis. Francis Barry and Ste-phen Sherrill Jr. steered me to useful sources in New York City government, as former Mayor Dick Riordan and David Crane did in California government.

My colleagues at Covington & Burling were an extraordinary resource: Rod DeArment and Dan Bryant on how Capitol Hill actually works; John Dugan, on the paradoxes of financial regu-lation; Bill Massey, on infrastructure regulation; George Framp-ton, on environmental review; . . . I know I've left some out. Scott Smith has been consistently supportive. Librarians Karen Schu-bart and Nicholas Perugini found all kinds of obscure sources, and Anne Fitch helped keep it all straight.

A number of friends and colleagues were close readers. Ron Faucheux at Clarus Research was a thoughtful reader of many drafts, and provided wisdom on the workings of Washington. Tony Kiser and Henry Reath suffered through early drafts, as they have with my prior books. John Guare was extraordinarily gener-ous in his reactions, and got roped into helping with the sub-title. Bob Hemm, a gifted analytical thinker, helped me develop the progression of the argument on the framework of law. Mark Schultz was consistently original in his comments. Sean Brady, Stuart Cohen, Michael Formachelli, Richard Gould, Simon Head, Fritz Hobbs, Dennis Howe, Jeffrey Leeds, Charles Nesbit, Bobby Scott, Barbara Wiechmann, and my brother John Allen Howard offered good suggestions. My daughter Charlotte Howard, a jour-nalist with healthy skepticism, pointed me to new sources and was a regular sounding board.

The expanding Common Good family was an extraordinary resource, especially Henry Miller at Goodman Media. Bill Brody, Perry Golkin, Jim O'Shaughnessy, and Missie Rennie Taylor were encouraging and opened many doors. Bob Dilenschneider was characteristically generous in his ideas and contacts. My friends who support the work of Common Good hold on to their wallets when they see me coming, but continue to generously support our campaign to redesign legal structures to unleash human freedom and ingenuity.

The TED family has proved the power of community. I have learned much from the amazing thinkers that come together in that magical tent, too many to name. Those who have become active with Common Good include Bruno Bowden, Michael Donovan, Mats Lederhausen, Craig Nevill-Manning, Alan Siegel, Katie Stanton, and Tony Tjan. Chris Anderson has done more to spread these ideas than I would have thought humanly possible. Moral authority, as I argue in the book, is like a force of nature, almost unstoppable.

The W. W. Norton team was consistently thoughtful and flexible. My editor, Starling Lawrence, is justifiably famous for his judgment. Ryan Harrington was consistently responsive, and helped me deal painlessly with the obscure concerns of publishers. Copy editor Stephanie Hiebert was sharp as a knife. Ken Godat, overnight, designed a forceful cover.

My agent and friend Andrew Wylie has made all this possible by believing in me from the beginning, twenty years ago. He is also a close reader and offered valuable suggestions to early drafts.

Luck goes a long way, and I have been lucky in the people in my life. My mentors taught me so much: My father, Reverend John Howard, taught me the meaning in helping others, and my mother, Charlotte Howard, taught everyone about limitless human willpower; Eugene Wigner, my boss at the Oak Ridge National Lab, encouraged me to follow my instincts (only decades later did I learn that his mentor was Michael Polanyi, one of the main resources for this book); John Warden taught me how to write boldly; Kent Barwick is a model of gracious willpower, never taking no for an answer; Andrew Heiskell was a role model for so many things, including effective leadership; and Arthur Schlesinger, attached to me through our marriages to close cousins, became my greatest resource, encouraging me to pursue this inquiry wherever it might lead. Growing up, I never imagined I could be blessed with such inspiring, generous friends as these and others too numerous to name.

Finally, I thank my lovely and long-suffering wife Alexandra and our four amazing children—Olivia, Charlotte, Lily, and Alexander, who are each purposeful, funny, and not sufficiently respectful. The two that have married have brought remarkable men into the fold—Ernie Sabine and Dan Osnoss—balancing the odds a little in family gatherings. Sometimes I have to pinch myself.

Thank you all.

NOTES

These notes are linked to the text by page number and key phrase. Key phrases enclosed in quotation marks represent exact wording from quoted material; those without quotation marks are the author's exact wording. Bracketed language identifies general topics that do not exactly match wording in the text. These endnotes are also available at www.ruleofnobody.com.

Preface

1 [Franklin Township flooding]: Rick Epstein, "Franklin Township Official Bemoans $12K in Paperwork to Remove Tree from Creek," *Hunterdon County Democrat*, February 17, 2012.

1 "government must go away completely": Jon Stewart, in his interview of the author on *The Daily Show with Jon Stewart*, Comedy Central, November 18, 2010, http://www.thedailyshow.com/watch/thu-november-18-2010/exclusive---philip-k--howard-extended-interview.

2 $5 billion to weatherize some 607,000 homes: Michael Grunwald, *The New New Deal* (New York: Simon & Schuster, 2012), 305–10. See US Government Accountability Office, *Recovery Act: Progress and Challenges in Spending Weatherization Funds*, GAO-12-195 (Washington, DC: GAO, 2011), 5–7, http://www.gao.gov/assets/590/587064.pdf; Louise Radnofsky, "A Stimulus Project Gets All Caulked Up," *Wall Street Journal*, September 21, 2010, http://online.wsj.com/article/SB10001424052748704488404575441410775239560.html?mod=WSJ_hpp_LEFTTopStories.

2 costs taxpayers about 20 percent more: James Sherk, "Examining the Department of Labor's Implementation of the Davis-Bacon Act," Heritage Foundation, April 28, 2011, http://www.heritage.org/research/testimony/2011/04/examining-the-department-of-labors-implementation-of-the-davis-bacon-act.

2 the actual total was twelve: US Department of Energy, Office of Inspector General, Office of Audit Services. *Special Report: Progress in Implementing the Department of Energy's Weatherization Assistance Program under the American Recovery and Reinvestment Act*, OAS-RA-10-04 (Washington, DC: US Department of Energy, 2010), 2, http://energy.gov/sites/prod/files/igprod/documents/OAS-RA-10-04.pdf.

Part I: The Rule of Nobody

The Rule of Nobody

7 [Bayonne Bridge]: Most facts about the Bayonne Bridge process came from interviews with Joann Papageorgis and review of project files in 2012 and 2013. The final environmental assessment can be found at http://www.regulations.gov/#!documentDetail;D=

USCG-2012-1091-0118. A fact sheet can be found at http://www.uscg.mil/d1/prevention/bridges/BayonneBridge_FactSheet_ENG_v8.pdf. See also "Bayonne Bridge Navigational Clearance Program—Draft Environmental Assessment," US Coast Guard, January 4, 2013, http://www.regulations.gov/#!documentDetail;D=USCG-2012-1091-0002. According to the US Coast Guard, the $1 billion Bayonne Bridge project would save an average of $169 million per year over fifty years.

9   [environmental requirements]: Agency guidelines for the implementation of the National Environmental Policy Act (NEPA) are issued by the White House Council on Environmental Quality. They are available at http://ceq.hss.doe.gov/nepa/regs/ceq/toc_ceq.htm.

10 [environmental objections]: Letter dated December 8, 2011, from William J. Schulte (Eastern Environmental Law Center) to Commander Gary Kasoff, US Coast Guard. See Steve Strunsky, "Attempt to Raise Bayonne Bridge Roadway Puts Politicians, Environmental Groups at Odds," *Star Ledger*, July 27, 2012, http://www.nj.com/news/index.ssf/2012/07/attempt_to_raise_bayonne_bridg.html. For quality of life in Newark, see "Building Bridges," *Need to Know*, PBS, January 18, 2013: video, http://www.pbs.org/wnet/need-to-know/economy/video-building-bridges/16069; transcript, http://www.pbs.org/wnet/need-to-know/uncategorized/transcript-january-18-2013/16072.

11 [Obama expediting the project]: White House, Office of the Press Secretary, "We Can't Wait: Obama Administration Announces 5 Major Port Projects to Be Expedited," news release, July 19, 2012.

11 "shoddy review": Jeff Tittel from the Sierra Club, as quoted in Steve Strunsky, "Fast-Tracking Raising of Bayonne Bridge a Bad Idea, N.J. Sierra Club Pres. Says," *Star Ledger*, July 20, 2012, http://www.nj.com/news/index.ssf/2012/07/fast-tracking_raising_of_bayon.html. See also the December 8, 2011, letter from William J. Schulte to Coast Guard Commander Gary Kasoff, http://cleanandsafeports.org/wp-content/uploads/2012/07/20111208-CHPs-Comments-Re-Bayonne-Bridge-Project1.pdf.

12 "a basic impasse still exists": EPA Preliminary Remarks, Bayonne Bridge Navigation Clearance Project Preliminary Draft Environmental Assessment, August 16, 2012, http://www.regulations.gov/api/contentStreamer?objectId=0900006481218c1e&disposition=attachment&contentType=pdf. EPA repeated its objections in remarks dated December 6, 2012, after the Port Authority had commissioned a study on the effects of allowing more efficient ships in the harbor.

12 [Coast Guard approval]: US Coast Guard, "Finding of No Significant Impact for Proposed Modification of the Bayonne Bridge across the Kill Van Kull between Bayonne, Hudson County, New Jersey and Staten Island, Richmond County, New York," http://www.uscg.mil/hq/cg4/cg47/docs/FONSI_SIGNED_9MAY13.doc.pdf.

12 [over eight years for highway projects]: Petra Todorovich and Daniel Schned, *Getting Infrastructure Going: Expediting the Environmental Review Process* (New York: Regional Plan Association, 2012), 6, http://www.rpa.org/library/pdf/RPA-Getting-Infrastructure-Going.pdf.

12 [Goethals Bridge]: The Goethals Bridge review began in 2003 and still was not complete in mid-2013. The Port Authority web page on the Goethals Bridge states that the environmental review was completed in 2010, after six and a half years. But this statement does not include a variety of related approvals.

13 [antiquated electrical grid]: US Department of Energy, *Large Power Transformers and the U.S. Electric Grid*, June 2012, http://energy.gov/sites/prod/files/Large%20Power%20Transformer%20Study%20-%20June%202012_0.pdf. See also US Energy Information Administration, "How Much Electricity Is Lost in Transmission and Distribution in the United States?" http://www.eia.gov/tools/faqs/faq.cfm?id=105&t=3, and other information in the EIA's "Frequently Asked Questions" web page.

14 "rule by Nobody": Hannah Arendt, "A Special Supplement: Reflections on Violence," *New York Review of Books*, February 27, 1969: "Bureaucracy . . . could be properly called the rule

by Nobody. Indeed, if we identify tyranny as the government that is not held to give account of itself, rule by Nobody is clearly the most tyrannical of all, since there is no one left who could even be asked to answer for what is being done." See also Hannah Arendt, *The Human Condition* (Chicago: University of Chicago Press, 1958), 40: "The rule by nobody is not necessarily no-rule; it may indeed . . . be one of its cruelest and most tyrannical versions."

15   not by the whim of some official: The traditional limitation of state power is that there must be "no offense without a law" (*nullum crimen sine legem*). John Locke's conception is that the Rule of Law aimed to "make sure power does not catch us unawares." See discussion in John Braithwaite, "Rules and Principles: A Theory of Legal Certainty," *Australian Journal of Legal Philosophy* 27 (2002): 47–82.

15   National Environmental Policy Act: 42 USC § 4331(a) (1969). "The Congress . . . declares that it is the continuing policy of the Federal Government, in cooperation with State and local governments, and other concerned public and private organizations, to use all practicable means and measures, including financial and technical assistance, in a manner calculated to foster and promote the general welfare, to create and maintain conditions under which man and nature can exist in productive harmony, and fulfill the social, economic, and other requirements of present and future generations of Americans."

15   "Government in all its actions": Friedrich Hayek, *The Road to Serfdom* (London: Routledge & Sons, 1944), 75. Hayek stated a similar confined view of the authority of judges: "When we obey laws, in the sense of general abstract rules . . . we are not subject to another man's will and are therefore free. It is because the judge who applies them has no choice in drawing the conclusions that follow from the existing body of rules and the particular facts of the case, that it can be said that laws and not men rule." Friedrich Hayek, *The Constitution of Liberty* (Chicago: University of Chicago Press 1960), 153.

16   "Let all the laws be clear": Voltaire, as quoted in John R. Howe, *Language and Political Meaning in Revolutionary America* (Amherst: University of Massachusetts Press, 2004), 38.

16   A teacher in Chicago: John Stewart, "Class Disrupted: Disorder and Its Effects on Learning and School Culture" (paper presented at Common Good Conference, Washington, DC, October 31, 2007).

17   [New York law prohibiting facility closure]: Associated Press, "Gov.-Elect Andrew Cuomo Warns of Tough Choices in New York's Future," November 22, 2010, http://www.syracuse.com/news/index.ssf/2010/11/gov-elect_andrew_cuomo_warns_o.html. ("'We're paying 30 staff people to baby-sit an empty building,' Cuomo said.") See also Russell Sykes, "Unions v. NY Youth," *New York Post*, March 22, 2012, http://www.nypost.com/p/news/opinion/oped columnists/unions_ny_youth_spvTW1YdtBRilUsrfv3jpL.

17   [Medicare history]: Robert Ball, as quoted in M. G. Gluck and V. Reno, eds., *Reflections on Implementing Medicare* (Washington, DC: National Academy of Social Insurance, 2001). Legislative carelessness was there in the beginning. In the legislative push to create Medicare in 1965, one key part (reimbursement of doctor's fees, known as Part B) was inserted over a weekend with no advance planning, at the instruction of Wilbur Mills, the powerful head of the House Ways and Means Committee. Staffers simply marked up a standard Aetna policy without, as the main drafter put it, "appreciating the implications of its basic assumptions" (ibid., 3). See also Robert M. Ball, "The First 60 Days of Medicare," *Journal of the National Medical Association* 58: 475–79 (November 1966); Robert M. Ball, "What Medicare's Architects Had In Mind," *Health Affairs* 14: 62–72 (1995).

17   "energetic gaming strategies": Theodore R. Marmor, *The Politics of Medicare*, 2nd ed. (New York: Aldine Transaction, 2000), 97. See also D. Peter Birkett, *Psychiatry in the Nursing Home* (Binghamton, NY: Haworth, 2001), 58: "In the early days of Medicare notorious examples of 'gang visits' abounded. The doctor would visit a nursing home containing 100 or more patients, not leave the administrator's office, yet charge for having seen all the patients."

18 [Medicare mud wrestling]: See Steven Brill, "Bitter Pill: Why Medical Bills Are Killing Us," *Time*, March 4, 2013.

18 [Medicare waste]: Robert Pear, "Health Official Takes Parting Shot at 'Waste,'" *New York Times*, December 3, 2011, http://www.nytimes.com/2011/12/04/health/policy/parting-shot-at-waste-by-key-obama-health-official.html: "The official in charge of Medicare and Medicaid for the last 17 months says that 20 percent to 30 percent of health spending is 'waste' that yields no benefit to patients, and that some of the needless spending is a result of onerous, archaic regulations enforced by his agency . . . If his estimate is right, Medicare and Medicaid could save $150 billion to $250 billion a year by eliminating waste, which he defines as 'activities that don't have any value.'"

18 70 percent of federal tax revenue: See the Heritage Foundation's report: William W. Beach and Patrick D. Tyrrell, *The 2012 Index of Dependence on Government*, SR-104 (Washington, DC: Heritage Center for Data Analysis, 2012), https://thf_media.s3.amazonaws.com/2012/pdf/sr104.pdf.

19 [New York City civil service rules]: Stephen Goldsmith and Stephen Dobrowsky, separate interviews by author, 2011.

19 [federal IT technician]: Interview with affected federal employee, by Betselot Zeleke (a researcher for the author), 2011.

19 Accountability is virtually nonexistent: Stephen Dobrowsky, interview by author, 2011. In California, a nurse's aide who stole money from patients and a hospital employee who beat a disabled patient with a shoe could not be held accountable. Their firings were overturned by the state Personnel Board, which determined that the firings were not consistent with "progressive discipline." See Jack Dolan, "Little-Known State Board Overturns Employee Terminations," *Los Angeles Times*, November 3, 2011.

19 [math on public employees]: The number of government employees in 2011 was 22.3 million (2.9 million federal and 19.4 million state and local). US Census Bureau, "Federal Government Civilian Employment," March 2011, http://www2.census.gov/govs/apes/11fedfun.pdf; and US Census Bureau, "2011 Public Employment and Payroll Data, State and Local Governments: United States Total," http://www2.census.gov/govs/apes/11stlus.txt.

The total compensation and benefits of public employees in 2011 (the latest year for which information is available) was $1,551,439 million ($476,991 million federal, plus $1,074,448 million state and local). See "Compensation of Employees: Federal General Government (B568RC0A144NBEA)," Bureau of Economic Analysis, March 31, 2013, http://research.stlouisfed.org/fred2/series/B568RC0A144NBEA; and "Compensation of Employees: State and Local General Government (B251RC0A144NBEA)," Bureau of Economic Analysis, March 31, 2013, http://research.stlouisfed.org/fred2/series/B251RC0A144NBEA.

The approximate amount spent by government in 2011 (the latest year for which complete information is available) was calculated by taking all government expenditures at all levels—$5,300.6 billion—and backing out employee compensation ($1,551,439 million) and the major transfer payments: Medicare ($479,923 million); Medicaid ($274,964 million); Social Security ($724,923 million); and debt service ($577,559 million—$453,987 million federal, plus $123,572 million state and local), for total remaining expenditures of $1,691,792 million, excluding personnel costs, major transfer payments, and interest. See Office of Management and Budget, "Historical Tables," tables 15.2 and 8.5, http://www.whitehouse.gov/omb/budget/historicals, accessed August 2013; and Jeffrey L. Barnett and Phillip M. Vidal. "State and Local Government Finances Summary: 2011," G11-ALFIN (Washington, DC: US Census Bureau, July 2013), 7, http://www2.census.gov/govs/local/summary_report.pdf.

20 The failures . . . are hardly surprising: See Philippe Nonet and Philip Selznick, *Law and Society in Transition: Toward Responsive Law* (New York: Harper & Row, 1978), 64: "Detaching legal thought from social reality," Nonet and Selznick note with academic understatement, works "to the detriment of practical problem-solving."

20 [doubling down on rigidities]: See Paul C. Light, *Thickening Government: Federal Hierarchy and*

the Diffusion of Accountability (Washington, DC: Brookings Institution Press, 1995). Sociologist Michel Crozier pointed out the tendency of bureaucracy to feed itself in his 1964 landmark study: "Finally, when one rule prevents adequate dealing with one case, its failure will not generate pressure to abandon the rule, but, on the contrary, will engender pressure to make it more complete, more precise, and more binding." Michel Crozier, *The Bureaucratic Phenomenon* (Chicago: University of Chicago Press, 1964), 187. See also James M. Buchanan, *The Limits of Liberty: Between Anarchy and Leviathan* (Indianapolis, IN: Liberty Fund, 2000; originally published 1975 by University of Chicago Press), 91: "If something is wrong, have government regulate it. If the regulators fail, regulate them, and so on down the line."

20 [Morristown soup kitchen]: William McGurn, "Government vs. Soup Kitchen," *Wall Street Journal*, November 22, 2011.

21 [Bethesda lemonade stand]: Emily Maltby, "Lemonade Stand Gets Squeezed," *Wall Street Journal*, June 17, 2011, http://blogs.wsj.com/in-charge/2011/06/17/lemonade-stand-gets-squeezed. See also Michael Laris, "Near U.S. Open, Montgomery Tries to Put the Squeeze on Lemonade Stands," *Washington Post*, June 17, 2011, http://www.washingtonpost.com/local/dc-politics/montgomery-tries-to-put-the-squeeze-on-lemonade-stand/2011/06/17/AGJ9fWZH_story.html.

21 [lemonade stand shutdowns across the country]: Erik Kain, "The Inexplicable War on Lemonade Stands," *Forbes*, August 3, 2011, http://www.forbes.com/sites/erikkain/2011/08/03/the-inexplicable-war-on-lemonade-stands. See also Erik Kain, "Twelve-Year-Old's Green Tea Stand Shut Down in Massachusetts," *Forbes*, August 25, 2011, http://www.forbes.com/sites/erikkain/2011/08/25/massachusetts-state-police-shut-down-twelve-year-olds-green-tea-stand.

21 Opening a new restaurant: Diane Cardwell, "A New Team Helps Steer Restaurateurs through a Thicket of Red Tape," *New York Times*, December 27, 2010, http://www.nytimes.com/2010/12/28/nyregion/28permits.html. The emergency manager appointed to take over bankrupt Detroit, Kevyn Orr, "found 'bureaucracy on steroids'—for example, 'more than two dozen layers of approval for planning and zoning.'" George F. Will, "Kevyn Orr, Motown's One-Man Show," *Washington Post*, August 2, 2013, http://www.washingtonpost.com/opinions/george-will-kevyn-orr-motowns-one-man-show/2013/08/02/5d0a0672-facd-11e2-a369-d1954abcb7e3_story.html.

22 Retired scientists can't teach: See http://www.theatlantic.com/national/archive/2013/01/teacher-bar-exams-would-be-a-huge-mistake/267133, citing "Report to the President: Prepare and Inspire: K-12 Education in Science, Technology, Engineering, and Math (STEM) for America's Future," President's Council of Advisors on Science and Technology, September 2010, http://www.whitehouse.gov/sites/default/files/microsites/ostp/pcast-stem-ed-final.pdf. Almost any volunteer activity for schools or government arouses the ire of public employee unions, who often claim that volunteers violate union agreements. In Wausau, Wisconsin, for example, the union filed a grievance to prevent an elderly resident from serving as a volunteer crossing guard for the local elementary school. See Meg Bonacorsi, "Union Has Issues with Volunteer Crossing Guard," WAOW.com, January 27, 2010, http://www.waow.com/Global/story.asp?S=11891208.

22 The inexorable growth of bureaucratic requirements: Stephen Rathgeb Smith, "Civic Infrastructure in America," in *Civil Society, Democracy, and Civic Renewal*, ed. Robert Fullinwider (New York: Rowman and Littlefield, 1999), 144–45. See also Michael Lipsky, *Street-Level Bureaucracy: Dilemmas of the Individual in Public Services* (New York: Russell Sage Foundation, 1980); Robert J. Chaskin, "Bureaucracy and Democracy in a Community Planning Context," *Journal of Planning Education and Research* 24 (2005): 408–19; and Marc Hertogh, "Through the Eyes of Bureaucrats: How Front-Line Officials Understand Administrative Justice," in *Administrative Justice in Context*, ed. Michael Adler (Oxford: Hart, 2010), 203–26 (describing how a crime-ridden neighborhood in the Netherlands was stabilized by giving local officials more autonomy from bureaucratic requirements).

22   to ignore what's legally required: See Steven Maynard-Moody and Michael C. Musheno, *Cops, Teachers, Counselors: Stories from the Front Lines of Public Service* (Ann Arbor: University of Michigan Press, 2003); and Hertogh, "Through the Eyes," *supra* note for page 22, p. 204. See also Lipsky, *Street-Level Bureaucracy, supra* note for page 22, p. 71: "To deliver street-level policy through bureaucracy is to embrace a contradiction. On the one hand, service is delivered by people to people, invoking a model of human interaction, caring, and responsibility. On the other hand, service is delivered through a bureaucracy, invoking a model of detachment and equal treatment."

22   The system wears people down: See Cary Cherniss, *Professional Burnout in Human Service Organizations* (Westport, CT: Praeger, 1980). In hierarchical bureaucracies, burnout is often "caused by emotional drain due to routine, monotony, and lack of control." Wilmar B. Schaufeli, Christina Maslach, and Tadeusz Marek, eds., *Professional Burnout: Recent Developments in Theory and Research* (Washington, DC: Taylor & Francis, 1993), 132. The first listed cause of "burnout" by the Mayo Clinic is "lack of control." Mayo Clinic, "Job Burnout: How to Spot It and Take Action," http://www.mayoclinic.com/health/burnout/WL00062, accessed July 2013. For a description of Pavlov's experiments, see Michael Polanyi, *Personal Knowledge: Towards a Post-critical Philosophy* (Chicago: University of Chicago Press, 1958), 367.

22   "tired of feeling powerless": Adam K. Edgerton, "Why I Quit Teaching," *Huffington Post*, September 5, 2012.

23   "The guy standing there": Joe Tanner, interview by author, 2008. Leaving soldiers free to make decisions on the battlefield is a basic tenet of military organization. Since at least the turn of the twentieth century, the US Army field service regulations have specified that "an order shall not trespass upon the province of a subordinate. It should contain everything beyond the independent authority of the subordinate, but nothing more." Colonel Clinton J. Ancker III, "The Evolution of Mission Command in U.S. Army Doctrine, 1905 to the Present," *Military Review*, March/April 2013, 43.

23   "at least nine-tenths": Chester Irving Barnard, *The Functions of the Executive* (Cambridge, MA: Harvard University Press, 1938), 232.

23   "will give full scope": Peter F. Drucker, *Management*, rev. ed. (New York: Collins, 2008), 267. Thomas Edison put the point his way: "Nothing that's good works by itself . . . You've got to make the damn thing work." See generally Harold Evans, *They Made America* (Boston: Little, Brown, 2004), 169.

24   Centralized legal dictates: Tocqueville talks extensively about the evils of centralized administration. See Alexis de Tocqueville, *Democracy in America*, ed. Phillips Bradley (New York: Vintage, 1990), 1:86–92, 2:300–320. He distinguishes between centralized legal goals, which can enhance freedom, and dictating to people how people meet those goals: "It is especially dangerous to enslave men in the minor details of life. For my own part, I should be inclined to think freedom less necessary in great things than in little ones . . . Subjection in minor affairs . . . does not drive men to resistance, but it crosses them at every turn, till they are led to surrender the exercise of their own will. Thus their spirit is gradually broken and their character enervated" (ibid., 2:320).

25   "A government ill-executed": Alexander Hamilton, "No. 70," in Hamilton, Madison, and Jay, *Federalist*, 341.

26   "Policy problems are multiplying faster": Donald F. Kettl, "Administrative Accountability and the Rule of Law," *PS: Political Science and Politics* 42, no. 1 (January 2009): 16.

Rethinking the Rule of Law

26   The Rule of Law: For a comprehensive account of the Rule of Law, see Brian Z. Tamanaha, *On the Rule of Law: History, Politics, Theory* (Cambridge: Cambridge University Press, 2004).

26   [requirements of the Rule of Law]: Scholars and philosophers have posited numerous

variations of the requirements of the Rule of Law. For example, see Lon Fuller, *The Morality of Law* (New Haven, CT: Yale University Press, 1969), listing eight factors, most of which I believe can be incorporated into the doctrines of predictability and nonarbitrariness. See also discussion in Jeremy Waldron, "Is the Rule of Law an Essentially Contested Concept (in Florida)?" *Law and Philosophy*, no. 2 (March 2002): 137–64.

27 [the Rule of Law as boundary conditions]: See, for example, Isaiah Berlin, "Two Concepts of Liberty," in Berlin, *The Proper Study of Mankind: An Anthology of Essays*, ed. Henry Hardy and Roger Hausheer (New York: Farrar, Straus and Giroux, 1998), 236; Michael Oakeshott, "The Rule of Law," in *On History and Other Essays* (Indianapolis, IN: Liberty Fund, 1999), 129–78.

27 Liberals self-righteously cling to the status quo: Representative Keith Ellison (D-MN) in 2013 claimed that President Obama's attempts to alter Social Security payment metrics represent an attempt "to take apart everything that helps make American lives better." See Lloyd Grove, "Pelosi Joins Obama as Target of Liberals' Anger over Budget," *Daily Beast*, April 11, 2013.

28 "starving the beast": See Bruce Bartlett, "'Starve the Beast': Origins and Development of a Budgetary Metaphor," *Independent Review* 12, no. 1 (Summer 2007): 5–26.

29 "wise legal policy to use rules": Joseph Raz, "Legal Principles and the Limits of Law," *Yale Law Journal* 81, no. 5 (April 1972): 841.

29 "peace of mind is promoted": Tom Campbell, *Prescriptive Legal Positivism: Law, Rights and Democracy* (London: UCL, 2004), 36.

29 "This step has enormous virtues": Cass R. Sunstein, "Problems with Rules," *California Law Review* 83, no. 4 (July 1995): 1022.

29 "rationalized completeness": Louis L. Jaffe, "The Effective Limits of the Administrative Process: A Reevaluation," *Harvard Law Review* 67, no. 7 (May 1954): 1135.

29 nursing homes in America: See Anita Bercovitz et al., "End-of-Life Care in Nursing Homes: 2004 National Nursing Home Survey," *National Health Statistics Reports* no. 9 (October 8, 2008), http://www.cdc.gov/nchs/data/nhsr/nhsr009.pdf.

30 [nursing home regulations]: All of the state nursing home regulations for Kansas can be viewed online: Kansas Department on Aging, "Statutes and Regulations for the Licensure and Operation of Nursing Facilities," http://www.hpm.umn.edu/nhregsplus/NHRegs_by_State/Kansas/KS%20Complete%20Regs.pdf, accessed June 2013. Regulations from other states can also be viewed online, through the University of Minnesota School of Public Health's website: "NH Regulations Plus," http://www.hpm.umn.edu/nhregsplus, accessed June 2013. In the case of Kansas, none of the regulations can be waived.

31 "either natural or artificial illumination": Occupational Safety & Health Administration, "Safety and Health Regulations for Construction," § 1926.26, https://www.osha.gov/pls/oshaweb/owadisp.show_document?p_table=STANDARDS&p_id=10612, accessed June 2013.

31 [Medicare reimbursement categories]: Anna Wilde Mathews, "Walked into a Lamppost? Hurt While Crocheting? Help Is on the Way," *Wall Street Journal*, September 13, 2011, http://online.wsj.com/article/SB10001424053111904103404576560742746021106.html. See also the *Wall Street Journal*'s interactive web page "A Code for What Ails You": http://graphicsweb.wsj.com/documents/MEDICALCODES0911/#term=Bitten.

32 [day care center rules]: Tim Hoover, "Early State Proposal Would Ramp Up Rules for Child Care Centers to Earn License," *Denver Post*, July 12, 2011.

32 thirty-seven pages of regulatory fine print: See *Rules Regulating Child-Care Centers (Less than 24-Hour Care)* (Denver: Colorado Department of Human Services, Division of Child Care, 2012), 29, http://www.colorado.gov/cs/Satellite?blobcol=urldata&blobheadername1=Content-Disposition&blobheadername2=Content-Type&blobheadervalue1=inline%3B+filename%3D%227.702+Center.pdf%22&blobheadervalue2=application%2Fpdf&blobkey=id&blobtable=MungoBlobs&blobwhere=1251820002192&ssbinary=true.

33 [Maryland school rules]: Eric Owens, "Maryland School District Outlaws Hugging, Homemade Food, Pushing Kids on Swings," *Daily Caller*, March 19, 2013, http://dailycaller .com/2013/03/19/maryland-school-district-outlaws-hugging-homemade-food-pushing-kids-on-swings.

33 "eliminate[d] the human element": David Kairys, "Searching for the Rule of Law," *Suffolk University Law Review* 36, no. 2 (2003): 319.

34 "if the laws be so voluminous": James Madison, "No. 62," in Hamilton, Madison, and Jay, *Federalist*, 304.

34 Modern law is too detailed: The logic of rationalized completeness drives rules light-years away from information that might be useful to a real person or problems. The worker safety regulations require thick volumes of "material safety data sheets," known as MSDS, to be accessible to all workers for all products that might be hazardous in any way, without distinguishing remote from realistic dangers. An MSDS sheet on bricks (mandatory for construction sites) helps workers identify a brick (a "hard ceramic body . . . with no odor") and provides its boiling point (above 3500 degrees Fahrenheit), among other useless information. See Philip K. Howard, *The Death of Common Sense: How Law Is Suffocating America* (New York: Random House, 1994), 12–15, 36–38.

34 "Some of the standards are completely forgotten": John Braithwaite and Valerie Braithwaite, "The Politics of Legalism: Rules versus Standards in Nursing-Home Regulation," *Social & Legal Studies* 4, no. 3 (1995): 320.

35 "I run a lot of decisions by legal counsel": Frederick M. Hess, "Cages of Their Own Design," *Educational Leadership* 67, no. 2 (October 2009), http://m.ascd.org/EL/Article/859b4bbf2 0eb3210VgnVCM100000250210acRCRD.

35 "culture of can't": Frederick M. Hess and Whitney Downs, "The Culture of 'Can't' in American Schools," *Atlantic*, April 12, 2012, http://www.theatlantic.com/national/ archive/2012/04/the-culture-of-cant-in-american-schools/255757. See also Chester E. Finn, Jr., "Why School Principals Need More Authority," *Atlantic*, April 4, 2012.

35 When California allowed schools to apply for waivers: Levin, H. M. (2006). "Why Is This So Difficult?" in *Educational Entrepreneurship: Realities, Challenges, Possibilities*, ed. F. M. Hess (Cambridge, MA: Harvard Education Press, 2006), 173–74.

35 [disorder in schools]: See generally Richard Arum, *Judging School Discipline: The Crisis of Moral Authority* (Cambridge, MA: Harvard University Press, 2003), 169: "It is this hesitation, doubt and weakening of conviction . . . that has undermined the effectiveness of school discipline." See also David L. Kirp, "Proceduralism and Bureaucracy: Due Process in the School Setting," *Stanford Law Review* 28, no. 5 (May 1976), 841–76. For a vivid description of the decline in school culture at one school, see Gerald Grant, *The World We Created at Hamilton High* (Cambridge, MA: Harvard University Press, 1988).

35 [girl rejecting pill]: Connie Leonard, "Jeffersonville Middle School Student Suspended for Touching Pill," Wave 3 News, February 25, 2010, http://www.wave3.com/Global/story .asp?S=12047295.

36 cheese slice: Stephen Goldsmith (former New York City deputy mayor), interview by author, 2011.

36 large legal staffs can't keep it all straight: See J. B. Ruhl and James Salzman, "Mozart and the Red Queen: The Problem of Regulatory Accretion in the Administrative State," *Georgetown Law Journal* 91 (2003): 792. See also the following comparative study of environmental regulation in Japan and the US: Kazumasu Aoki, Lee Axelrad, and Robert A. Kagan, "Industrial Effluent Control in the United States and Japan," in Axelrad and Kagan, *Regulatory Encounters*, 64–95. See also Eugene Bardach and Robert A. Kagan, *Going by the Book: The Problem of Regulatory Unreasonableness* (Philadelphia: Temple University Press, 1982).

36 "enforced or invoked selectively": Lipsky, *Street-Level Bureaucracy*, *supra* note for page 22, p. 14. See also "The Dodd-Frank Act: Too Big Not to Fail," *Economist*, February 18, 2012, discussing the complexity of the 848-page Dodd-Frank law: "Officials are being given the

power to . . . make arbitrary or capricious rulings. The lack of clarity which follows from the sheer complexity of the scheme will sometimes, perhaps often, provide cover for such capriciousness."

37 "habit of citing the same ones": Braithwaite, "Rules and Principles," *supra* note for page 15, p. 63.

37 at the mercy of any official: In his critique of the American criminal justice system, William Stuntz concluded that "too much law amounts to no law at all: when legal doctrine makes everyone an offender, the relevant offenses have no meaning independent of law enforcers' will. The formal rule of law yields the functional rule of official discretion." William J. Stuntz, *The Collapse of American Criminal Justice* (Cambridge, MA: Belknap Press, 2011), 3. See also Aharon Barack (former president of the Israel Supreme Court), *Judicial Discretion*, trans. Yadin Kaufmann (New Haven, CT: Yale University Press, 1989), 261: "Law without discretion ultimately yields arbitrariness."

37 "bankrupt, morally as well as financially": Peter F. Drucker, "Really Reinventing Government," *Atlantic Monthly*, February 1995.

37 "merely a puzzle to be solved": Vaclav Havel, *The Art of the Impossible: Politics as Morality in Practice* (New York: Knopf, 1994), 91s.

38 "effective government": Drucker, "Really Reinventing," *supra* note for page 37.

39 Observers tell horror stories: Interview with former manager of a nursing home, by author, 2012.

39 "NCLB's fixation on testing": Randi Weingarten, "Picking Up the Pieces of No Child Left Behind," *Atlantic*, April 9, 2012. See also Andy Hargreaves and Dennis Shirley, "Beyond Standardization: Powerful New Principles for Improvement," *Phi Delta Kappan* 90, no. 2 (October 2008): 135–43. Finland, which has top-ranked schools, has more or less the opposite approach from NCLB, hiring highly qualified teachers and giving them substantial autonomy. See Pasi Sahlberg and Andy Hargreaves, *Finnish Lessons: What Can the World Learn from Educational Change in Finland?* (New York: Teachers College Press, 2011). See generally Amanda Ripley, *The Smartest Kids in the World* (New York: Simon & Schuster, 2013).

39 Focusing on compliance actually impairs: Polanyi, *Personal Knowledge*, *supra* note for page 22, pp. 18–24, 49–65, 212–45, 299–324.

39 Focus on A, and you cannot see B: Robert K. Merton, "Bureaucratic Structure and Personality," *Social Forces* 18, no. 4 (May 1940): 562.

39 "tacit knowledge": Polanyi, *Personal Knowledge*, *supra* note for page 22, p. 92.

39 shuts the mental door: See Ibid., 56: "Subsidiary awareness and focal awareness are mutually exclusive. If a pianist shifts his attention from the piece he is playing to the observation of what he is doing with his fingers while playing it, he gets confused and may have to stop."

40 "Once regulations become as voluminous": John G. Kemeny, *Report of the President's Commission on the Accident at Three Mile Island* (New York: Pergamon, 1979), 9. See discussion in Joseph V. Rees, *Hostages of Each Other: The Transformation of Nuclear Safety since Three Mile Island* (Chicago: University of Chicago Press, 1994), 192.

40 [Appalachian children]: Nicholas D. Kristof, "Profiting from a Child's Illiteracy," *New York Times*, December 7, 2012. Undermining purpose is a common effect of metric-driven accountability. See Dennis F. Thompson, "Moral Responsibility of Public Officials: The Problem of Many Hands," *American Political Science Review* 74, no. 4 (December 1980), 905, 914, recounting a study about how the metrics of a Job Corps program gave officials an incentive to discriminate against applicants whom the program was designed to help: "Because the performance of officials in the Job Corps program was measured by the number of trainees who received a job after completing the program, officials tended to recruit those youths who already seemed disposed to succeed in a job; these turned out to be youths with a more middle-class than lower-class orientations."

40 [agencies wasting money at year's end]: See Charles Peters, *How Washington Really Works*

(New York: Basic Books, 1992), 45: "One of the notorious results of the fear of budget cuts is the end-of-the-year spending spree."

41 Law truly rules: "In summary, it is exactly a rule's rigidity, even in the face of applications that would ill suit its purpose, that renders it a rule." Fredrick Schauer, "Formalism," *Yale Law Journal* 97, no. 4 (March 1998): 509, 510.

41 "frozen decisions": See Herbert Simon, "Decision-Making and Organizational Design: Man-Machine Systems for Decision-Making," in *Organizational Theory: Selected Readings*, ed. D. S. Pugh (Baltimore: Penguin, 1971), 189–212. See also discussion in Ralph P. Hummel, *The Bureaucratic Experience: The Post-modern Challenge*, 5th ed. (Armonk, NY: M. E. Sharpe, 2008), 141.

41 [Chris Christie quip]: This aside was overheard by a senior executive involved in the train tunnel project.

41 [*Deepwater Horizon*]: Tim Harford, *Adapt: Why Success Always Starts with Failure* (New York: Farrar, Straus and Giroux, 2011), 187, 218.

42 "die with their rights on": Lloyd I. Sederer, "Dying with Your Rights On: Mental Illness, Civil Rights, and Saving Lives," *Huffington Post*, June 7, 2011. Widespread confusion concerning the scope of privacy rights of mass murderer Seung-Hui Cho was cited as a contributing factor in the massacre at Virginia Tech in 2007; Virginia Tech Review Panel, "Mass Shootings at Virginia Tech, April 16, 2007: Report of the Virginia Tech Review Panel, Presented to Timothy M. Kaine, Governor, Commonwealth of Virginia," August 2007, http://www.governor.virginia.gov/tempcontent/techPanelReport-docs/FullReport.pdf.

42 "over-complex regulation": Niall Ferguson, *The Great Degeneration: How Institutions Decay and Economies Die* (New York: Penguin, 2013), p. 54.

42 [Kalid al-Mihdhar]: Thomas H. Kean and Lee H. Hamilton, *The 9/11 Commission Report: Final Report of the National Commission on Terrorist Attacks upon the United States* (New York: W. W. Norton, 2004), 271. See discussion in William D. Eggers and John O'Leary, *If We Can Put a Man on the Moon . . . : Getting Big Things Done in Government* (Boston: Harvard Business Press, 2009), 174–75.

43 [pruning dumb regulations]: Barack Obama, "Toward a 21st-Century Regulatory System," *Wall Street Journal*, January 18, 2011. The head of the Office of Information and Regulatory Affairs during President Obama's first term, Cass Sunstein, initiated thoughtful reforms, which are described in his book *Simpler: The Future of Government* (New York: Simon & Schuster, 2013). These reforms, however, do not take on the broad paralysis caused by a regulatory system based on an assumption of rationalized completeness. As liberal commentator Joe Klein notes, "His people can tell you the number of unnecessary regulations they've eliminated. It barely scratches the surface of what needs to be done—there is no creative destruction in government, regulations pile up on top of each other like silt, generation after generation." Joe Klein, "More Brill, More Obamacare Incompetence," *In the Arena* (blog), April 4, 2013, http://swampland.time.com/2013/04/04/more-brill-more-obamacare-incompetence. The underlying flaws of America's regulatory system remain unaddressed. See William H. Simon, "The Republic of Choosing: A Behaviorist Goes to Washington" (review of *Simpler: The Future of Government*), *Boston Review*, July 8, 2013, http://bostonreview.net/us-books-ideas/cass-sunstein-simpler-future-government-republic-choosing.

43 treated a milk spill the same as an oil spill: Andrew Restuccia, "Obama Touts EPA Effort to Exempt Milk from Oil-Spill Rules," *Hill*, January 24, 2012, http://thehill.com/blogs/e2-wire/e2-wire/206337-obama-touts-epa-effort-to-exempt-milk-from-oil-spill-rules.

43 "to bundle up yesterday in neat packages": Peter F. Drucker, *The Age of Discontinuity: Guidelines to Our Changing Society*, 2nd ed. (New Brunswick, NJ: Transaction, 1992), 222.

44 "highest possible degree of responsibility": James Madison, "Speech in Congress on Presidential Removal Power," in Madison, *Writings*, 435.

45   no longer were willing to give people authority: David Brooks, "The Follower Problem," *New York Times*, June 11, 2012.

45   [criticism of Brooks]: See, for example, Matt Welch, "David Brooks Authoritarianism Watch," *Hit & Run* (blog), Reason.com, June 13, 2012, http://reason.com/blog/2012/06/13/david-brooks-authoritarianism-watch; and Radley Balko, "David Brooks: Know Your Betters," *Agitator*, June 13, 2012.

46   "The flight from the individual": George F. Kennan, "America's Administrative Response to Its World Problems," *Daedalus* 87, no. 2 (Spring 1958): 17.

Regulating by Personal Responsibility

47   Australia radically overhauled its regulation: Braithwaite and Braithwaite, "Politics of Legalism," *supra* note for page 34, pp. 310–25.

47   "could be checked with a ruler": Braithwaite and Braithwaite, "Politics of Legalism," *supra* note for page 34, p. 310.

47   "Rather embarrassed": Ibid., 311.

48   mired in a bureaucratic rut: Professor Braithwaite, often together with his wife (psychology professor Valerie Braithwaite) and other collaborators, has written numerous articles on nursing homes—American, Australian, and English—over the years. Most of his conclusions are distilled in a more recent book: John Braithwaite, Toni Makkai, and Valerie A. Braithwaite, *Regulating Aged Care: Ritualism and the New Pyramid* (Cheltenham, UK: Edward Elgar, 2007).

48   sleeping residents degraded the enjoyment: Braithwaite, Makkai, and Braithwaite, *Regulating Aged Care*, *supra* note for page 48, p. 228.

48   "a great deal of falsification of records": Ibid., 47.

48   "Principles do not work that way": Ronald M. Dworkin, "The Model of Rules," *University of Chicago Law Review* 35, no. 1 (Autumn 1967): 36.

49   not on paperwork compliance: Studies of US nursing homes repeatedly show that overbearing regulation is counterproductive. See Marshall B. Kapp, "Resident Safety and Medical Errors in Nursing Homes," *Journal of Legal Medicine* 24, no. 1 (2003): 52. "Nearly half or more of nursing homes also cited regulations (56%) . . . as barriers to adoption [of culture change]." Michelle M. Doty, Mary Jane Koren, and Elizabeth L. Sturla, *Culture Change in Nursing Homes: How Far Have We Come?* (New York: Commonwealth Fund, 2007), 17. See also discussion in Marshall B. Kapp, "Nursing Home Culture Change: Legal Apprehensions and Opportunities," *Gerontologist*, October 24, 2012 [Epub ahead of print], 3.

50   the principal "protects his faculty": Sara Lawrence-Lightfoot, *The Good High School: Portraits of Character and Culture* (New York: Basic Books, 1983), 68.

50   Doing what's right . . . requires trade-offs: See discussion and sources in notes for pages 39–45, *supra*.

50   Within minutes of walking into a school: John Chubb, interview by author, 2007.

51   [no specific rules for airworthiness]: Paul M. Romer, "Process, Responsibility, and Myron's Law," in *In the Wake of the Crisis: Leading Economists Reassess Economic Policy*, ed. Olivier J. Blanchard et al. (Cambridge, MA: MIT Press, 2012), 116–17.

51   the child was electrocuted: Jane Golden (Children's Aid Society), interview by author, 2011.

51   Utah child welfare law: See Kathleen G. Noonan, Charles F. Sabel, and William H. Simon, "Legal Accountability in the Service-Based Welfare State," *Law & Social Inquiry* 34, no. 3 (Summer 2009): 537–38. Central administration gives "frontline offices and workers relatively broad discretion in applying the principles," Professors Sabel, Simon, and Noonan report, allowing it to "monitor [their] success in achieving the goals" and "learn from local practice while correcting its mistakes."

52   main source of American exceptionalism: See Evans, *They Made America*, *supra* note for page 23.

52   "Trust thyself": Ralph Waldo Emerson, "Self-Reliance," in Emerson, *Essays & Lectures*, 260.

52   "fit only to enervate": Tocqueville, *Democracy in America, supra* note for page 24, vol. 1, p. 87.

52   "it must be free in its gait": Ibid., 90.

52   A study of good nursing homes in the US: See Sarah Forbes-Thompson, Tona Leiker, and Michael R. Bleich, "High-Performing and Low-Performing Nursing Homes: A View from Complexity Science," *Health Care Management Review* 32, no. 4 (October 2007): 341–51. The study found that "high performing homes suggest that fewer, more flexible rules when grounded in trusting relationships and a clear mission, will empower staff and allow greater creativity in meeting resident needs." The key to a good nursing home was the culture in which people focused on being helpful, not compliant: "The seemingly small gestures in high-performing homes, such as acknowledging a person by name, giving tokens of appreciation, or helping out on the unit, were foundational to creating positive relationships and a healthy work environment." Interviews of personnel in good nursing homes were characterized by quotations such as these: "We listen to each other. We help each other out."

53   [study on parental participation]: Robert D. Putnam, *Bowling Alone: The Collapse and Revival of American Community* (New York: Simon & Schuster, 2000), 304, describing a study by James P. Comer: *School Power: Implications of an Intervention Project* (New York: Free Press, 1980), 126–28.

53   key ingredient of civic culture: See Tocqueville, *Democracy in America, supra* note for page 24, vol. 1, pp. 84–94. "The most powerful and perhaps the only means that we still possess of interesting men in the welfare of their country is to make them partakers in the government" (ibid., 243). "It is incontestable that the people frequently conduct public business very badly . . . The humblest individual who cooperates in the government of society acquires a certain degree of self-respect; and as he possesses authority, he can command the services of minds more enlightened than his own" (ibid., 251).

53   "take pride in their common project": Michael J. Sandel, *Democracy's Discontent: America in Search of a Public Philosophy* (Cambridge, MA: Belknap Press, 1996), 206.

53   "[she] likes being where she is": Philip W. Jackson, Robert E. Boostrom, and David T. Hansen, *The Moral Life of Schools* (San Francisco: Jossey-Bass, 1993), 115.

53   Most regulatory detail is aimed: See Kansas Department on Aging, "Statutes and Regulations," *supra* note for page 30.

54   "Facilities and equipment should be reasonably suited": The American National Standards Institute (http://www.ansi.org) promulgates standards of design and labeling for tools, equipment, and materials—ranging from, say, the design of power-driven brushing tools to the proper warning labels to use on packages containing radioactive materials.

54   OSHA "tries to do the impossible": Drucker, *Management, supra* note for page 23, p. 164. "The most effective way to produce safety," Drucker concluded, " is to eliminate unsafe behavior." Ibid. The danger in furniture factories, for example, comes from fumes of "glue guns," which over time destroy the nerve endings of workers. The workers often look like "upright cadavers," according to a 2013 exposé by the *New York Times*, and are permanently disabled. But OSHA has done little to protect them, because it's hard to constantly monitor ventilation in the factories and use of protective masks. Ian Urbina, "As OSHA Emphasizes Safety, Long-Term Health Risks Fester," *New York Times*, March 30, 2013. OSHA's regulations can be found at http://www.osha.gov/law-regs.html. Instead, OSHA "constantly nips at firms with flea-bite fines." Ian Ayres and John Braithwaite, *Responsive Regulation: Transcending the Deregulation Debate* (New York: Oxford University Press, 1992), 49.

54   [Alcoa]: William H. Simon, "Optimization and Its Discontents in Regulatory Design," *Regulation & Governance* 4, no. 1 (2010): 7.

54   Safety in nuclear submarines: Drucker, "Really Reinventing Government," *supra* note for page 37.

54   "usual process of unconscious trial and error": Polanyi, *Personal Knowledge, supra* note for page 22, p. 65.

54   "The simpler the better": Nassim Nicholas Taleb, *Antifragile: Things That Gain from Disorder* (New York: Random House, 2012), 11.

55   Accountability all around: See Russell Hardin, "The Street-Level Epistemology of Trust," *Politics & Society* 21 (1993): 152–53: "First, you trust someone if you have adequate reason to believe it will be in that person's interest to be trustworthy in the relevant way at the relevant time." See discussion in Mark E. Warren, "Democratic Theory and Trust," in *Democracy and Trust*, ed. Mark E. Warren (Cambridge: Cambridge University Press, 1999), 310–45. See also Tocqueville, *Democracy in America, supra* note for page 24, vol. 1, p. 209: As long as the citizens in a democracy can remove officials, there is "no reason to fear any abuse of their authority."

55   That's what power is: Robert E. Goodin, *Political Theory and Public Policy* (Chicago: University of Chicago Press, 1982), 71: "Power is the essence of politics, and the essence of power lies in restricting the choices available to others."

55   A rules-based system centralizes decisions: Nonet and Selznick observe that a "regime of rules limits the discretion of lower echelons, thereby concentrating authority at the top." Nonet and Selznick, *Law and Society in Transition, supra* note for page 20, 14. Michael Lerner discusses how rules can provide an "aroma of fairness" while in fact they "legitimize domination." See Michael Lerner, *Surplus Powerlessness: The Psychodynamics of Everyday Life . . . and the Psychology of Individual and Social Transformation* (Amherst, NY: Humanity Books, 1991), 54–58.

56   Special interests are also control freaks: See Adam Smith, *The Theory of Moral Sentiments* (London: A. Millar, 1790), part 6, sec. 2, chap. 1: "The man of system . . . seems to imagine that he can arrange the different members of a great society with as much ease as the hand arranges the different pieces upon a chess-board. He does not consider that the pieces upon the chess-board have no other principle of motion besides that which the hand impresses upon them; but that, in the great chess-board of human society, every single piece has a principle of motion of its own, altogether different from that which the legislature might chuse to impress upon it." See also discussion in Samuel Fleischacker, *A Third Concept of Liberty: Judgment and Freedom in Kant and Adam Smith* (Princeton, NJ: Princeton University Press, 1999), 163.

56   "cannot be left to their own devices": Marcia Lowry, as quoted in Noonan, Sabel, and Simon, "Legal Accountability," *supra* note for page 51, p. 531. See also Ross Sandler and David Schoenbrod, *Democracy by Decree: What Happens When Courts Run Government* (New Haven, CT: Yale University Press, 2003), describing how advocates for special-needs students use a decades-old court decree to control the minute details of special education in New York City. Special education in New York, Sandler and Schoenbrod conclude, has become "a huge, gold-plated dysfunctional cog in a rusty educational machine," consuming almost 30 percent of the total city school budget for a small fraction of students who are actually learning-disabled (ibid., 92).

56   "unintelligible any way you read it": "The Dodd-Frank Act," *supra* note for page 36. The *Economist* also quotes Professor Jonathan Macey: "Laws classically provide people with rules. Dodd-Frank is not directed at people. It is an outline directed at bureaucrats and it instructs them to make still more regulations and to create more bureaucracies . . . Officials are being given the power to . . . make arbitrary or capricious rulings. The lack of clarity which follows from the sheer complexity of the scheme will sometimes, perhaps often, provide cover for such capriciousness."

56   as rigid and porous as the tax code: The entire 848-page Dodd-Frank Wall Street Reform and Consumer Protection Act can be found at http://www.sec.gov/about/laws/wall streetreform-cpa.pdf.

58   agreed to put aside sanctions for rule noncompliance: See US Department of Labor,
     Occupational Safety and Health Administration, *Reflections on OSHA's History*, OSHA
     3360 (Washington, DC: OSHA, 2009), 39–41, https://www.osha.gov/history/OSHA_
     HISTORY_3360s.pdf.

58   "less hierarchical in nature": Grainne de Burca and Joanne Scott, *Law and New Governance
     in the EU and the US* (Oxford: Hart, 2006), 2.

58   escalating toward sanctions: In *Responsive Regulation*, Professors Ian Ayres and John
     Braithwaite recommend a pyramid of regulatory enforcement with six levels of inter-
     vention, starting with persuasion, moving to a warning letter and eventually to harder
     sanctions, such as fines, and ultimately, shuttering a business. Ayres and Braithwaite,
     Responsive Regulation, supra note for page 54, p. 35.

59   rewards the innovator: See John Mikler, *Greening the Car Industry: Varieties of Capitalism
     and Climate Change* (Cheltenham, UK: Edward Elgar, 2009), 105–7; and Osamu Kimura,
     "Japanese Top Runner Approach for Energy Efficiency Standards," SERC Discussion
     Paper SERC09035 (CRIEPI, 2010), http://www.climatepolicy.jp/thesis/pdf/09035dp
     .pdf. See also Aoki, Axelrad, and Kagan, "Industrial Effluent Control," *supra* note for
     page 36. The study concluded that Japanese environmental regulation, based on prin-
     ciples and ongoing dialogue, was more certain and effective than rules-based US regu-
     lation. It was also much simpler: "The book of effluent control regulations in Japan is
     'this thin,' [an] environmental manager told us, holding two fingers an inch apart. The
     material she had to master in the United States, in contrast, filled a four foot bookshelf
     in her office" (ibid., 82).

59   [Bavarian statutes]: For the rest-home statute, see article 3, principles 3, 6, and 4, respec-
     tively, of the "Gesetz zur Regelung der Pflege-, Betreuungs- und Wohnqualität im Alter
     und bei Behinderung," July 8, 2008, http://www.gesetze-bayern.de/jportal/portal/page/
     bsbayprod.psml?showdoccase=1&doc.id=jlr-PflWoQualGBY2008rahmen&doc.part=X.
     All German laws are formally promulgated in federal or state law gazettes and are
     generally available online at the website of the pertinent state or federal ministry. For
     the section of the school statute allowing principals, under broad principles, to "work
     together in trust" with other participants in the "school community," see article 2, sec-
     tion 4, of the "Bayerisches Gesetz über das Erziehungs- und Unterrichtswesen (Bay-
     EUG)," May 31, 2000, http://www.gesetze-bayern.de/jportal/portal/page/bsbayprod.
     psml?showdoccase=1&doc.id=jlr-EUGBY2000rahmen&doc.part=X. For the section of the
     school statute authorizing each school to create its own "house law," see article 3, sec-
     tion 4, of the house law (*Hausordnung*) of the 450-year-old Wilhelm's Academic School
     (*Wilhelmsgymnasium*) in Munich, http://www.wilhelmsgymnasium.de/hausordnung,
     accessed May 2013.

59   [FSA principles]: For a summary of the FSA's principles-based initiative, see Julia Black,
     Martyn Hopper, and Christa Band, "Making a Success of Principles-Based Regulation,"
     Law and Financial Markets Review 1, no. 3 (April 2007).

59   "people who have no principles": Hector Sants, "Delivering Intensive Supervision and
     Credible Deterrence" (speech, Reuters Newsmakers, London, March 12, 2009).

60   "rebalancing away from prescriptive rules": Andrew Haldane, "The Dog and the Frisbee"
     (paper presented at the Federal Reserve Bank of Kansas City's 36th Economic Policy
     Symposium, Jackson Hole, WY, August 31, 2012), http://www.kansascityfed.org/publicat/
     sympos/2012/ah.pdf. Similarly, Professor Julia Black, of the London School of Econom-
     ics, emphasizes the imperative of regulatory flexibility, as well as the constant question-
     ing of assumptions: "The final insight that we can take from the experience . . . is that
     regulators need to observe and adapt, to engage in self-critical learning . . . in short, to
     be reflexive." Julia Black, "Paradoxes and Failures: 'New Governance' Techniques and the
     Financial Crisis," *Modern Law Review* 75, no. 2 (2012): 1062.

60 "institutionalizing systems that pursue": Braithwaite, Makkai, and Braithwaite, *Regulating Aged Care, supra* note for page for page 48, p. 176.

The Framework of Law, Properly Understood

62 "frontiers, not artificially drawn": Berlin, "Two Concepts," *supra* note for page 27, p. 236. John Locke emphasized that the goal of law is to preserve an open field of freedom, not tell people what to do: "The end of law is not to abolish or restrain, but to preserve and enlarge freedom." John Locke, *The Second Treatise on Civil Government* (Amherst, MA: Prometheus, 1986), 33.

62 "a negative, rather than a positive, determination": George F. Kennan, "On American Principles," *Foreign Affairs* 74, no. 2 (March/April 1995): 119. See also Eugene J. McCarthy, "Freedom and Political Authority," *ALA Bulletin* 47, no. 10 (November 1953): 466: "It is the responsibility of government to defend the outer walls."

63 Spontaneity . . . disappeared: Hannah Arendt, "What Is Authority?" in Arendt, *Between Past and Future*, 96.

65 carries legal weight: Someone with authority typically is free to make a choice, within legal boundaries, on the basis of what he thinks is right, not what he can prove. "Authority," Hannah Arendt observes, "is incompatible . . . with a process of argumentation." Ibid., 93. The wisdom or fairness of the decision can still be checked up the line, but the basis for review is not objective proof and argument, but what the higher authority believes is right or fair under applicable legal standards.

65 "Discretion, like the hole in a doughnut": Ronald M. Dworkin, *Taking Rights Seriously* (Cambridge, MA: Harvard University Press, 1978), 31.

65 "standards of sense and fairness": Ibid., 33.

65 "The first requirement": Oliver Wendell Holmes, *The Common Law* (Clark, NJ: Lawbook Exchange, 2005), 41. If the job of judges is be sensitive to "prevailing standards of right conduct," as Cardozo put it, then it's doubly true that officials engaged in regulatory oversight and public services should be guided and held accountable by social norms of reasonableness. Benjamin N. Cardozo, *The Nature of the Judicial Process* (New Haven, CT: Yale University Press, 1921), 63.

66 Law will deter officials: See Jean Hampton, "Democracy and the Rule of Law," in *The Rule of Law*, ed. Ian Shapiro, Nomos 36 (New York: New York University Press, 1994), 24.

66 "authoritative grounds": Nonet and Selznick, *Law and Society in Transition, supra* note for page 20, p. 81, note 12. Thomas Hobbes, the consummate pragmatist, understood that a law unavoidably hinges on human judgment; Thomas Hobbes, *Leviathan*, ed. E. M. Curley (Indianapolis, IN: Hackett, 1994), 180: "All laws, written, and unwritten, have need of interpretation." He therefore leapt to the conclusion that law was just putty in the hands of whoever was in charge. Better, Hobbes concluded in *Leviathan*, just to cede authority to a monarch. But law constrains officials more than Hobbes gave it credit for. The main constraint is cultural. Officials can't get away with unreasonable or abusive interpretations of law if other judges and officials—and ultimately the public—believe in the importance of law and have a different view of the underlying purpose of the law in question.

66 "departs from the reason of law": Timothy A. O. Endicott, "The Impossibility of the Rule of Law," *Oxford Journal of Legal Studies* 19, no. 1 (Spring 1999): 1–18.

66 Social norms achieve validity: Jürgen Habermas, *The Inclusion of the Other: Studies in Political Theory* (Cambridge, MA: MIT Press, 1998), 3–5. For this summary description I am indebted to the introduction by the editors, Ciaran Cronin and Pablo de Grieff.

66 "infused with the glow of principle": Cardozo, *Nature of the Judicial Process, supra* note for page 65, p. 93.

67   The "principle becomes fully manifest": Hannah Arendt, "What Is Freedom?" in Arendt, *Between Past and Future*, 152.

67   "conduct that the rule was intended to avoid": Richard A. Posner, *Economic Analysis of Law* (Austin: Wolters Kluwer, 2007), 587. See also Michel de Montaigne, "Of Experience," in De Montaigne, *Complete Works*, 993: "Therefore I do not much like the opinion of the man who thought by a multiplicity of laws to bridle the authority of judges, cutting up their meat for them. He did not realize that there is as much freedom and latitude in the interpretation of laws as in their creation." In a recent book, Ralph Nader waits less than three pages before lashing out against precise rules in the tax code: "The more complex the laws are, the more shenanigans the corporations are likely to attempt." Ralph Nader, *The Seventeen Solutions: Bold Ideas for Our American Future* (New York: Harper, 2012), 3. In addition, see Doreen McBarnet and Christopher Whelan, "The Elusive Spirit of the Law: Formalism and the Struggle for Legal Control," *Modern Law Review* 54, no. 6 (December 1991).

68   The frailty of human judgment: The authoritative book on the flaws in human reasoning is Daniel Kahneman, *Thinking, Fast and Slow* (New York: Farrar, Straus and Giroux, 2011). For books on the mystery of human accomplishment, see Gary Klein, *Intuition at Work: Why Developing Your Gut Instinct Will Make You Better at What You Do* (New York: Doubleday, 2003); Mike Rose, *The Mind at Work: Valuing the Intelligence of the American Worker* (New York: Viking, 2004); Hubert Dreyfus, *Mind over Machine* (New York: Free Press, 1986); and Polanyi, *Personal Knowledge*, *supra* note for page 22. See also Kenneth R. Hammond, *Human Judgment and Social Policy* (Oxford: Oxford University Press 1996).

68   There's a wisdom in crowds: See generally James Surowiecki, *The Wisdom of Crowds* (New York: Anchor, 2005). See also Tracey L. Meares, "It's a Question of Connections," *Valparaiso Law Review* 31 (1997): 594: "Social norms are better and more effective constraints on behavior than law ever could hope to be."

69   "windowsill height shall not exceed": Kansas Department on Aging, "Statutes and Regulations," *supra* note for page 30.

69   *minimize uncertainty:* See Endicott, "Impossibility," *supra* note for page 66 (arguing that law should aim to minimize arbitrariness, not maximize certainty).

69   "Standards that capture lay intuitions": Richard A. Posner, *The Problems of Jurisprudence* (Cambridge, MA: Harvard University Press, 1990), 48.

69   A study of juvenile justice in Britain: See Nicola Lacey, "Jurisprudence of Discretion," in *The Uses of Discretion*, ed. Keith Hawkins, Oxford Socio-Legal Studies (Oxford: Clarendon, 1992), 380.

69   American judges and German bank regulators: For the American example, see Orley Ashenfelter, Theodore Eisenberg, and Stewart J. Schwab, "Politics and the Judiciary: The Influence of Judicial Background on Case Outcomes," *Journal of Legal Studies* 24 (1995): 257–81. See also Cass Sunstein et al., *Are Judges Political?: An Empirical Analysis of the Federal Judiciary* (Washington, DC: Brookings Institution Press, 2006). For the German example, see Edward L. Rubin, "Discretion and Its Discontents," *Chicago-Kent Law Review* 72 (1997), 1299–366.

69   "more precision than the subject matter admits": Aristotle, *The Nicomachean Ethics*, trans. W. D. Ross (Oxford: Oxford University Press, 1940). See discussion in Ken Kress, "Legal Indeterminacy," *California Law Review* 77, no. 2 (March 1989): 283.

69   officials can predictably enforce: Aristotle, *Politics*, Book III, 16: "Where it seems that the law cannot draw a boundary, it would seem impossible for a human being to identify one. Yet the law trains officials for that very purpose, and appoints them to judge and to regulate that which it leaves undetermined, as rightly they can" (quoted from Endicott, "Impossibility," *supra* note for page 66, p. 13). Professor Ofer Raban explains that "indeterminate legal standards often produce more certainty and predictability than any alternative bright-line rule because they replicate, one for one, the social, moral, economic

or political norm that already prevails, and which . . . cannot be reduced to clear and unambiguous language." Ofer Raban, "The Fallacy of Legal Certainty: Why Vague Legal Standards May Be Better for Capitalism and Liberalism," *Boston University Public Interest Law Journal* 19, no. 2 (Spring 2010): 175–91.

70 "some things that the process cannot do reliably": Braithwaite and Braithwaite, "Politics of Legalism," *supra* note for page 34, 326.

70 "it would soon be bankrupt": Ibid. John Braithwaite and Valerie Braithwaite posit a "reliability paradox: reliability is more likely to be achieved when reliability is not the central objective." Focusing on substance will have the effect of better reliability. Australia is more reliable than the US because it is "broad, vague, subjective and undefined with regard to protocols." Ibid., 310–11.

70 "already in ethical difficulty": Jeremy Waldron, "Vagueness in Law and Language: Some Philosophical Issues," *California Law Review* 82, no. 3 (May 1994): 535.

71 "can go scot free": John Dewey, "Logical Method and Law," *Cornell Law Quarterly* 10 (1924): 17, 26.

71 "guided discretion": See Tracey L. Meares and Dan M. Kahan, "When Rights Are Wrong: The Paradox of Unwanted Rights," in Meares and Kahan, *Urgent Times*, 27–29. See discussion in William H. Simon, "Solving Problems vs. Claiming Rights," *William and Mary Law Review* 46, no. 1 (2004): 149.

71 federal criminal sentencing guidelines: Until the Supreme Court in 2005 declared rigid guidelines unconstitutional, judges from every ideological perspective had attacked the sentencing rules as being contrary to basic principles of justice because they did not permit "the saving grace of humane discretion." Adam Gopnick, "The Caging of America," *New Yorker*, January 30, 2012, reviewing Stuntz, *Collapse of American Criminal Justice, supra* note for page 37. See also John S. Martin Jr., "Why Mandatory Minimums Make No Sense," *Notre Dame Journal of Law, Ethics & Public Policy* 18, no. 2 (2004): 311–12: "Judges no longer have to take moral responsibility for the sentence they impose." See generally Kate Stith and Jose A. Cabranes, *Fear of Judging* (Chicago: University of Chicago Press, 1998), 5: "Judges, prosecutors, defense attorneys, and probation officers find themselves operating in a labyrinthine system of rules devised by distant and alien administrative agency. The rules themselves, which generally ignore the individual characteristics of defendants, often seem to sacrifice comprehensibility and common sense on the altar of pseudo-scientific uniformity."

72 retirement of commercial airline pilots: Colin S. Diver, "The Optimal Precision of Administrative Rules," *Yale Law Journal* 93, no. 1 (November 1983): 65–109.

73 [B-17 crash]: Atul Gawande, *The Checklist Manifesto: How to Get Things Right* (New York: Metropolitan, 2010), 32–34. Dr. Gawande has made significant contributions to our understanding of the opportunities and problems of medical protocols, and also of skewed incentives that drive up health care costs, especially in his revelatory essay on the self-interested variations in health care costs in nearby communities in Texas: Atul Gawande, "The Cost Conundrum," *New Yorker*, June 1, 2009.

73 [complicated versus complex]: "To run a system that's complex. . ." comes from Brenda Zimmerman, as quoted in David Segal, "It's Complicated: Making Sense of Complexity," *New York Times*, May 1, 2010. See also Frances Westley, Brenda Zimmerman, and Michael Patton, *Getting to Maybe: How the World Is Changed* (Toronto: Vintage Canada, 2007). Professor Zimmerman's distinction reveals why Dr. Gawande overshoots the mark in his enthusiasm for checklists. Checklists can be lifesaving in "complicated" situations and deadly in "complex" situations, such as, say, the *Deepwater Horizon* or Three Mile Island incidents. Dr. Gawande cites, as a success of checklists, the January 2009 crash landing on the Hudson River of a US Airways plane that had lost its power in both engines. He is correct that disciplined training and protocols kept order in the cockpit; the purpose of

training is to internalize choices so that they become automatic. But the "miracle on the Hudson" happened because Captain "Sully" Sullenberger focused on flying the plane, not on a checklist for how to fly the plane. As William Langewiesche put it in his account of the incident: "There was no time for the ditching checklist . . . Across a lifetime of flying, Sullenberger had developed an intimacy with these machines that is difficult to convey. He did not sit in airplanes so much as put them on. He flew them in a profoundly integrated way, as an expression of himself." William Langewiesche, *Fly by Wire: The Geese, the Glide, the Miracle on the Hudson* (New York: Farrar, Straus and Giroux, 2009), 177. Captain Sullenberger himself described the final moments this way: "The earth and the river were rushing towards us. I was judging our descent rate and our altitude visually. At that instant, I judged it was the right time. I began the flare for landing. I pulled the side-stick back, farther back, finally full aft, and held it there as we touched the water." This was not someone dutifully checking the boxes, but a skilled professional drawing on all his experience to avoid a disaster. See Philip K. Howard, "Problems with Protocols" (review of *The Checklist Manifesto*), *Wall Street Journal*, January 20, 2010.

73 Most government oversight: There's a theory of complexity that arose out of computer science, known as "fuzzy thinking" or "fuzzy logic," which posits that precision and relevance are mutually exclusive in complex activities. A precise rule, by this theory, will rarely accomplish what most people would consider appropriate with complex choices. See Bart Kosko, *Fuzzy Thinking* (New York: Hyperion, 1993). Professor Kenneth Hammond addresses a similar point by distinguishing between highly controlled situations, such as an assembly line or a rail line, and complex situations in which variables are often uncertain. "Rigorous systems" can be highly efficient in the appropriate situation but can lead to a train wreck (literally and figuratively) when one small thing goes wrong. Human systems are sloppier, but less dangerous. Hammond, *Human Judgment, supra* note for page 68, p. 175.

74 nonbinding rules can often be useful: See Braithwaite, "Rules and Principles," *supra* note for page 15. Like judges with the sentencing guidelines, physicians are passionate about the inappropriateness of rigid medical practice guidelines. See David Gelber, "Rigid Regulation Can Become Detrimental to Patient Care," *KevinMD.com* (blog), December 2, 2011, http://www.kevinmd.com/blog/2011/12/rigid-regulation-detrimental-patient-care.html. Dr. Gelber describes common situations in which the guidelines hurt patients, such as when a thirteen-year-old boy was dehydrated going into surgery because the guideline required a 500-cc pediatric IV fluid bag and the hospital had only 1,000-cc bags. Dr. Gelber pleaded with the nurse that the boy was larger than many adults, but the nurse refused to use the regular-sized bag. Dr. Gelber concludes, "Rigid regulation can become detrimental to healthcare . . . Clinical guidelines may be helpful but it must be remembered that they are guidelines only."

Ending Bureaucratic Amorality

74 "an act of intellectual probity": Polanyi, *Personal Knowledge, supra* note for page 22, p. 271.

75 "Each citizen will rationally pursue": Donald J. Black, "The Mobilization of Law," *Journal of Legal Studies* 2, no. 1 (1973): 138.

75 the many ways teachers can be fair or unfair: Jackson, Boostrom, and Hansen, *Moral Life of Schools, supra* note for page 53.

76 "Laws on paper are meaningless": Lawrence M. Friedman, "Legal Rules and the Process of Social Change," *Stanford Law Review* 19, no. 4 (April 1967): 786.

76 "can never be knowable in advance": Hans-Georg Gadamer, *Truth and Method*, trans. Joel Weinsheimer and Donald G. Marshall, 2nd ed. (New York: Continuum, 1998), 317.

77 institutions are inherently less moral: Reinhold Niebuhr, *Moral Man and Immoral Society: A Study in Ethics and Politics*, rev. ed. (New York: Scribner, 1960). See discussion in Robert Heineman, *Authority and the Liberal Tradition: From Hobbes to Rorty*, 2nd ed. (New

Brunswick, NJ: Transaction, 1994), 143–47. See generally Thompson, "Moral Responsibility," *supra* note 89, describing the causes of a famous mining disaster in 1947, known as the blast at Centralia No. 5. "As one strives to fix responsibility for the disaster, again and again one is confronted, as were the miners, not with any individual but with a host of individuals fused into a vast, unapproachable, insensate organism. Perhaps this immovable juggernaut is the true villain of the piece." John Bartlow Martin, "The Blast at Centralia No. 5," in Richard Stillman, *Public Administration: Concepts and Cases*, 9th ed. (Belmont, CA: Wadsworth Cengage Learning, 2009), 43. See also David Luban, Alan Strudler, and David Wasserman, "Moral Responsibility in the Age of Bureaucracy," *Michigan Law Review* 90, no. 8 (July 1992): 2356.

78 "helping them hold on to memories of the past": Timothy Diamond, "Social Policy and Everyday Life in Nursing Homes," in *The Worth of Women's Work*, ed. Anne Statham, Eleanor M. Miller, and Hans O. Mauksch (Albany: State University of New York Press, 1988), 48. See Marshall B. Kapp, "Quality of Care and Quality of Life in Nursing Facilities: What's Regulation Got to Do with It?" *McGeorge Law Review* 31, no. 3 (2000): 731: "Regulatory requirements may be essential to inspire, but can never substitute for, the sense of moral obligation that, in the final analysis, must lie at the heart of protecting and promoting the well-being of our most vulnerable citizens."

78 [Foner's nursing home study]: Nancy Foner, "The Hidden Injuries of Bureaucracy: Work in an American Nursing Home," *Human Organization* 54, no. 3 (1995): 229–37.

80 "banality of evil": Hannah Arendt, *Eichmann in Jerusalem: A Report on the Banality of Evil* (New York: Penguin, 2006).

80 "Most evil is done": Hannah Arendt, *The Life of the Mind*, ed. Mary McCarthy (New York: Mariner, 1981), 180. See also Robert Michels, *Political Parties: A Sociological Study of the Oligarchical Tendencies of Modern Democracy*, trans. Eden and Cedar Paul (New York: Free Press, 1962), 189: "Bureaucracy is the sworn enemy of individual liberty . . . The bureaucratic spirit corrupts character and engenders moral poverty."

80 "bureaucratic virtuoso": Merton, "Bureaucratic Structure," *supra* note for page 39.

80 these destructive values are increasingly embraced: See Marshall B. Kapp, "Resident Safety and Medical Errors in Nursing Homes," *Journal of Legal Medicine* 24, no. 1 (2003): 52. When I interviewed Professor Kapp in 2012, he discussed how a budding "culture movement" in nursing home management has trouble getting off the ground because caregivers find themselves constantly pulled back by the rules into a compliance mind-set. See Doty et al., *Culture Change*, *supra* note page 49, p. 17: "Nearly half or more of nursing homes also cited regulations (56%) . . . as barriers to adoption [of culture change]."

80 federal procurement practices: Steven Kelman, *Procurement and Public Management: The Fear of Discretion and the Quality of Government Performance* (Washington, DC : AEI Press, 1990).

81 "We will not hesitate to sue": Amy Goldsmith, as quoted in Strunsky, "Attempt to Raise," *supra* note for page 10. The lawsuit to stop the Bayonne Bridge project was filed on July 31, 2013. See "Lawsuit Challenges Bayonne Bridge Project," Journal of Commerce, August 1, 2013, http://www.joc.com/port-news/us-ports/port-new-york-new-jersey/lawsuit-challenges-bayonne-bridge-project_20130801.html.

81 [suing the dry cleaner]: See Henri E. Cauvin, "Court Rules for Cleaners in $54 Million Pants Suit," *Washington Post*, June 26, 2007. For the arc of the two-year saga to win the case, see Philip K. Howard, *Life without Lawyers* (New York: W. W. Norton, 2009), 72–73.

82 "lack of good": Aquinas, *St. Thomas Aquinas: Philosophical Texts*, ed. Thomas Gilby (London: Oxford University Press, 1951), 167.

82 [fired St. Louis cafeteria worker]: Ryan Sullivan, "Mo. Cafeteria Worker Loses Job After Giving Meals to Students in Need," MyFox8.com, December 14, 2012, http://myfox8.com/2012/12/14/mo-cafeteria-worker-loses-job-after-giving-meals-to-student-in-need.

82 [fired Florida lifeguard]: Ihosvani Rodriguez, "Hallandale Beach Lifeguard Fired after Participating in Beach Rescue," *Sun Sentinel* (Fort Lauderdale), July 3, 2012.

83 "to alienate the worker": William H. Simon, "Legality, Bureaucracy, and Class in the Welfare System," *Yale Law Journal* 92, no. 7 (June 1983): 1204.

83 "indifference, impersonality, and irresponsibility": Ibid., 1198.

83 "There is nothing I can do": Ibid., 1199.

84 "never . . . to give a straightforward answer": Charles Dickens, *Little Dorrit*, ed. Harvey Peter Sucksmith and Dennis Walder, Oxford World's Classics (Oxford: Oxford University Press, 2012), 120.

84 [Omar in Iraq]: "Taking Names," *This American Life*, NPR, June 28, 2013, http://www .thisamericanlife.org/radio-archives/episode/499/transcript. See Kirk Johnson, *To Be a Friend Is Fatal* (New York: Scribner, 2013).

85 "paper errors": Simon, "Legality, Bureaucracy, and Class," *supra* note for page 83, p. 1209.

85 there's a "moral force to immorality": Polanyi, *Personal Knowledge, supra* note for page 22, pp. 227–28.

86 The moral vacuum is now filled with opportunists: "Fundamentalists rush in," Michael Sandel observes, "where liberals fear to tread." Sandel, *Democracy's Discontent, supra* note for page 53, p. 322. See also Leszek Kolakowski, *Modernity on Endless Trial* (Chicago: University of Chicago Press, 1990), 162–74 (discussing "the self-poisoning of open society").

86 "People feel their only public duty": Stanley Hauerwas, *A Community of Character: Toward a Constructive Christian Social Ethic* (Notre Dame, IN: University of Notre Dame Press, 1991), 79. See also Alasdair C. MacIntyre, *After Virtue: A Study in Moral Theory* (Notre Dame, IN: University of Notre Dame Press, 1984). See Alasdair MacIntyre, "Regulation: A Substitute for Morality," *Hastings Center Report* 10, no. 1 (February 1980): 31–33: "When there is continuous resort to the law, it is generally a sign that moral relations have to some large degree broken down. It is a sign that the motives which make us invoke the law are those of fear and self-interest. And when fear and self-interest have to be brought into play, law itself tends to be morally discredited."

86 not even a vocabulary for public virtue: See Mary Ann Glendon, *Rights Talk: The Impoverishment of Political Discourse* (New York: Free Press, 1991), 14: "Lacking a grammar of cooperative living, we are like a traveler who can say a few words to get a meal and a room in a foreign city, but cannot converse with its inhabitants."

86 either "a totalitarian strategy": Hauerwas, *Community of Character, supra* note for page 86, p. 86. Reinhold Niebuhr makes a similar point: "A consistent pessimism in regard to men's rational capacity for justice invariably leads to absolutist political theories." Reinhold Niebuhr, "The Children of Light and the Children of Darkness," in Niebuhr, *Essential Reinhold Niebuhr*, 160.

87 "That is the protocol we followed": "Bakersfield Police Investigating Glenwood Gardens After Woman Refused CPR, Died," *23ABC News*, March 4, 2013, http://www. turnto23.com/news/local-news/bakersfield-police-investigating-glenwood-gardens-after-woman-refused-cpr-died.

87 Americans are abandoning our values: See Robert B. Denhardt, *In the Shadow of Organization* (Lawrence: Regents Press of Kansas, 1981), 32: "We originally sought to construct social institutions that would reflect our beliefs and values; now there is a danger that our values may reflect our institutions. Here we encounter a most serious problem: as we continue to permit organizations to structure our lives, rather than vice-versa, we may become locked in their grasp."

87 [Alameda firefighters]: Angela Hill, "Man Drowns After Walking Fully Clothed into Bay off Alameda Beach," *Oakland Tribune*, May 29, 2011, http://www.insidebayarea.com/news/ ci_18172320. See also Alan Wang, "Alameda Police, Firefighters Watch as Man Drowns," KGO-TV (San Francisco, CA), May 30, 2011, http://abclocal.go.com/kgo/story?section=new

s%2Flocal%2Feast_bay&id=8161285; CNN, "Authorities Make Changes After First Responders Watch Man Drown," CNN.com, June 1, 2011, http://www.cnn.com/2011/US/06/01/california.drowning/index.html; and Associated Press, "Firefighters Watch Man Drown Himself in San Francisco Bay," *New York Post*, June 1, 2011, http://www.nypost.com/p/news/national/firefighters_watch_man_drown_himself_COyFnjoaSEctUKIvgha1yL ("'The incident yesterday was deeply regrettable,' [interim Alameda (CA) Fire Chief Mike D'Orazi] said. 'But I can also see it from our firefighters' perspective. They're standing there wanting to do something, but they are handcuffed by policy at that point.'").

87 "Well, if I was off duty": Wang, "Alameda Police," *supra* note for page 87.

88 moral tapestry of a strong culture: See Lord John Fletcher Moulton, "Law and Manners," *Atlantic Monthly*, July 1924. A British minister during the First World War, Lord Moulton described the vital role of the "domain of Manners," a world of public values that exists between conduct that is legally mandated and conduct that is merely a matter of personal preference: "Between 'can do' and 'may do' ought to exist the whole realm which recognizes the sway of duty, fairness, sympathy, taste, and all the other things that make life beautiful and society possible."

88 "Above all, laws work best": Amitai Etzioni, "Social Norms: Internalization, Persuasion, and History," *Law & Society Review* 34, no. 1 (2000): 165.

88 "law floats in a sea of ethics": Earl Warren, address at the Jewish Theological Seminary of America Annual Awards Dinner (November 11, 1962), quoted in Fred J. Cook, "The Corrupt Society," *Nation* 196 (1963): 453, 454.

89 The only purpose of government: Brian Z. Tamanaha, "How an Instrumental Rule of Law Corrodes the Rule of Law," *DePaul Law Review* 56 (2007): 14: "A constant refrain in the history of the rule of law ideal is that the law is, and should be, for the common good." See Cardozo, *Nature of the Judicial Process*, *supra* note for page 65, p. 66: "The final cause of law is the welfare of society." See also Tocqueville, *Democracy in America*, *supra* note for page 24, vol. 1, p. 91 footnote: "The end of good government is to ensure the welfare of a people and not merely to establish order in the midst of its misery."

89 The touchstone of every public choice: The validity of any claimed right, philosopher Joseph Raz observes, hinges on whether "by protecting the right of the individual one protects the common good." Raz, "Rights and Individual Well-Being," in *Ethics in the Public Domain: Essays in the Morality of Law and Politics* (Oxford: Clarendon, 1995), 53. See also John Stuart Mill, *On Liberty*, ed. David Bromwich and George Kateb (New York: Penguin, 2007), 16: "The only purpose for which power can be rightfully exercised over any member of a civilized community, against his will, is to prevent harm to others. His own good . . . is not sufficient warrant." For a discussion of the moral validity of assertions of individual rights, see Howard, *Life without Lawyers*, *supra* note for page 81, 49–67. For a discussion of the moral validity of laws, see Part II herein.

89 "a veil of ignorance": John Rawls, *A Theory of Justice* (Cambridge, MA: Belknap Press, 1971).

90 profoundly anti-majoritarian: Brian Z. Tamanaha, "The Dark Side of the Relationship between the Rule of Law and Liberalism," *New York University Journal of Law & Liberty* 3, no. 3 (2008): 516–47.

90 dissuade rational people from acting badly: See Hardin, "Street-Level Epistemology," *supra* note for page 55. See also Jean Cohen, "Trust, Voluntary Association and Workable Democracy," in *Democracy and Trust*, ed. Mark Warren (Cambridge: Cambridge University Press, 1999), 222: "If one knows one can expect impartiality from a judge, care and concern from a doctor, protection from police, concern for the common good from the legislatures, and so on, then one can develop confidence (instead of cynicism) that shared norms and cultural values will orient the actions of powerful others."

91 Even when disputes have metastasized: Oliver Wendell Holmes, "Codes, and the Arrangement of the Law," *American Law Review* 5, no. 1 (October 1870): 1.

91 "designed to alleviate individual need": Simon, "Legality, Bureaucracy, and Class," *supra*
    note for page 83, p. 1269. Ibid, p. 1242: "The answer to the question of trust is that pub-
    lic officials can be trusted to adhere to applicable standards when they are socialized
    through professional training to do so, when they are active participants in a vital pro-
    fessional culture, when they are subject to pressure from peers to do so, when they have
    a duty to justify their decisions to citizens affected by them, and when they receive rela-
    tively high status and reward." See also Edward S. Corwin, as quoted in John A. Rohr,
    "Professionalism, Legitimacy, and the Constitution," *Public Administration Quarterly* 8, no.
    4 (Winter 1985): 401: "The world of administration . . . reposes in great measure on the
    loyalty and competence of individual bureaucrats, qualities that thrive best in condi-
    tions making for independence of judgment and pride in a job well done." Ibid., 416:
    "Without some sort of principled autonomy, professionalism in Public Administration
    is no profession at all."
92 remarkably consistent job: See M. P. Baumgartner, "The Myth of Discretion," in *The
    Uses of Discretion*, ed. Keith Hawkins, Oxford Socio-Legal Studies (Oxford: Clarendon,
    1992), 129: Leaving aside a few hot-button issues, American judges of different ideologi-
    cal bent generally rule in ways, as one study found, that are "remarkably patterned and
    consistent."
92 forest rangers: Herbert Kaufman, *The Forest Ranger: A Study in Administrative Behavior*, 2nd
    ed. (Washington, DC: RFF Press, 2006; originally published 1960 by Johns Hopkins Press).
92 the importance of professionalism: Edmund L. Andrews, "Former Bush Aide Isn't Keeping
    to the Script," *New York Times*, August 23, 2004, http://www.nytimes.com/2004/08/23/
    politics/23budget.html, quoting Douglas Holtz-Eakin. This story, and the role of profes-
    sionals, is set forth in Michael Schudson, "The Trouble with Experts—And Why Democ-
    racies Need Them," *Theory and Society* 35, no. 5/6 (December 2006): 491–506.
93 "unique potential of children": Lipsky, *Street-Level Bureaucracy, supra* note for page 22, p. 15.
93 [social challenges require active participation]: See Havel, *Art of the Impossible, supra* note
    for page 37, pp. 147–48: "A modern democratic state cannot consist merely of civil service,
    political parties, and private enterprises. It must offer citizens a colorful array of ways to
    become involved, both privately and publicly, and must develop very different types of
    civic coexistence, solidarity, and participation. In a richly layered civil society, a vital and
    inimitable role is played not only by the organs of administration and nonprofit orga-
    nizations, but also by the churches, the trade unions, the widest possible array of civic
    associations, groups, and clubs. A genuine civil society is, moreover, the best insurance
    against various types of social tension and political or social upheavals: it makes it pos-
    sible for various problems to be solved immediately, when and where they arise, before
    they can turn septic somewhere under the skin of society."
93 Reducing bullying in schools: Jessie Klein, "Opinion: Victim or Bully? Schools Need to
    Create More Choices," *Newsday*, April 18, 2010, http://www.newsday.com/opinion/oped/
    opinion-victim-or-bully-schools-need-to-create-more-choices-1.1866593.
93 "subsidiarity": See generally Domènec Melé, "Exploring the Principle of Subsidiarity in
    Organisational Forms," *Journal of Business Ethics* 60, no. 3 (September 2005): 293–305. See also
    Pope John Paul II (pope), "'*Centesimus Annus*': Encyclical Letter . . . ," May 1, 1991, http://www
    .vatican.va/holy_father/john_paul_ii/encyclicals/documents/hf_jp-ii_enc_01051991_
    centesimus-annus_en.html: "A community of a higher order should not interfere in
    the internal life a community of a lower order, depriving the latter of its functions,
    but rather should support it in case of need and help to coordinate its activity with the
    activities of the rest of society, always with a view to the common good." In addition, see
    Adam Smith, "Book IV, Chapter V," in *An Inquiry into the Nature and Causes of the Wealth of
    Nations*, ed. Edwin Cannan (Chicago: University of Chicago Press, 1976), 38: "But the law
    ought always to trust people with the care of their own interest, as in their local situa-

tions they must generally be able to judge better of it than the legislator can do." See also discussion in Fleischacker, *Third Concept of Liberty*, *supra* note for page 56, p. 131.

93   It is now a core tenet: Subsidiarity has been formally adopted as a governing principle of the European Union. See Article 5(3) of the Maastricht Treaty, which established the EU in 1992, as amended by the 2007 Treaty of Lisbon. For a discussion of Cameron's "Big Society," see Matt Chorley, "The Pub Society: Cameron Relaunches Big Society with £250million Fund to Help Locals Rescue Bars, Shops and Swimming Pools," *Daily Mail*, June 6, 2013, http://www .dailymail.co.uk/news/article-2336913/David-Cameron-relaunches-Big-Society- 250m-fund-let-locals-rescue-bars-shops-swimming-pools.html. For the communitarian movement, see the Institute for Communitarian Policy Studies' website: http://www. gwu.edu/~ccps. A more detailed discussion of this idea can be found in Amitai Etzioni, *The New Golden Rule* (New York: Basic Books, 1996); Benjamin R. Barber, *A Place for Us* (New York: Hill and Wand, 1998), 70: "The true enemy of civil society is, in fact, neither government nor corporations per se, but bureaucracy, dogmatism, unresponsiveness, totalism, bloat, unaccountability, absolutism, and inertia wherever they are found."

93   "fresh thinking and flexible action": Lipsky, *Street-Level Bureaucracy*, *supra* note for page 22, p. 161. See also Jeremy Waldron, "The Concept and the Rule of Law," *Georgia Law Review* 43, no. 1 (Fall 2008): 23: "A mode of governing people that treats them with respect," legal philosopher Jeremy Waldron explains, requires allowing them to present "a view or perspective of their own to present on the application of the norm to their conduct and situation."

94   The overt paternalism of the welfare system: Simon, "Legality, Bureaucracy, and Class," *supra* note for page 83, pp. 1198, 1202, 1207.

94   "Just give us responsibility": Richard Buery, interview by author, 2013.

95   Subsidiarity should be a core value: See Peter F. Drucker, "Individual Freedom and Effective Government in a Society of Super-powers," in Drucker et al., *Power and Democracy in America* (Notre Dame, IN: University of Notre Dame Press, 1961), 13: "Effective national government . . . demands that local tasks be done locally; today they fall by default to the national government where they can only be done badly, but also where their very existence inhibits true policy, true government and national leadership." See also Charles F. Sabel and William H. Simon, "Minimalism and Experimentalism in the Administrative State," *Georgetown Law Journal* 100, no. 1 (2011): 90: "Tailoring also requires an understanding of local context. A child welfare worker putting together a plan for an obese child may be able to include a bicycle in the plan if she knows that the family's church can be persuaded to come up with one if credibly assured that it will fill an important need. Police dealing with a high-crime neighborhood can be more effective if they learn from local residents that a poorly maintained house from which drugs are sold is a magnet for nonresident deviants."

95   "moderating effect of community involvement": Nonet and Selznick, *Law and Society in Transition*, *supra* note for page 20, p. 15.

95   *because* people inevitably disagree: Isaiah Berlin, "The Pursuit of the Ideal," in Berlin, *Proper Study of Mankind*, *supra* note for page 27, p. 15.

History of Human Choice in American Law

96   judges "do not make law": See Harlan F. Stone, *Law and Its Administration* (New York: Columbia University Press, 1915), 22–23; and Zechariah Chafee Jr., "Do Judges Make or Discover Law?" *Proceedings of the American Philosophical Society* 91, no. 5 (1947): 405–20.

97   "play any tune upon it they pleased": William Manning, as quoted in Saul Cornell, *The Other Founders: Anti-Federalism and the Dissenting Tradition in America, 1788-1828* (Chapel Hill: University of North Carolina Press, 1999), 229.

97   "abolish all inferior governments": Brutus, "Letter XI," in Hamilton, Madison, and Jay, *Federalist*, 504–5.

98   "to the public detriment": James Madison, "No. 41," in Hamilton, Madison, and Jay, *Federalist*, 195.

98   [anti-federalist quotations]: See Howe, *Language and Political Meaning, supra* note for page 16, pp. 206–7.

98   "unavoidable inaccuracy": James Madison, "No. 37," in Hamilton, Madison, and Jay, *Federalist*, 172.

99   "It is a great mistake": John Francis Mercer, as quoted in Howe, *Language and Political Meaning, supra* note for page 16, p. 218.

99   "a mere machine": Thomas Jefferson, as quoted in Gordon S. Wood, *Empire of Liberty: A History of the Early Republic, 1789–1815* (Oxford: Oxford University Press, 2009), 403.

99   "'the parent of new perplexities'": St. George Tucker, as quoted in Wood, *Empire of Liberty, supra* note for page 99, p. 405.

99   [Mather]: These quotations come from Wood, *Empire of Liberty, supra* note for page 99, p. 405.

100   The legal philosophy of laissez-faire: For a discussion of philosophy and Supreme Court rulings , see Heineman, *Authority, supra* note for page 77, pp. 91–107.

100   "the great objection": James Kent, Chancellor of New York, as quoted in Morton Keller, *Affairs of State: Public Life in Late Nineteenth Century America* (Cambridge, MA: Belknap Press, 1977), 347.

100   "All barrels": William J. Novak, "Common Regulation: Legal Origins of State Power in America," *Hastings Law Journal* 45 (1994): note 48.

101   A 1911 Wisconsin law: Friedman, "Legal Rules," *supra* note for page 76, pp. 794–95.

101   Sherman Antitrust Act: "Every person who shall monopolize, or attempt to monopolize, or combine or conspire with any other person or persons, to monopolize any part of the trade or commerce among the several States, or with foreign nations, shall be deemed guilty of a felony."

101   "mechanical jurisprudence" and "traffic officers": Roscoe Pound, "Mechanical Jurisprudence," *Columbia Law Review* 8 (1908): 605; Roscoe Pound, "Law and Social Change," *Indiana Law Journal* 3, no. 3 (1927): article 1.

101   "No discretion as to scope": Ernst Freund, "The Law of Administration in America," *Political Science Quarterly* 9, no. 3 (September 1894): 403, 410.

102   "faithless administrators": Daniel R. Ernst, "Ernst Freund, Felix Frankfurter and the American Rechtsstaat: A Transatlantic Shipwreck, 1894–1932," Georgetown Law Faculty Publications and Other Works 18, p. 34, http://scholarship.law.georgetown.edu/facpub/18.

102   "The bestowal of administrative discretion": Ibid., 29, quoting John Henry Wigmore.

102   "opened the doors to arbitrariness": Ibid., 30, quoting Felix Frankfurter.

102   "'men bred to the facts'": Ibid., 36, quoting James Landis.

102   Brownlow report: *Report of the President's Committee on Administrative Management* (Washington, DC: US Government Printing Office, 1937), 65.

103   The old guard kept pushing back: Reuel E. Schiller, "'Saint George and the Dragon': Courts and the Development of the Administrative State in Twentieth-Century America," *Journal of Policy History* 17, no. 1 (2005): 113. In a 1938 report, the American Bar Association characterized administrative discretion as "a Marxian idea much in vogue now among a type of American writers"; *Report of the Special Committee on Administrative Law*, ABA Reports, publication no. 63 (Washington, DC: American Bar Association, 1938), 339–40. See discussion in George B. Shepherd, "Fierce Compromise: The Administrative Procedure Act Emerges from New Deal Politics," *Northwestern University Law Review* 90 (1996): 1591.

103   [1946 Administrative Procedure Act]: See Shepherd, "Fierce Compromise," *supra* note for page 103; and Reuel E. Schiller, "The Era of Deference: Courts, Expertise, and the Emergence of New Deal Administrative Law," *Michigan Law Review* 106 (2007): 399–440.

104 [Landis report to JFK]: James M. Landis, *Report on Regulatory Agencies to the President-Elect* (Washington, DC: US Government Printing Office, 1960).

104 "Nothing is impossible": The official was James H. Boren, founder of the National Association of Professional Bureaucrats, which I believe is meant to be a parody of such an organization. James H. Boren, "Arcane and Proud of It," *New York Times*, June 4, 1998, http://www.nytimes.com/1998/06/04/opinion/arcane-and-proud-of-it.html. Almost as apt is "the Peters Principle," invented by *Washington Monthly* founder Charles Peters: "The Peters Principle—take care to distinguish it from the less persuasive Peter Principle—provides that organizations cease to function effectively when employees spend more than 15.8 percent of their time attending meetings or writing memoranda." Peters, *How Washington Really Works*, supra note for page 40, p. 50.

104 "'the most intelligent cannot disturb'": Kennan, "America's Administrative Response," *supra* note for page 46, p. 12. For a history of legal changes since the 1960s, see, for example, Philip K. Howard, "History of American Law since 1968," in *Oxford Companion to American Law*, ed. Kermit L. Hall (New York: Oxford University Press, 2002), 392–96; John D. Skrentny, *The Minority Rights Revolution* (Cambridge, MA: Harvard University Press, 2004).

105 "new property": Charles A. Reich, "The New Property," *Yale Law Journal* 73, no. 5 (April 1964): 733–87.

105 [Supreme Court expansion of due process]: Howard, "History of American Law," *supra* note for page 104.

105 "an inclusiveness that divides": Hugh Heclo, "Sixties Civics," in *The Great Society and the Hightide of Liberalism*, ed. Sidney M. Milkis and Jerome M. Mileur, Political Development of the American Nation: Studies in Politics & History (Amherst: University of Massachusetts Press, 2005), 65.

106 [taking over Kansas City schools]: Charles Chieppo, "School Reform That Money Can't Buy," Governing.com, September 27, 2011, http://www.governing.com/blogs/bfc/kansas-city-desegregation-school-reform-accountability-performance.html.

106 [Boston busing]: Eggers and O'Leary, *If We Can Put*, supra note for page 42, pp. 82–85. See also Katherine Q. Seelye, "Decades after Clashes, Boston Again Debates Busing," *New York Times*, October 4, 2012.

106 "Choosing among values": Charles Wyzanski, "Equal Justice through Law," *Tulane Law Review* 47 (1973): 951–960.

107 "legal process movement": The book that articulated the new approach was Henry M. Hart and Albert M. Sacks, *The Legal Process: Basic Problems in the Making and Application of Law*, ed. William N. Eskridge and Philip P. Frickey (Westbury, NY: Foundation Press, 1994).

107 "greatest inventions of modern government": Kenneth Culp Davis, *Discretionary Justice: A Preliminary Inquiry* (Urbana: University of Illinois Press, 1979), 65.

107 *Federal Register* nearly quadrupled in length: Ten Thousand Commandments (http://www.tenthousandcommandments.com) has compiled a historical table of the size of the *Federal Register*: Clyde Wayne Crews Jr., *An Annual Snapshot of the Federal Regulatory State*, 20th Anniversary Edition, 2013, http://cei.org/sites/default/files/Wayne%20Crews%20-%2010,000%20Commandments%202013.pdf.

107 Forest rangers used to have: See, for example, Kaufman, *Forest Ranger*, supra note for page 92. See also Al Gore, *Common Sense Government* (New York: Random House, 1995) (introduction by Philip K. Howard).

108 "contrast[ing] legality with discretion": Simon, "Legality, Bureaucracy, and Class," *supra* note for page 83, p. 1223.

108 Lawsuits exploded: George Priest, "The Modern Transformation of Civil Law," *Buffalo Law Review* 54 (2006): 957; Philip K. Howard, *The Collapse of the Common Good* (New York: Ballantine, 2002), 3–70; Walter Olson, *The Litigation Explosion* (New York: Truman Talley, 1992).

109   *Chevron* decision: Chevron U.S.A. Inc. v. Natural Resources Defense Council, Inc., 467 U.S. 837 (1984).

109   rulings encouraging federal judges: See discussion in Philip K. Howard, "Making Civil Justice Sane," *City Journal*, Spring 2006.

109   "distrust of motive": Heclo, "Sixties Civics," *supra* note for page 105, p. 64. Ibid., 70: "In the latter years of Ronald Reagan's presidency, negotiations with the Soviet Union popularized the motto 'trust but verify.' Sixties civics represented the mirror image of that idea: distrust but demand. On reflection, the former appears a hopeful view, the latter a rather resigned morbidity."

109   One high-ranking . . . official: See Howard, *Death of Common Sense, supra* note for page 34, pp. 71–73 (discussing the resignation of Budget Director Philip Michael).

109   prohibition on "direct dealing": Stephen Goldsmith, interview by author, 2011.

109   [definitions in the Affordable Care Act]: "High school" is from 42 USC § 18201(4) (2010); see "42 USC § 18201—Definitions," Legal Information Institute, Cornell University Law School, http://www.law.cornell.edu/uscode/text/42/18201, accessed June 2013. The "didactic" language comes from Affordable Care Act, Pub. L. No. 111-148, § 5505, 124 Stat. 119, 591 (2010); see "Compilation of Patient Protection and Affordable Care Act," Office of Legislative Council, May 2010, http://housedocs.house.gov/energycommerce/ppacacon. pdf. The X-ray language is at 42 USC § 1395w-4 (b)(4)(B) (2010); see "42 USC § 195w-4— Payment for Physicians' Services," Legal Information Institute, Cornell University Law School, http://www.law.cornell.edu/uscode/text/42/1395w-4, accessed June 2013.

Government by Real People, Not Theories

110   everyone follows a theory slavishly: Jonathan Swift, *Gulliver's Travels*, ed. Albert Rivero (New York: W. W. Norton, 2002), 146–63.

111   "rules announced and fixed beforehand": Hayek, *Road to Serfdom, supra* note for page 15.

112   recertified for land-based rescue: Wang, "Alameda Police," *supra* note for page 87.

112   "Keep your government hands off my Medicare": Philip Rucker, "Sen. DeMint of S.C. Is Voice of Opposition to Health Care Reform," *Washington Post*, July 28, 2009.

112   "'Does anybody govern?'": Samuel P. Huntington, "The United States," in Crozier et al., *Crisis of Democracy*, 92.

113   rarely provable: See Tamanaha, *On the Rule of Law, supra* note for page 26, p. 123: "The idea of 'the rule of law, not man,' powerful as it is, has been forever dogged by the fact that laws are not self-interpreting or applying."

113   "mere obedience to a rule": Benjamin N. Cardozo, *The Growth of the Law* (New Haven, CT: Yale University Press, 1924), 87.

113   "No scientist": Jacques Barzun, *A Stroll with William James* (Chicago: University of Chicago Press, 1983), 162. In *The Moral Life of Schools*, Professor Philip Jackson and colleagues emphasized the intangible factors that distinguished good from bad teachers; Jackson, Boostrom, and Hansen, *Moral Life of Schools, supra* note for page 53, p. 48: "What we reject about the words objective and subjective is the implication that one refers to something real and the other does not."

113   "look to custom": Cardozo, *Nature of the Judicial Process, supra* note for page 65, p. 60.

113   "moral risk cannot be avoided": Isaiah Berlin, "The Pursuit of the Ideal," in Berlin, *Proper Study of Mankind, supra* note for page 27, p. 15.

114   Authority "is lost when a person betrays": Havel, *Art of the Impossible, supra* note for page 37, p. 201.

114   But authority is also essential in a crowded society: See Yves Simon, *Philosophy of Democratic Government* (Notre Dame, IN: University of Notre Dame Press, 1993), 71: "Autonomy renders authority necessary and authority renders autonomy possible." See also William A. Frank, "Authority and the Common Good in Democratic Governance," *Review of Metaphysics* 60, no. 4 (June 2007): 823–24: "The need for authority responds as much to the plenitude

of human genius and undeterminable richness of possibilities for action," Professor Frank observes, as to deficiencies in human behavior. "Not every defeat of authority," Justice Robert H. Jackson observed, "is a gain for individual freedom." Jackson, "The Task of Maintaining Our Liberties," *American Bar Association Journal* 39 (November 1953): 961–65.

114 individual freedom is weak tea: John H. Schaar, "Liberty/Authority/Community in the Political Thought of John Winthrop," *Political Theory* 19, no. 4 (November 1991): 512: "Those who think that deliverance from all authority means full human emancipation have not, perhaps, thought the matter through, for to be without authority in this world is to be insignificant in this world. It means you do not matter to anyone." See also Tocqueville, *Democracy in America, supra* note for page 24, vol. 1, p. 250: "If an American were condemned to confine his activity to his own affairs, he would be robbed of one half of his existence."

115 But joint endeavors: See Niebuhr, "Children of Light," *supra* note for page 86, p. 162: "The community requires liberty as much as does the individual, and the individual requires community more than bourgeois thought comprehended." David Hume discussed the need for authority to make common choices this way: "Two neighbors may agree to drain a meadow which they possess in common . . . But 'tis very difficult and, indeed, impossible, that a thousand persons shou'd agree in any such action; it being difficult for them to concert so complicated a design, and still more difficult for them to execute it; while each seeks a pretext to free himself of the trouble and expence; and wou'd lay the whole burden on others. Political society easily remedies both these inconveniences . . . Thus bridges are built; harbours open'd; ramparts rais'd; canals form'd; fleets equip'd; and armies disciplin'd." David Hume, *A Treatise of Human Nature*, ed. L. A. Selby-Bigge and P. H. Nidditch, 2nd ed. (Oxford: Clarendon, 1978), 538–39.

115 "simultaneous recession of both freedom and authority": Arendt, "What Is Authority?" *supra* note for page 63, p. 100. See also Ibid., 97: "The liberal writer is apt to pay little attention" to the "distinction between legitimate and illegitimate power . . . because of his conviction that all power corrupts and that the constancy of progress requires constant loss of power, no matter what it's origin may be."

115 No authority "means to be confronted anew": Ibid., 141. The classic study of a culture without authority or public morality is Edward Banfield, *The Moral Basis of a Backward Society* (New York: Free Press, 1958). Professor Banfield studies a village in southern Italy in which community norms have all but disappeared, and there is no mechanism for action in the common good. It is a community in which there are "no leaders and no followers," and no one gets what they view as their "fair share" (ibid., 97–98).

115 a kind of marketplace for good ideas: "The rule that functions," as Justice Cardozo put it, "will produce a title deed to recognition." Cardozo, *Nature of the Judicial Process, supra* note for page 65, pp. 102–3.

115 "Authority implies an obedience": Arendt, "What Is Authority?" *supra* note for page 63, p. 474.

115 "the hierarchy itself": Ibid., 463. See Cardozo, *Nature of the Judicial Process, supra* note for page 65, p. 135: "You may say there is no assurance that judges will interpret the mores of the day more wisely and truly than other men. I am not disposed to deny this, but in my view it is quite beside the point. The point is rather that this power of interpretation must be lodged somewhere."

116 the Sovern Commission: State-City Commission on Integrity in Government. *Report and Recommendations Relating to City Procurement and Contracts* (November 19, 1986), 67.

116 The safest system: See generally Frank Anechiarico and James B. Jacobs, *The Pursuit of Absolute Integrity: How Corruption Control Makes Government Ineffective* (Chicago: University of Chicago Press, 1996).

116 "escaping from the old ones": John Maynard Keynes, *The General Theory of Employment, Interest, and Money* (New York: Harcourt, Brace & World, 1965), viii. John Schaar describes the problem of old ideas this way: "Perhaps we really are in crisis, but mistake its true nature. The crisis may be in our whole way of seeing and being in the world. But if that is

so, in the very nature of things we would be the last to know it, for we are the crisis." John
H. Schaar, *Legitimacy in the Modern State* (New Brunswick, NJ: Transaction, 1981), 333.

116   Wittgenstein: For a discussion of Wittgenstein and legal indeterminacy, see Margaret
Jane Radin, "Reconsidering the Rule of Law," *Boston University Law Review* 69 (July 1989):
1–31; and Daniel G. Stroup, "Law and Language: Cardozo's Jurisprudence and Wittgenstein's Philosophy," *Valparaiso University Law Review* 18, no. 2 (Winter 1984): 371.

116   "Words do not determine meaning": Waldron, "Vagueness in Law," *supra* note for page 70,
p. 510.

117   "all other goals are useless": Drucker, "Individual Freedom and Effective Government,"
supra note for page 95, p. 11.

117   "not a magic that somehow absolves us": Jeremy Waldron, "The Rule of Law and the
Importance of Procedure," in *Getting to the Rule of Law*, ed. James E. Fleming, Nomos: Year-
book of the American Society for Political and Legal Philosophy 50 (New York: New York
University Press, 2011), 25.

118   "unreasonable searches and seizures": U.S. Const. amend. IV.

118   Hayek recanted: Friedrich A. Hayek, *Law, Legislation and Liberty*, vol. 1 (Chicago: University
of Chicago Press, 1973), 116: "Although legislation can certainly increase the certainty of
the law on particular points, I am now persuaded that this advantage is more than offset
if its recognition leads to the requirement that *only* what has thus been expressed in
statutes should have the force of law. It seems to me that judicial decision may in fact be
more predictable if the judge is also bound by generally held views of what is just, even
when they are not supported by the letter of the law."

118   society without responsibility: The classic book on how freedom from responsibility
might be more attractive than freedom itself is Erich Fromm's *Escape from Freedom* (New
York: Henry Holt, 1994). Management expert Warren Bennis has also written about the
self-destructive attractions of bureaucracy; see Warren Bennis, *The Essential Bennis* (San
Francisco: Jossey-Bass, 2009), 162: "Bureaucracies are beautiful mechanisms for the evasion of responsibility and guilt."

119   "government is the shepherd": Tocqueville, *Democracy in America, supra* note for page 24,
vol. 2, p. 319.

Part II: Restoring Human Control of Democracy

Democracy without Leaders

127   "EPA is hobbled": National Academy of Public Administration, *Setting Priorities, Get-
ting Results: A New Direction for the Environmental Protection Agency* (Washington, DC: The
Academy, 1995), 1. See discussion in OECD, *Regulatory Reform in the United States* (Paris:
OECD, 1999), 48.

127   "excessive detail, legalism, and rigidity": OECD, *Regulatory Reform, supra* note for page 127,
p. 128.

128   There are eighty-two teacher training programs: US Government Accountability Office,
*Opportunities to Reduce Potential Duplication in Government Programs, Save Tax Dollars, and
Enhance Revenue*, GAO-11-318SP (Washington, DC: GAO, 2011), 144–50, http://www.gao
.gov/new.items/d11318sp.pdf. See also Ed O'Keefe, "GAO: Overlapping Government
Programs Cost Billions," *Washington Post*, February 28, 2012, http://www.washington
post.com/blogs/federal-eye/post/gao-overlapping-government-programs-cost-bil
lions/2012/02/27/gIQAnSPdeR_blog.html.

128   The US ranks behind sixteen other countries: International Finance Corporation, "Making a Difference for Entrepreneurs," *Doing Business* 2011, http://www.doingbusiness
.org/~/media/fpdkm/doing%20business/documents/annual-reports/english/db11-full
report.pdf. See discussion in Ferguson, *Great Degeneration, supra* note for page 42, pp. 101–2.

128   required forty-seven approvals: "Bayonne Bridge Navigation Clearance Project—Updated Permit/Approvals List," revised April 16, 2012. See also references at page 11.

128   small businesses . . . find themselves whipsawed: According to a 2010 report from the Small Business Administration, regulation is 80 percent more costly to small employers than to large employers: Nicole V. Crain and W. Mark Crain, *The Impact of Regulatory Costs on Small Firms*, SBAHQ-08-M-0466 (SBA Office of Advocacy, 2010), http://www.sba.gov/sites/default/files/The%20Impact%20of%20Regulatory%20Costs%20on%20Small%20Firms%20(Full).pdf.

128   wrap her home in red tape: "Exclusive: Long Beach Woman 'Fed Up' with Feds Wraps Storm-Damaged Home in Red Tape," *CBS New York*, February 5, 2013, http://newyork.cbslocal.com/2013/02/05/exclusive-long-beach-woman-fed-up-with-feds-wraps-storm-damaged-home-in-red-tape.

129   "a large and needless deterrent": Matthew Yglesias, "Starting a Business Is a Huge Pain," *Slate*, February 1, 2013, http://www.slate.com/articles/business/small_business/2013/02/starting_my_small_business_cities_make_it_incredibly_hard_to_get_a_business.single.html. Blackstone weighed in on the evil of regulation for its own sake: "Nay, that even laws themselves, whether made with or without our consent, if they regulate and constrain our conduct in matters of mere indifference, without any good end in view, are laws destructive of liberty." William Blackstone, *Commentaries on the Laws of England in Four Books* (Philadelphia: Robert Bell, 1771), 126.

129   "We've got fifty state regulators": Amy Friend, as quoted in Robert G. Kaiser, *Act of Congress: How America's Essential Institution Works, and How It Doesn't* (New York: Knopf, 2013), 193.

129   "one-stop shopping": See OECD, "Implementing Administrative Simplification in OECD Countries," http://www.oecd.org/mena/governance/37026688.pdf, accessed May 2013.

129   [Germany's administrative code]: "Administrative Procedure Act (*Verwaltungsverfahrensgesetz*, VwVfG)," § 75 (1). English translation ("Section 75: Legal Effects of Planning Approval") available at http://www.iuscomp.org/gla/statutes/VwVfG.htm, accessed July 2013.

129   [India's bureaucracy]: Nandita Bose, "Held Up by Red Tape and Graft," *New York Times*, May 6, 2013, http://www.nytimes.com/2013/05/07/business/global/07iht-inside07.html?pagewanted=all&_r=0.

130   "an 18-foot chart": See discussion in OECD, *Regulatory Reform, supra* note for page 127, p. 42.

130   [Common Good inventory of school bureaucracy]: Danielle Rhoades, "New Study Reveals How the Burden of Law Is Paralyzing America's Schools" (press release), *Common Good*, November 29, 2004; David Andretta, "Regs Stifle Schools, Study Says," *New York Post*, November 30, 2004, http://www.nypost.com/p/news/item_OrHlysXVYvje1KNTrTwopM. See also Melissa Junge and Sheara Krvaric, "Federal Compliance Works against Education Policy Goals," *Education Outlook* no. 6 (July 2011): 4, http://www.aei.org/files/2011/07/28/EDU-2011-06-g.pdf: "Title I alone contained 588 discrete compliance requirements."

130   [New York City civil service]: Stephen Goldsmith and Stephen Dobrowsky, separate interviews by author, 2011; and review of union contracts. The clerical workers union contract, for example, contains this language: "Where new equipment . . . is installed . . . the Employer agrees to reopen this Agreement for the sole purpose of negotiating with the Union on the practical effect, if any, such equipment has on the affected employees." The culture in many public offices is divorced from the idea of public duty. Charlie Peters tells the story of the regional head of FEMA who went on holiday the day following the 1989 California earthquake because, as he explained, he had nonrefundable plane tickets. Charles Peters, *How Washington Really Works, supra* note for page 40, p. 59. An acquaintance who ran a humanitarian emergency relief department in the Pentagon was surprised when, soon after a large bombing in Kosovo, most of her staff walked off the job. When she asked how they could leave at such a time, they responded matter-of-factly that their workday ended at five o'clock. The absence of accountability, whether formal or informal, inevitably corrodes the culture of any joint endeavor. See sources cited in

Philip K. Howard, "The Freedom to Judge Others," in Howard, *Life without Lawyers, supra* note for page 81, pp. 122–49. See also Marshall Dimock, "Bureaucracy Self-examined," in *Reader in Bureaucracy*, ed. Robert K. Merton (New York: Macmillan, 1952), 400: "When an individual in an organization feels utterly secure, the sense of struggle which produces much of the world's best effort is lost. Lassitude results. Laziness gradually translates itself into managerial slothfulness, one of bureaucracy's worst faults."

131   sweetheart pensions: See Daniel DiSalvo, "The Trouble with Public Sector Unions," *National Affairs*, Fall 2010, http://www.nationalaffairs.com/publications/detail/the-trou ble-with-public-sector-unions; and Philip K Howard, "The Public-Union Albatross," *Wall Street Journal*, November 9, 2011, http://online.wsj.com/article/SB100014240529702 04190704577024321510926692.html. See also Marc Lacey, "School Official Finds Retire- ment Is Just a Higher Pay Grade," *New York Times*, April 1, 2011, http://www.nytimes .com/2011/04/02/us/02superintendent.html (a school superintendent in Phoenix retires with a $100,000 pension and is rehired the next day with his $150,000 salary).

131   [public service in other countries]: See John Halligan, ed., *Civil Service Systems in Anglo- American Countries* (London: Edward Elgar, 2004). For a summary of civil service rules in European countries, see DGAFP (Direction Générale de l'Administration et de la Fonc- tion Publique), "Administration and the Civil Service in the EU 27 Member States," 2008, http://www.fonction-publique.gouv.fr/files/files/publications/etudes_perspectives/ Administration_and_the_Civil_service_in_the_27_EU_Member_states.pdf.

131   "expulsion of the fittest": Sam Schwartz, interview by author, 2008.

131   "Think of city government as a big bus": Los Angeles Deputy Mayor Michael Keeley, as quoted in William D. Eggers and John O'Leary, *Revolution at the Roots: Making Our Govern- ment Smaller, Better, and Closer to Home* (New York: Free Press, 1995), 150.

132   "Is it still the right mission?": Drucker, *Management, supra* note for page 23, p. 164.

132   would emerge unscathed: See Richard B. Stewart, "Madison's Nightmare," *University of Chicago Law Review* 57, no. 2 (Spring 1990): 342–46.

132   "almost lawless passion for lawmaking": Henry Steele Commager, *The American Mind: An Interpretation of American Thought and Character since the 1880's* (New Haven, CT: Yale Uni- versity Press, 1950), 363.

132   "will increasingly penalise the United States": OECD, *Regulatory Reform, supra* note for page 127, p. 94.

133   "Members of Congress don't 'do' law": Congressman Jim Cooper, interview by author, 2013.

133   "They don't really understand the issues": Kaiser, *Act of Congress, supra* note for page 129, p. 112.

133   [Pelosi's statement about ACA]: "Pelosi: We Have to Pass Health Care So You Can Find Out What Is in It," *Real Clear Politics*, March 9, 2010, http://www.realclearpolitics.com/ video/2010/03/09/pelosi_we_have_to_pass_health_care_so_you_can_find_out_what_ is_in_it.html.

133   "an enormous shift in responsibility": Edward M. Kennedy, *True Compass: A Memoir* (New York: Twelve, 2009), 486. See discussion in Kaiser, *Act of Congress, supra* note for page 129, p. 112.

134   The internal rules of Congress: See Thomas E. Mann and Norman J. Ornstein, *The Broken Branch: How Congress Is Failing America and How to Get It Back on Track* (Oxford: Oxford Uni- versity Press, 2006).

134   Campaign finance rules act as mortar: See Lawrence Lessig, *Republic, Lost: How Money Corrupts Congress—and a Plan to Stop It* (New York: Twelve, 2011); Robert G. Kaiser, *So Damn Much Money: The Triumph of Lobbying and the Corrosion of American Government* (New York: Knopf, 2009).

134   Nearly nine out of ten Americans: In January 2013, Gallup found 91 percent of Ameri- cans in favor of background checks for firearms purchases: Lydia Saad, "Americans Back Obama's Proposals to Address Gun Violence," *Gallup Politics*, January 23, 2013, http://

www.gallup.com/poll/160085/americans-back-obama-proposals-address-gun-violence. aspx. Sixty-five percent of Americans favored the actual bill proposed: Frank Newport, "Americans Wanted Gun Background Checks to Pass Senate," *Gallup Politics*, April 29, 2013, http://www.gallup.com/poll/162083/americans-wanted-gun-background-checks-pass-senate.aspx.

135 On litigation reform: Meeting by author with a senior Democratic congressman, 2005.

135 The power of a small group: See generally Jonathan Rauch, *Government's End: Why Washington Stopped Working* (New York: PublicAffairs, 1999).

135 to protest discrimination against large cars: Peters, *How Washington Really Works*, *supra* note for page 40, p. 36.

135 anchored in the status quo: Political leaders are lagging indicators, but they, too, are starting to comprehend the reality of no forward movement. Former Speaker of the House Nancy Pelosi, in 2013, remarked, "This is an environment that is almost rigged, intentionally or not, wittingly or not, rigged so that the status quo just goes on." Laura Bassett, "Nancy Pelosi: Congress Is 'Rigged' to Maintain the Status Quo," *Huffington Post*, June 5, 2013, http://www .huffingtonpost.com/2013/06/05/nancy-pelosi-congress-rigged_n_3391936.html.

137 "A political system that expects failure": Gerald F. Seib, "Oil Woes Fail to Stir Leadership," *Wall Street Journal*, June 24, 2008.

137 the other side "on the ropes": Jeffrey Leeds, conversation with author, 2013.

137 "they wanted to score political points": Kaiser, *Act of Congress*, *supra* note for page 129, p. 381.

138 the White House could blame Democrats: Interview by author with staffer who wished to remain anonymous, 2005.

138 EPA should be a cabinet-level department: E. Donald Elliott (former EPA general counsel), interview by author, 2009.

138 "We need to keep the issue for our side": Ronald Faucheux (former chief of staff to a Democratic senator), interview by author, 2011.

138 The shocking humiliations: Philip G. Zimbardo, *The Lucifer Effect: Understanding How Good People Turn Evil* (New York: Random House, 2007), 324–443.

138 Reacting to . . . Simpson-Bowles: Jordan Fabian, "Pelosi: Fiscal Panel Proposal 'Is Simply Unacceptable,'" *Hill*, November 10, 2010, http://thehill.com/blogs/blog-briefing-room/news/128701-pelosi-fiscal-panel-proposal-simply-unacceptable; Philip K. Howard, "One Nation, under Too Many Laws," *Washington Post*, December 12, 2010.

139 "bipartisan conspiracy": Marshall made this remark in a presentation at a Common Good forum, "Is Leadership Possible," held at the New York Times Building in New York City, October 20, 2010.

139 "an end in itself": See Kaiser, *Act of Congress*, *supra* note for page 129, p. 51.

139 $1.6 million job: Congressman Jim Cooper, interview by author, 2013. See also Drew Griffin and David Fitzpatrick, "Retiring Congresswoman Leads 2013 Lobbying Revolving Door," CNN.com, January 22, 2013, http://ac360.blogs.cnn.com/2013/01/22/retiring-congresswoman-leads-2013-lobbying-revolving-door.

140 "deviant subculture": Anthony Giddens and Philip W. Sutton define a deviant subculture as one "whose members have values which differ substantially from those of the majority in a society." Giddens and Sutton, *Sociology*, 7th ed. (Cambridge: Polity Press, 2013), glossary, http://www.polity.co.uk/giddens7/studentresource/glossary/default.asp#d.

140 The values of government are not congruent with: See Theda Skocpol, *The Missing Middle: Working Families and the Future of American Social Policy* (New York: W. W. Norton, 2000), 141: "Nothing they do there," a friend of Professor Skocpol's from Maine said about Washington, "ever makes any difference for people like me."

140 "vetocracy": Francis Fukuyama, "Oh for a Democratic Dictatorship and Not a Vetocracy," *Financial Times* (London), November 22, 2011.

140 [Affordable Care Act giveaways]: See "42 USC § 280g-15: State Demonstration Programs

to Evaluate Alternatives to Current Medical Tort Litigation," Legal Information Institute, Cornell University Law School, http://www.law.cornell.edu/uscode/text/42/280g-15, accessed July 2013.

141   "Most members like to duck tough issues": Congressman Barney Frank, as quoted in Kaiser, *Act of Congress*, *supra* note for page 129, p. 170.

142   bad cultures generally must first collapse: See Joseph A. Tainter, *The Collapse of Complex Societies* (Cambridge: Cambridge University Press, 1988). See also Hugh Trevor-Roper, introduction, in Edward Gibbon, *The Decline and Fall of the Roman Empire*, Everyman's Library (New York: Knopf, 1993), 1:xciv: "Once active virtue is lost in a society it is hard to recover, perhaps impossible without radical social change; and the survival of nations may sometimes depend on the life of one man."

A New Charter for Public Leadership

144   Institutions tend to take a life of their own: The larger an organization, the more resistant it is to change. Michael T. Hannan and John Freeman, "Structural Inertia and Organizational Change," *Sociological Review* 49, no. 2 (April 1984), 1949–64. See also Paul C. Light, *A Government Ill Executed: The Decline of the Federal Service and How to Reverse It* (Cambridge, MA: Harvard University Press, 2008).

144   "All experience hath shewn": The text of the Declaration of Independence can be found at http://www.archives.gov/exhibits/charters/declaration_transcript.html.

144   governments rarely reform themselves: Gibbon attributed Rome's collapse mainly to the deadening effects of central control. See Hugh Trevor-Roper, introduction, in Gibbon, *Decline and Fall*, *supra* note for page 142, vol. 1, p. xci: "The centralization, the immobility, the monopoly of the Roman Empire had gradually destroyed the pluralism, stifled those ideas, and so progress had been retarded, public virtue had declined, and in the end an inert, top heavy political structure had fallen to external blows which a healthier organism could have survived." For a survey of social collapse, see Tainter, *Collapse of Complex Societies*, *supra* note for page 142.

144   stick-slip phenomenon: Frank M. Baumgartner and Bryan D. Jones, "From There to Here: Punctuated Equilibrium to the General Punctuation Thesis to a Theory of Government Information Processing," *Journal of Policy Studies* 40, no. 1 (2012); Frank R. Baumgartner and Bryan D. Jones, *Agendas and Instability in American Politics*, 2nd ed. (Chicago: University of Chicago Press, 2009).

145   "I have a dream": Martin Luther King Jr., "I Have a Dream" (speech, March on Washington, Lincoln Memorial, Washington, DC, August 28, 1963), http://www.archives.gov/press/exhibits/dream-speech.pdf.

146   The shift from democracy toward dictatorship: Polybius, *The Histories*, ed. Robin Waterfield and B. C. McGing, Oxford World's Classics (Oxford: Oxford University Press, 2010), 376, 378. Hannah Arendt viewed bureaucracy, not democracy, as the last stage of the government before it reverted to monarchy. See Arendt, *Human Condition*, *supra* note for page 14, p. 40, describing bureaucracy, or "no-man rule," as "the last stage of government in the nation state just as one-man rule . . . was its first."

147   School bureaucracy is a fortress: See notes for pages 35–36, *supra*. See also, for example, Bonacorsi, "Union Has Issues," *supra* note for page 22 (public union files grievance to bar volunteer school crossing guard).

147   too expensive to operate small nursing homes: Braithwaite, Makkai, and Braithwaite, *Regulating Aged Care*, *supra* note for page 48, pp. 20–22.

147   [development of the Uniform Commercial Code]: See, for example, Lawrence M. Friedman, "Business Law in an Age of Change," in *American Law in the 20th Century* (New Haven, CT: Yale University Press, 2002), 377–98.

148   *Corpus Juris Civilis*: D. J. Osler, "Budaeus and Roman Law," *Ius Commune* 13 (1985): 195, 201, http://data.rg.mpg.de/iuscommune/ic13_osler.pdf.

148   "a kind of cancer": *Justinian's Institutes*, trans. Peter Birks and Grant McLeod (Ithaca, NY: Cornell University Press, 1987), 11.

148   [Portalis's recodification of French law]: James R. Maxeiner, "Costs of No Codes," *Mississippi College Law Review* 31 (2013): 363, 379–80. See *Preliminary Address on the First Draft of the Civil Code*, Canada Department of Justice, http://www.justice.gc.ca/eng/rp-pr/csj-sjc/ilp-pji/code/index.html, accessed July 2013. Inspired by the success of France's recodification, many other European countries embarked on similar efforts. See, for example, Konrad Zweigert and Hein Kötz, *An Introduction to Comparative Law*, 3rd ed., trans. Tony Weir (Oxford: Clarendon, 1998), 98; and Xavier Blanc-Jouvan, *Worldwide Influence of the French Civil Code, on the Occasion of Its Bicentennial Celebration*, Cornell Law School Berger International Speaker Papers 3, September 27, 2004, http://scholarship.law.cornell.edu/biss_papers/3.

148   presided over by Napoleon himself: H. A. L. Fisher, "The Codes," in *Cambridge Modern History* (New York: MacMillan, 1906), 9:151.

148   "It is for the judge and the jurist": Portalis, quoted in Jean Louis Bergel, "Principal Features and Methods of Codification," *Louisiana Law Review* 48 (1988): 1073. Napoleon considered the new code his greatest accomplishment. See also Ibid., 1078–79: "While in exile in Saint Helena, Napoleon said, 'My true glory is not that I have won forty battles. Waterloo will blow away the memory of these victories. What nothing can blow away, what will live eternally is my Civil Code.'"

148   [nineteenth-century codification movement]: See, for example, Lawrence M. Friedman, "Procedure and Practice: An Age of Reform," in Friedman, *A History of American Law*, 3rd ed. (New York: Touchstone, 2005), 293–308; and Charles M. Cook, *The American Codification Movement: A Study of Antebellum Legal Reform* (Westport, CT: Greenwood Press, 1981).

150   [infrastructure project approvals in Germany]: The Independent Institute for Environmental Issues (Unabhängiges Institut für Umweltfragen, or UfU) reports that in Germany, most proceedings are concluded within twelve months, and even complicated infrastructure projects rarely take more than two years. See "Ablauf des Planfeststellungsverfahrens," UfU, http://www.aarhus-konvention.de/einmischen/oeffentlichkeitsbeteiligung/planfeststellungsverfahren/ablauf-planfeststellungsverfahren.html, accessed May 2013.

150   "whole of Government": See OECD, "Recommendation of the Council on Regulatory Policy and Governance," 2012, http://www.oecd.org/gov/regulatory-policy/49990817.pdf. Governments should "ensure that regulation serves whole-of-government policy."

151   "slough off from government": Peter F. Drucker, William V. D'Antonio, and Howard J. Ehrlich, *Power and Democracy in America* (Notre Dame, IN: University of Notre Dame Press, 1961), 13.

151   The problem of obsolete law: The British legal historian F. W. Maitland observed that "one of the primary functions of a Legislature is . . . to sweep into the dustbin that rubbish that inevitably accumulates in the course of legal history." Maitland, as quoted in Frank Gahan, "The Codification of Law," *Transactions of the Grotius Society* 8 (1922): 112. See also Paul H. Kocher, "Francis Bacon on the Science of Jurisprudence," *Journal of the History of Ideas* 18, no. 1 (January 1957). Bacon wanted to recodify laws "being so many in number that neither common people can half practice them, nor the lawyer sufficiently understand them" (ibid., 4). He continued, "purge out multiplicity of laws, clear the incertainty of them . . . define the jurisdiction of your courts" (ibid.).

151   "A little rebellion now and then": Thomas Jefferson, "Letter to James Madison," in Jefferson, *Writings* (New York: Library of America, 1984), 882. Judge Guido Calabresi identified the growing pile of obsolete law as a threat to governance in his 1982 book, *A Common Law for the Age of Statutes* (Boston: Harvard University Press, 1985), proposing that federal courts could take it upon themselves to eliminate obsolete laws. I doubt that judges would feel comfortable discarding statutes except in the most obvious cases—say, a statute dealing with horses and buggies. See discussion

between Judge Calabresi and the author at Philip K. Howard, "Should the Courts Be Allowed to Repeal Obsolete Law?" *Atlantic*, March 20, 2012, http://www.theatlantic .com/national/archive/2012/03/should-the-courts-be-allowed-to-repeal-obsolete-law/254454.

152 "the infirmities most besetting": James Madison, "Letter to John Cartwright," in *Selections from the Private Correspondence of James Madison: From 1813 to 1836* (Washington: J. C. McGuire, 1824), 53. See also John Jay, in *The Speeches of the Different Governors, to the Legislature of the State of New York* (Albany, NY: J. B. van Steenbergh, 1825), 48: "Laws and regulations, however carefully devised, frequently prove defective in practice."

152 [states circumventing sunset laws]: Chris Mooney, "A Short History of Sunsets," *Legal Affairs*, January/February 2004, http://www.legalaffairs.org/issues/January-February-2004/story_mooney_janfeb04.msp: "In 1978, *The New York Times* reported that under Colorado's sunset law $212,000 in state funding was spent to review 13 agencies. This led to the termination of just three small agencies, a savings of $6,810. Colorado wasn't unique: In Nebraska and Louisiana, every agency scheduled to expire was re-established by the legislature. "In Alabama, even the process was an utter embarrassment: 'The House of Representatives ran through the nearly 300 separate sunset resolutions in quick succession,' noted *The Washington Monthly* at the time. 'Many representatives left the chamber, giving their young pages instructions on how to vote for them.'"

152 Texas Sunset Advisory Commission: Sunset Advisory Commission, *Sunset in Texas*, January 2012, http://www.sunset.state.tx.us/suntx.pdf.

152 certified only four nurses in the state: Eggers and O'Leary, *If We Can Put, supra* note for page 42, p. 176.

153 regulations . . . 7 feet high: Matt Nesto, "Obamacare: 3-Years-Old and Still Growing," *Yahoo! Finance*, March 22, 2013, http://finance.yahoo.com/blogs/breakout/obamacare-3-years-old-still-growing-134029965.html.

153 One proposal on the table: This proposal is known as the REINS bill. Regulations from the Executive in Need of Scrutiny (REINS) Act, H.R. 10, 112th Cong. (2011). See Jonathan R. Siegel, "The REINS Act and the Struggle to Control Agency Rulemaking," *New York University Journal of Legislation and Public Policy* 16 (2013): 131 (arguing that the REINS Act would be "hopelessly impractical," given to gamesmanship and partisan excess).

154 [legislative veto]: The legislative veto was invalidated in INS v. Chadha, 462 U.S. 919 (1983), on the basis, among others, that all legislative acts must be "presented" to the president for his signature or veto.

154 could incarcerate terrorist suspects: Joseph Margulies, *Guantánamo and the Abuse of Presidential Power* (New York: Simon & Schuster, 2006).

154 There is a comparable controversy: See Robert J. Delahunty and John Yoo, "Dream On: The Obama Administration's Non-enforcement of Immigration Laws, the DREAM Act, and the Take Care Clause," *Texas Law Review* 91, no. 4 (2013): 781–857.

154 power to do the rudimentary tasks: Most debate is on the terms of history and theory, not practicality of modern governing. For different views, compare Steven G. Calabresi and Christopher S. Yoo, *The Unitary Executive: Presidential Power from Washington to Bush* (New Haven, CT: Yale University Press, 2008), with Bruce Ackerman, *The Decline and Fall of the American Republic* (Cambridge, MA: Harvard University Press, 2010).

154 The President lacks the ability: See Terry M. Moe and Scott A. Wilson, "Presidents and the Politics of Structure," *Law and Contemporary Problems*, Regulating Regulation: The Political Economy of Administrative Procedures and Regulatory Instruments: Part 2, 57, no. 2 (Spring 1994): 19: "The continuing problem for presidents, though, is that they have too little control, not too much, and they need to build an institution that helps them do a better job of overcoming the tremendous obstacles to leadership the system places in their way."

155 other public officials existed only because: George Washington, "Letter to Count de

Moustier, May 25, 1789, Gilder Lehrman Collection Documents, http://www.pbs.org/
georgewashington/collection/pres_1789may25.html.

155 "If any power whatsoever": Madison, "Speech in Congress," *supra* note for page 44, p. 456.
See also Peters, *How Washington Really Works, supra* note for page 40, p. 159: "If elections
are going to mean anything . . . the administration must be given the authority to hire
and fire not just cabinet members and agency heads, but also enough other officials, high
and low, to allow the president to move the machinery of government." In addition, see
Commager, *American Mind, supra* note for page 132, pp. 310–35.

156 "Poor Ike": Richard E. Neustadt, *Presidential Power and the Modern Presidents: The Politics of
Leadership from Roosevelt to Reagan* (New York: Free Press, 1990), 10.

156 Civil Works Administration: Harold Meyerson, "Work History," *The American Prospect*,
May 2, 2010, http://prospect.org/article/work-history-0: "Putting millions of people to
work in a space of two months was an amazing achievement. The 4.26 million Americans
employed by the CWA constituted roughly 3.5 percent of the nation's population of 125
million people. Today, the Census Bureau estimates that America is home to 309 million.
If a modern-day public-works program were employed on the same scale, it would employ
10.8 million Americans." See also Charles Peters and Timothy Noah, "Wrong Harry: Four
Million Jobs in Two Years? FDR Did It in Two Months," *Slate*, January 26, 2009, http://
www.slate.com/articles/news_and_politics/chatterbox/2009/01/wrong_harry.html.

157 "the imperial presidency": See Arthur M. Schlesinger, *The Imperial Presidency* (Boston:
Houghton Mifflin, 1973).

157 One by one Congress removed: For a history of presidential efforts to reform the executive branch in the twentieth century, see Brian Balogh, Joanna Grisinger, and Philip
Zelikow, *Making Democracy Work: A Brief History of Twentieth-Century Federal Executive Reorganization*, Miller Center Working Paper in American Political Development (Charlottes-
ville, VA: Miller Center for Public Affairs, University of Virginia, 2002), http://www
.hennessyaward.org/images/Hoover%20Commission/main_content.pdf.

157 known as FACA: Jay S. Bybee, "Advising the President: Separation of Powers and the Federal Advisory Committee Act," *Yale Law Journal* 104 (1994): 51.

157 Ares I rocket program: Mark K. Matthews, "NASA's Ares Rocket Dead, but Congress Lets
You Pay $500 Million More for It," *Orlando Sentinel*, December 26, 2010, http://articles.
orlandosentinel.com/2010-12-26/news/os-nasa-ares-rocket-constellation-20101227_1_
constellation-moon-program-nasa-s-ares-new-nasa-plan.

157 "line-item veto": Clinton v. City of New York, 524 U.S. 417 (1998).

158 [1883 civil service law]: Paul P. van Riper, *History of the United States Civil Service* (Evanston,
IL: Row, Peterson, 1958), 105–9.

159 "unites all power in the same hands": Alexander Hamilton, "No. 71," in Hamilton, Madison, and Jay, *Federalist*, 350. See William Paley, *The Works of William Paley in Five Volumes*
(Boston: Joshua Belcher, 1811), 3:400, as quoted in Hayek, *Constitution of Liberty, supra* note
for page 15, p. 173: "The first maxim of a free state is, that the laws be made by one set
of men, and administered by another: in other words, that the legislative and judicial
characters be kept separate."

159 "executive power in his hands": Locke, *Second Treatise of Government*, 89.

159 "no right to diminish or modify his executive authority": Madison, "Speech in Congress,"
supra note for page 44, p. 456.

159 "partial intermixture": Alexander Hamilton, "No. 66," in Hamilton, Madison, and Jay, *Federalist*, 322.

160 Never, ever, give . . . honest feedback: See Walter Olson, *The Excuse Factory* (New York: Free
Press, 1997). See also Howard, *Collapse of the Common Good, supra* note for page 108, pp.
173–98.

160 legal minefield: See Simon, "Solving Problems," *supra* note for page 71, p. 151: "The Ameri-

can tort system has radical deficiencies that one would expect liberals to decry. The system provides no benefits at all to most injured people . . . The awards that the system does make are staggeringly arbitrary, depending on the actual or anticipated judgments . . . of panels of lay decisionmakers . . . operating under vague instructions and without any knowledge of decisions in other cases. The system's effect in deterring bad conduct seems weak, and in some respects, perverse . . . Less than fifty percent of the total payments by defendants go to claimants, in some categories, much less . . . 'Close to two-thirds of insurance company expenditures in asbestos suits (including cases settled before trial) ended up in the pockets of lawyers and experts for both sides rather than in those of asbestos victims and their families.'" See James R. Maxeiner, *Failures of American Civil Justice in International Perspective* (Cambridge: Cambridge University Press, 2011), comparing American justice with justice in Germany and South Korea.

160 Fear of lawsuits: "I should dread a lawsuit beyond almost anything except sickness and death." Learned Hand, "Deficiencies of Trials to Reach to the Heart of the Matter," in *Lectures on Legal Topics, 1921–1922* (New York: Macmillan, 1926).

160 90 percent of the time expended: Gail Charnley and E. Donald Elliott, "Risk Versus Precaution: Environmental Law and Public Health Protection," *Environmental Law Reporter* 32 (March 2002): 10363, 10364.

161 Letting any self-interested party: See Jeremy Rabkin, "The Secret Life of the Private Attorney General," *Law and Contemporary Problems* 61, no. 1 (Winter 1998): 179: One of the new legal concepts to emerge from the 1970s is the notion that a citizen can act as a "private attorney general," which Professor Rabkin describes as "someone who is understood to be suing on behalf of the public, but doing so on his own initiative, with no accountability to the government or the electorate." The court at least is impartial, but it, too, has no democratic accountability. See Sandler and Schoenbrod, *Democracy by Decree, supra* note for page 56. See generally Joanna Grisinger, *The Unwieldy American State: Administrative Politics since the New Deal* (Cambridge: Cambridge University Press, 2012).

161 nowhere suggests a judicial role: The National Environmental Policy Act of 1969 (NEPA) can be found at http://www.cr.nps.gov/local-law/fhpl_ntlenvirnpolcy.pdf. See Richard Lazarus, "The National Environmental Policy Act in the U.S. Supreme Court: A Reappraisal and a Peek behind the Curtains," *Georgetown Law Journal* 100, no. 5 (2012): 1507, 1515.

161 "These cases are only the beginning": Judge J. Skelly Wright, Calvert Cliffs Coordinating Council, Inc. v. Atomic Energy Commission 449 F.2d 1109 (D.C. Cir. 1971).

162 The drafters of NEPA were shocked: The enthusiastic rhetoric of the court also led the Council on Environmental Quality (CEQ) to write regulations that altered the public goal of the National Environmental Policy Act. The statute states that it seeks to "achieve a balance between population and resource use which will permit high standards of living and wide sharing of life's amenities." To that end, Congress required "a detailed statement by the responsible official . . . on the environmental impact" of major federal actions. See note for page 161, *supra*. After the *Calvert Cliffs* case, the CEQ wrote regulations that basically codified the judicial declarations. The statute's repeated statements about balancing economic considerations were replaced by more one-sided regulations, requiring environmental review to "state . . . all practicable means to avoid or minimize environmental harm." 40 C.F.R. 1505.2(c).

162 160 countries have since mandated: See Lazarus, "National Environmental Policy Act, *supra* note for page 161, 1510.

162 [German environmental review]: See note for page 150, *supra*.

163 all civil claims should undergo judicial scrutiny: E. Donald Elliott, "Twombley in Context: Why Federal Rule of Civil Procedure 4(b) is Unconstitutional," *Florida Law Review* 64, no. 4 (2012): 895. "A timid judge, like a biased judge, is intrinsically a lawless judge." Justice Felix Frankfurter, concurring in Wilkerson v. McCarthy (January 31, 1949).

164 "An equal right to oppress or interfere": Berlin, "Two Concepts," *supra* note for page 27, p. 234.

Citizen Supervision of Government

164 There's no fresh air . . . to purge the toxins: For a vivid portrait of mutant culture of Washington, see Daniel Leibovich, *This Town* (New York: Blue Rider Press, 2013).

164 "a republic, if you can keep it": Quote attributed to Benjamin Franklin in the "Papers of Dr. James McHenry on the Federal Convention of 1787," *American Historical Review* 11 (1906): 618: "A lady asked Dr. Franklin Well Doctor what have we got a republic or a monarchy. A republic replied the Doctor if you can keep it." See also Benjamin Franklin, "Letter to Messrs. The Abbes Chalut and Arnaud," in *The Works of Benjamin Franklin* (London: Benjamin Franklin Stevens, 1882), 10:297: "Let me add that only a virtuous people are capable of freedom."

165 "led by no permanent motive": Madison, "No. 62," *supra* note for page 34, pp. 302–3.

165 self-awareness requires the help of others: See, for example, Chris Argyris, *Integrating the Individual and the Organization* (Piscataway, NJ: Transaction, 1990), 25.

166 "The sovereign may confer power": Gibbon, *Decline and Fall, supra* note for page 142, vol. 1, p. 276.

166 There are plenty of interest groups: There's a lot of material here. See Kaiser, *So Damn Much Money, supra* note for page 134; Rauch, *Government's End, supra* note for page 135; Lessig, *Republic, Lost, supra* note for page 134. For a conservative perspective, see James V. DeLong, *Ending Big 'SIS' (the Special Interest State) and Renewing the American Republic* (North Charleston, SC: CreateSpace, 2012).

167 But each of these goals, if pushed too far: See Michel de Montaigne, *The Complete Works: Essays, Travel Journal, Letters* (New York: Knopf, 2003), 615: "It is ordinary to see good intentions, if they are carried out without moderation, push men to very vicious acts."

167 [German National Regulatory Control Council]: This advisory council (Normenkontrollrat, or NKR) is described in OECD, "Better Regulation in Europe: Germany," 54, 65–67, 116, 119, http://www.oecd.org/gov/regulatory-policy/betterregulationineuropegermany.htm, accessed July 2013. See also the NKR website (in German): http://www.normenkontrollrat .bund.de/Webs/NKR/DE.

168 a way of introducing fresh thinking: The Organisation for Economic Cooperation and Development (OECD) recommended in 2012 to all members that "a standing body charged with regulatory oversight should be established close to the centre of government to ensure that regulation serves whole-of-government policy. The specific institutional solution must be adapted to each system of governance." OECD, "Recommendation," *supra* note for page 150.

168 [Kennan's Council of State]: See George F. Kennan, "What Is to Be Done?" in Kennan, *Around the Cragged Hill*, 232–49.

168 "To meet the unprecedented challenges": Ibid., 248.

169 *euthyna*: Deirdre von Dornum, "The Straight and the Crooked: Legal Accountability in Ancient Greece," *Columbia Law Review* 97 (1997): 1483.

169 "Council of Censors": See "Constitution of Pennsylvania, September 28, 1776," Avalon Project, http://avalon.law.yale.edu/18th_century/pa08.asp, accessed May 2013.

169 Brownlow Committee: *Report of the President's Committee, supra* note for page 102, p. 21.

169 "liability to the watchful criticism": Mill, *On Liberty, supra* note for page 89, p. 173.

169 Plato's . . . "nocturnal council": Plato, "The Nocturnal Council," in Plato, *Laws*, 475–89.

169 its influence vanishes: E. Donald Elliott, "Portage Strategies for Adapting Environmental Law and Policy during a Logjam Era," *New York University Environmental Law Journal* 17 (2008): 24, 26–27, 50–53.

169 independent oversight committees: Canada has an independent quality control body, the Special Committee of Council, that reviews new regulations before they are adopted to ensure harmony with existing law and has the authority to reject them if they are deemed unsatisfactory. See http://www.oecd.org/mena/governance/38403668.pdf.

169 less likely to be suspicious: Officials are empowered when independent groups support their initiatives. Civic and advisory groups thus help solve the problem of legitimacy

that plagues leaders in the modern world. See Nonet and Selznick, *Law and Society in Transition, supra* note for page 20, p. 57: "He who exercises power to legitimate has his own problems of legitimacy" and needs "to convince the world . . . that his judgments are untainted by compromising associations."

170   incessant demands of self-interest: Self-interest is a reality of human nature, but democratic government is supposed to resist it. The game is lost when we capitulate to self-interest as the operating frame of reference for public choices. "Corruption can be held in check as long as it pays homage to the virtue of hiding itself." Jon Elster, *The Cement of Society: A Study of Social Order* (Cambridge: Cambridge University Press, 1989), 271. As Reinhold Niebuhr put it, "Evil is . . . the assertion of some self-interest without regard to the whole." Niebuhr, "Children of Light," *supra* note for page 86, p. 162.

170   "What manner of life there would be": Hobbes, *Leviathan, supra* note for page 66, p. 77.

171   many respected thinkers have tried to warn us: I have a fantasy about those wise jurists and philosophers, up there in some celestial metaphysical club, rolling their eyes as we burrow ever more deeply into bureaucracies instead of letting people take responsibility. I've asked them each to post a message taken from their actual writings. Here is a sampling:

Isaiah Berlin: "Systems are mere prisons of the spirit, and they lead not only to distortion in the sphere of knowledge, but to the erection of monstrous bureaucratic machines, built in accordance with the rules that ignore the teeming variety of the living world, the untidy and asymmetrical inner lives of men, and crush them into conformity." Berlin, *Proper Study of Mankind, supra* note for page 27, pp. 250–51.

Justice William Brandeis: "Those who won our independence believed that the final end of the state was to make men free to develop their faculties . . . they believed that the greatest menace to freedom is an inert people." Whitney v. California, 274 U.S. 357, 375 (1927) (Brandeis, J. Concurring).

Peter Drucker: "Freedom from the abuse of power is not enough for a free society. A free society rests on the freedom to make responsible decisions . . . Modern government has become ungovernable . . . Government agencies are all becoming autonomous ends in themselves and directed by their own desire for power." Drucker, Age of Discontinuity, *supra* note for page 43, pp. 258, 220.

Vaclav Havel: "Politicians seem to have turned into puppets that only look human and move in a giant rather inhuman theatre; they appear to have become merely cogs in a huge machine, objects of a major automation of civilization which has gotten out of control and for which nobody is responsible." Havel, Art of the Impossible, *supra* note for page 37, p. 126.

Friedrich Hayek: "The use of reason aims at control and predictability . . . We are not far from the point where the deliberate organized forces of society may destroy those spontaneous forces which have made advance possible." Hayek, Constitution of Liberty, *supra* note for page 15, p. 38.

Aldous Huxley: "'Don't you wish you were free, Lenina?' 'I don't know what you mean. I am free. Free to have the most wonderful time.'" Huxley, Brave New World (New York: Harper Perennial, 2010; originally published 1946 by Harper & Brothers), 99.

William James: "Refuse to believe, and you shall indeed be right, for you shall irretrievably perish. But believe, and again you shall be right, for you shall save yourself. You make one or the other of two possible universes true by your trust or mistrust—both universes having been only maybes, in this particular, before you contributed your act." James, The Will to Believe and Other Essays in Popular Philosophy (Cambridge, MA: Harvard University Press, 1979), 54.

George Kennan: "The basic assumption underlying this fear . . . of responsibility is surely the belief that such allotment lends itself to dictatorship and to curtailment of the liberties and rights of others. There is a feeling that concentration of authority is in some way 'undemocratic,' that the allotment to a single individual of the power to decide something is in some way incompatible with the spirit of the American political system. Ignored, of course, is the fact that authority is required to protect freedom just as it is required to assail freedom." Kennan, "America's Administrative Response," *supra* note for page 46, p. 17.

Michael Polanyi: "Human greatness . . . exists only for those committed to [it]. All manner of excellence that we accept for our guidance, and all obligations to which we grant jurisdiction over us, can be defined by our respect for human greatness." Polanyi, *Personal Knowledge, supra* note for page 22, p. 380.

They're all saying the same thing. No system will save us. Only real people, starting with the person in the mirror, have that power.

172 "A society based on the letter of the law": Aleksandr Solzhenitsyn, *Solzhenitsyn at Harvard: The Address, Twelve Early Responses, and Six Later Reflections*, ed. Ronald Berman (Washington, DC: Ethics and Public Policy Center, 1980), 8, 14.

172 Most Americans seem to be in a trance: See Lerner, *Surplus Powerlessness, supra* note for page 55, p. 2: "When people become powerless for any extended length of time, we become more willing to accept parts of the world we would otherwise reject . . . Powerlessness corrupts."

173 the force of movements grounded in moral arguments: See Anthony Appiah, *The Honor Code: How Moral Revolutions Happen* (New York: W. W. Norton, 2010), 53–100.

174 "If any action carries moral significance": Raz, *Ethics in the Public Domain, supra* note for page 89, 103.

174 "how the coming generation is to live": Dietrich Bonhoeffer, *Letters and Papers from Prison* (New York: Macmillan, 1972), 7. Bonhoeffer was executed in 1945 for participating in a plot to assassinate Hitler. Frederick Douglass has the same view of our moral obligation to the next generation: "You have no right to enjoy a child's share in the labor of your fathers, unless your children are to be blest by your labors. You have no right to wear out and waste the hard-earned fame of your fathers to cover your indolence." Douglass, as quoted in Jacob Needleman, *The American Soul: Rediscovering the Wisdom of the Founders* (New York: Tarcher, 2002), 247. Historian Niall Ferguson concludes that "the biggest challenge facing mature democracies is how to restore the social contract between the generations." Ferguson, *Great Degeneration, supra* note for page 42, pp. 43–44.

175 "worship the statue and forget the deity": Tocqueville, *Democracy in America, supra* note for page 24, vol. 1, p. 90.

176 "an absent or inattentive crowd": Ibid., 2:142.

176 "its force deserts it": Ibid., 1:90.

176 "Just powers": Declaration of Independence, http://www.archives.gov/exhibits/charters/declaration_transcript.html. Jefferson's opening words are worth reading again, with our present predicament in mind: "We hold these truths to be self-evident, that all men are created equal, that they are endowed by their Creator with certain unalienable Rights, that among these are Life, Liberty and the pursuit of Happiness.—That to secure these rights, Governments are instituted among Men, deriving their just powers from the consent of the governed,—That whenever any Form of Government becomes destructive of these ends, it is the Right of the People to alter or to abolish it, and to institute new Government, laying its foundation on such principles and organizing its powers in such form, as to them shall seem most likely to effect their Safety and Happiness."

Appendix: Bill of Responsibilities— Proposed Amendments to the Constitution

181 Historians of public service believe: See, for example, Commager, *American Mind, supra* note for page 132, pp. 310–35. Ibid., 318–19: "The remedy for corruption was so obvious

that it scarcely requisitioned political theory—the purification of politics, more commonly called civil service reform . . . Good government . . . would follow axiomatically from the merit system . . . They had no real faith in democracy . . . They were, in short, incapable of understanding the real nature of the fight that was going on around them . . . . An aura of unreality hangs over their history." Commager concludes that the "approach of the civil service reformers was clearly bankrupt" and quotes Walter Lippmann for the proposition that mechanical bureaucratic systems were hopeless, and that public choices must be made by real people, asserting their values in the political and cultural context of the time: "Because we have insisted on looking at . . . governing as a routine . . . politics has such a unreal relation to actual conditions . . . We have hoped for machine regularity when we needed human initiative and leadership." Ibid., 320. See also Van Riper, *History of the United States Civil Service, supra* note for page 158, pp. 533–64: "In any evaluation of the American civil bureaucracy it is crucial to understand that it is a *political* institution" (p. 562); "the great institutional curses of the federal service at the present time are over-centralization, over-proceduralization, over-departmentalization, and a much too rigid position classification system" (pp. 557–58); "neutrality and professionalism are extremely useful types of internal as opposed to external controls, but they are frail reeds in times of crisis and only modestly helpful during the ordinary course of events" (p. 551). Van Riper calls for a "representative bureaucracy . . . in which there is a minimum distinction between the bureaucrats . . . and the community . . . and [its] expectations of government" (p.552). For democracy to function, Van Riper concludes, we must develop an effective way of attracting, inspiring, and managing public employees: "He who administers the law is often more important than the law itself" (p. 533).

SELECTED BIBLIOGRAPHY

Ancker, Colonel Clinton J., III. "The Evolution of Mission Command in U.S. Army Doctrine, 1905 to the Present." *Military Review*, March/April 2013, 42–52.

Anechiarico, Frank, and James B. Jacobs. *The Pursuit of Absolute Integrity: How Corruption Control Makes Government Ineffective*. Chicago: University of Chicago Press, 1996.

Appiah, Anthony. *The Honor Code: How Moral Revolutions Happen*. New York: W. W. Norton, 2010.

Aquinas. *St. Thomas Aquinas: Philosophical Texts*. Edited by Thomas Gilby. London: Oxford University Press, 1951.

Arendt, Hannah. *Between Past and Future*. New York: Penguin, 1993.

Arendt, Hannah. *Eichmann in Jerusalem: A Report on the Banality of Evil*. New York: Penguin, 2006.

Arendt, Hannah. *The Human Condition*. Chicago: University of Chicago Press, 1958.

Arendt, Hannah. "A Special Supplement: Reflections on Violence." *New York Review of Books*, February 27, 1969.

Aristotle. *The Nicomachean Ethics*. Translated by W. D. Ross. Oxford: Oxford University Press, 1940.

Arum, Richard. *Judging School Discipline: The Crisis of Moral Authority*. Cambridge, MA: Harvard University Press, 2003.

Axelrad, Lee, and Robert A. Kagan, eds. *Regulatory Encounters: Multinational Corporations and American Adversarial Legalism*. Berkeley: University of California Press, 2000.

Ayres, Ian, and John Braithwaite. *Responsive Regulation: Transcending the Deregulation Debate*. New York: Oxford University Press, 1992.

Bailyn, Bernard, ed. *The Debate on the Constitution*. New York: Library of America, 1993.

Balogh, Brian, Joanna Grisinger, and Philip Zelikow. *Making Democracy Work: A Brief History of Twentieth Century Federal Executive Reorganization*. Miller Center Working Paper in American Political Development. [Charlottesville, VA]: Miller Center of Public Affairs, University of Virginia, 2002.

Banfield, Edward. *The Moral Basis of a Backward Society*. New York: Free Press, 1958.

Barber, Benjamin. *Strong Democracy: Participatory Politics for a New Age*. Berkeley: University of California Press, 2004.

Bardach, Eugene, and Robert A. Kagan. *Going by the Book: The Problem of Regulatory Unreasonableness*. Philadelphia: Temple University Press, 1982.

Barnard, Chester Irving. *The Functions of the Executive*. Cambridge, MA: Harvard University Press, 1968.

Barzun, Jacques. *From Dawn to Decadence: 500 Years of Western Cultural Life; 1500 to the Present*. New York: HarperCollins, 2000.

Barzun, Jacques. *A Stroll with William James*. Chicago: University of Chicago Press, 2002.

Baumgartner, Frank R., and Bryan D. Jones. *Agendas and Instability in American Politics*. 2nd ed. Chicago: University of Chicago Press, 2009.

Bellah, Robert N., Richard Madsen, William M. Sullivan, Ann Swidler, and Steven M. Tipton. *The Good Society*. New York: Vintage, 1991.

Bennis, Warren G. *Why Leaders Can't Lead*. San Francisco: Jossey-Bass, 1989.

Bergel, Jean Louis. "Principal Features and Methods of Codification." *Louisiana Law Review* 48 (1988): 1073–97.

Berlin, Isaiah. *The Proper Study of Mankind: An Anthology of Essays*. Edited by Henry Hardy and Roger Hausheer. New York: Farrar, Straus and Giroux, 2000.

Black, Donald J. "The Mobilization of Law." *Journal of Legal Studies* 2, no. 1 (1973): 125–49.

Black, Julia. "Paradoxes and Failures: 'New Governance' Techniques and the Financial Crisis." *Modern Law Review* 75, no. 2 (2012): 1037–63.

Bobbitt, Philip, and Guido Calabresi. *Tragic Choices*. New York: W. W. Norton, 1978.

Bonhoeffer, Dietrich. *Letters and Papers from Prison*. New York: Macmillan, 1972.

Bovens, Mark. *Quest for Responsibility: Accountability and Citizenship in Complex Organizations*. Cambridge: Cambridge University Press, 1998.

Braithwaite, John. "Rules and Principles: A Theory of Legal Certainty." *Australian Journal of Legal Philosophy* 27 (2002): 47–82.

Braithwaite, John, and Valerie Braithwaite. "The Politics of Legalism: Rules versus Standards in Nursing-Home Regulation." *Social & Legal Studies* 4, no. 3 (1995): 307–41.

Braithwaite, John, Toni Makkai, and Valerie A. Braithwaite. *Regulating Aged Care: Ritualism and the New Pyramid*. Cheltenham, UK: Edward Elgar, 2007.

Calabresi, Guido. *A Common Law for the Age of Statutes*. Boston: Harvard University Press, 1985.

Calabresi, Steven G., and Christopher S. Yoo. *The Unitary Executive: Presidential Power from Washington to Bush*. New Haven, CT: Yale University Press, 2008.

Cardozo, Benjamin N. *The Growth of the Law*. New Haven, CT: Yale University Press, 1924.

Cardozo, Benjamin N. *The Nature of the Judicial Process*. New Haven, CT: Yale University Press, 1921.

Commager, Henry Steele. *The American Mind: An Interpretation of American Thought and Character Since the 1880's*. New Haven, CT: Yale University Press, 1950.

Cornell, Saul. *The Other Founders: Anti-Federalism and the Dissenting Tradition in America, 1788–1828*. Chapel Hill: University of North Carolina Press, 1999.

Crozier, Michel. *The Bureaucratic Phenomenon*. Chicago: University of Chicago Press, 1964.

Crozier, Michel, Samuel P. Huntington, and Joji Watanuki. *The Crisis of Democracy: Report on the Governability of Democracies to the Trilateral Commission* (New York: New York University Press, 1975).

De Burca, Grainne, and Joanne Scott. *Law and New Governance in the EU and the US*. Oxford: Hart, 2006.

De Montaigne, Michel. *The Complete Works: Essays, Travel Journal, Letters*. New York: Knopf, 2003.

Dickens, Charles. *Little Dorrit*. Edited by Harvey Peter Sucksmith and Dennis Walder. Oxford World's Classics. Oxford: Oxford University Press, 2012.

Diver, Colin S. "The Optimal Precision of Administrative Rules." *Yale Law Journal* 93, no. 1 (November 1983): 65–109.

Doty, Michelle M., Mary Jane Koren, and Elizabeth L. Sturla. *Culture Change in Nursing Homes: How Far Have We Come?* New York: Commonwealth Fund, 2007.

Drucker, Peter F. *The Age of Discontinuity: Guidelines to Our Changing Society*. 2nd ed. New Brunswick, NJ: Transaction, 1992.

Drucker, Peter F. *Management*. Rev. ed. New York: Collins, 2008.

Drucker, Peter F., William V. D'Antonio, and Howard J. Ehrlich, eds. *Power and Democracy in America*. Notre Dame, IN: University of Notre Dame Press, 1961.

Durkheim, Emile. "Moral Obligation, Duty and Freedom." In *Emile Durkheim: Selected Writings*, edited by Anthony Giddens, 108–22. Cambridge: Cambridge University Press, 1972.

Dworkin, Ronald M. "The Model of Rules." *University of Chicago Law Review* 35, no. 1 (Autumn 1967): 14–46.

Dworkin, Ronald M. *Taking Rights Seriously*. Cambridge, MA: Harvard University Press, 1978.

Eggers, William D., and John O'Leary. *If We Can Put a Man on the Moon...: Getting Big Things Done in Government*. Boston: Harvard Business Press, 2009.

Elster, Jon. *The Cement of Society: A Study of Social Order*. Cambridge: Cambridge University Press, 1989.

Emerson, Ralph Waldo. *Essays & Lectures*. Edited by Joel Porte. New York: Library of America, 1983.

Endicott, Timothy A. O. "The Impossibility of the Rule of Law." *Oxford Journal of Legal Studies* 19, no. 1 (Spring 1999): 1–18.

Ernst, Daniel R. "Ernst Freund, Felix Frankfurter and the American Rechtsstaat: A Transatlantic Shipwreck, 1894–1932." Georgetown Law Faculty Publications and Other Works 18. http://scholarship.law.georgetown.edu/facpub/18.

Etzioni, Amitai. "Social Norms: Internalization, Persuasion, and History." *Law & Society Review* 34, no. 1 (2000): 157–78.

Ferguson, Niall. *The Great Degeneration: How Institutions Decay and Economies Die*. New York: Penguin, 2013.

Fleischacker, Samuel. *A Third Concept of Liberty: Judgment and Freedom in Kant and Adam Smith*. Princeton, NJ: Princeton University Press, 1999.

Foner, Eric. *The Story of American Freedom*. New York: W. W. Norton, 1998.

Foner, Nancy. "The Hidden Injuries of Bureaucracy: Work in an American Nursing Home." *Human Organization* 54, no. 3 (1995): 229–37.

Forbes-Thompson, Sarah, Tona Leiker, and Michael R. Bleich. "High-Performing and Low-Performing Nursing Homes: A View from Complexity Science." *Health Care Management Review* 32, no. 4 (October 2007): 341–51.

Frank, William A. "Authority and the Common Good in Democratic Governance." *Review of Metaphysics* 60, no. 4 (June 2007): 813–32.

Freund, Ernst. "The Law of Administration in America." *Political Science Quarterly* 9, no. 3 (September 1894): 403–25.

Freund, Ernst. "The Substitution of Rule for Discretion in Public Law." *American Political Science Review* 9, no. 4 (November 1915): 666–76.

Friedman, Lawrence M. *A History of American Law*. 3rd ed. New York: Touchstone, 2005.

Friedman, Lawrence M. "Legal Rules and the Process of Social Change." *Stanford Law Review* 19, no. 4 (April 1967): 786–840.

Fromm, Erich. *Escape from Freedom*. New York: Henry Holt, 1994.

Fuller, Lon. *The Morality of Law*. New Haven, CT: Yale University Press, 1969.

Gadamer, Hans-Georg. *Truth and Method*. Translated by Joel Weinsheimer and Donald G. Marshall. 2nd ed. New York: Continuum, 1998.

Gahan, Frank. "The Codification of Law." *Transactions of the Grotius Society* 8 (1922): 107–16.

Gibbon, Edward. *The Decline and Fall of the Roman Empire*. 3 vols. Everyman's Library. New York: Knopf, 1993.

Gilmore, Grant. *The Ages of American Law*. New Haven, CT: Yale University Press, 1979.

Glendon, Mary Ann. *Rights Talk: The Impoverishment of Political Discourse*. New York: Free Press, 1991.

Grant, Gerald. *The World We Created at Hamilton High*. Cambridge, MA: Harvard University Press, 1988.

Grunwald, Michael. *The New New Deal*. New York: Simon & Schuster, 2012.

Haldane, Andrew. "The Dog and the Frisbee." Paper presented at the Federal Reserve Bank of Kansas City's 36th Economic Policy Symposium, Jackson Hole, WY, August 31, 2012. http://www.kansascityfed.org/publicat/sympos/2012/ah.pdf.

Hamilton, Alexander, James Madison, and John Jay. *The Federalist, with "The Letters of Brutus"*.

Edited by Terence Ball. Cambridge Texts in the History of Political Thought. Cambridge: Cambridge University Press, 2003.

Hammond, Kenneth R. *Human Judgment and Social Policy*. Oxford: Oxford University Press, 1996.

Harford, Tim. *Adapt: Why Success Always Starts with Failure*. New York: Farrar, Straus and Giroux, 2011.

Harrison, Lawrence E., and Samuel P. Huntington. *Culture Matters: How Values Shape Human Progress*. New York: Basic Books, 2000.

Hart, H. L. A. *The Concept of Law*. Oxford: Clarendon, 1961.

Hart, Henry M., and Albert M. Sacks. *The Legal Process: Basic Problems in the Making and Application of Law*. Edited by William N. Eskridge and Philip P. Frickey. Westbury, NY: Foundation Press, 1994.

Hauerwas, Stanley. *A Community of Character: Toward a Constructive Christian Social Ethic*. Notre Dame, IN: University of Notre Dame Press, 1991.

Havel, Vaclav. *The Art of the Impossible: Politics as Morality in Practice*. New York: Knopf, 1997.

Hayek, Friedrich A. *The Constitution of Liberty*. Chicago: University of Chicago Press, 1960.

Hayek, Friedrich A. *Law, Legislation and Liberty*. Vol. 1. Chicago: University of Chicago Press, 1973.

Hayek, Friedrich. *The Road to Serfdom*. London: Routledge & Sons, 1944.

Heineman, Robert A. *Authority and the Liberal Tradition: From Hobbes to Rorty*. 2nd ed. New Brunswick, NJ: Transaction, 1994.

Hertogh, Marc. "Through the Eyes of Bureaucrats: How Front-Line Officials Understand Administrative Justice." In *Administrative Justice in Context*, edited by Michael Adler, 203–26. Oxford: Hart, 2010.

Hobbes, Thomas. *Leviathan*. Edited by E. M. Curley. Indianapolis, IN: Hackett, 1994.

Holmes, Oliver Wendell, Jr. *The Common Law*. Clark, NJ: Lawbook Exchange, 2005.

Howard, Philip K. *The Collapse of the Common Good*. New York: Ballantine, 2002.

Howard, Philip K. *The Death of Common Sense: How Law Is Suffocating America*. New York: Random House, 1994.

Howard, Philip K. "History of American Law since 1968." In *Oxford Companion to American Law*, edited by Kermit L. Hall, 392–96. New York: Oxford University Press, 2002.

Howard, Philip K. *Life without Lawyers*. New York: W. W. Norton, 2009.

Howe, John R. *Language and Political Meaning in Revolutionary America*. Amherst: University of Massachusetts Press, 2004.

Hume, David. *A Treatise of Human Nature*. Edited by L. A. Selby-Bigge and P. H. Nidditch. 2nd ed. Oxford: Clarendon, 1978.

Hummel, Ralph P. *The Bureaucratic Experience: The Post-modern Challenge*. 5th ed. Armonk, NY: M. E. Sharpe, 2008.

Jackson, Philip W., Robert E. Boostrom, and David T. Hansen. *The Moral Life of Schools*. San Francisco: Jossey-Bass, 1993.

Jaffe, Louis L. "The Effective Limits of the Administrative Process: A Reevaluation." *Harvard Law Review* 67, no. 7 (May 1954): 1105–135.

James, William. *Writings, 1878–1899*. Edited by Gerald E. Myers. New York: Library of America, 1992.

Jefferson, Thomas. *Writings*. Edited by Merrill D. Peterson. New York: Library of America, 1984.

Kagan, Robert A. *Adversarial Legalism: The American Way of Law*. Boston: Harvard University Press, 2003.

Kahneman, Daniel. *Thinking, Fast and Slow*. New York: Farrar, Straus and Giroux, 2011.

Kairys, David. "Searching for the Rule of Law." *Suffolk University Law Review* 36, no. 2 (2003): 307–29.

Kaiser, Robert G. *Act of Congress: How America's Essential Institution Works, and How It Doesn't*. New York: Knopf, 2013.

Kaiser, Robert G. *So Damn Much Money: The Triumph of Lobbying and the Corrosion of American Government*. New York: Knopf, 2009.

Kapp, Marshall B. "Nursing Home Culture Change: Legal Apprehensions and Opportunities." *Gerontologist*, October 24, 2012 [Epub ahead of print].

Kapp, Marshall B. "Quality of Care and Quality of Life in Nursing Facilities: What's Regulation Got to Do with It?" *McGeorge Law Review* 31, no. 3 (2000): 707–31.

Kaufman, Herbert. *The Forest Ranger: A Study in Administrative Behavior.* 2nd ed. Washington, DC: RFF Press, 2006. Originally published 1960 by Johns Hopkins Press.

Kean, Thomas H., and Lee H. Hamilton. *The 9/11 Commission Report: Final Report of the National Commission on Terrorist Attacks upon the United States.* New York: W. W. Norton, 2004.

Kelman, Steven. *Procurement and Public Management: The Fear of Discretion and the Quality of Government Performance.* Washington, DC: AEI Press, 1990.

Kemeny, John G. *Report of the President's Commission on the Accident at Three Mile Island.* New York: Pergamon, 1979.

Kennan, George F. "America's Administrative Response to Its World Problems." *Daedalus* 87, no. 2 (Spring 1958): 5–24.

Kennan, George F. *Around the Cragged Hill: A Personal and Political Philosophy.* New York: W. W. Norton, 1993.

Kennan, George F. "On American Principles." *Foreign Affairs* 74, no. 2 (March/April 1995): 116–26.

Kettl, Donald F. "Administrative Accountability and the Rule of Law." *PS: Political Science and Politics* 42, no. 1 (January 2009): 11–17.

Kirp, David L. "Proceduralism and Bureaucracy: Due Process in the School Setting." *Stanford Law Review* 28, no. 5 (May 1976): 841–76.

Klein, Gary. *Intuition at Work: Why Developing Your Gut Instinct Will Make You Better at What You Do.* New York: Doubleday, 2003.

Kolakowski, Leszek. *Modernity on Endless Trial.* Chicago: University of Chicago Press, 1990.

Kress, Ken. "Legal Indeterminacy." *California Law Review* 77, no. 2 (March 1989): 283–337.

Krygier, Martin. "Ethical Positivism and the Liberalism of Fear." In *Judicial Power, Democracy, and Legal Positivism*, edited by Tom Campbell and Jeffrey Goldsworthy, 59–87. Aldershot, UK: Ashgate, 2000.

Lawrence-Lightfoot, Sara. *The Good High School: Portraits of Character and Culture.* New York: Basic Books, 1983.

Lerner, Michael. *Surplus Powerlessness: The Psychodynamics of Everyday Life . . . and the Psychology of Individual and Social Transformation.* Amherst, NY: Humanity Books, 1991.

Lessig, Lawrence. *Republic, Lost: How Money Corrupts Congress—and a Plan to Stop It.* New York: Twelve, 2011.

Light, Paul C. *A Government Ill Executed: The Decline of the Federal Service and How to Reverse It.* Cambridge, MA: Harvard University Press, 2008.

Light, Paul C. *Thickening Government: Federal Hierarchy and the Diffusion of Accountability.* Washington, DC: Brookings Institution Press, 1995.

Lipsky, Michael. *Street-Level Bureaucracy: Dilemmas of the Individual in Public Services.* New York: Russell Sage Foundation, 1980.

Locke, John. *The Second Treatise on Civil Government.* Amherst, NY: Prometheus, 1986.

Luban, David, Alan Strudler, and David Wasserman. "Moral Responsibility in the Age of Bureaucracy." *Michigan Law Review* 90, no. 8 (July 1992): 2348–91.

MacIntyre, Alasdair C. *After Virtue: A Study in Moral Theory.* Notre Dame, IN: University of Notre Dame Press, 1984.

MacIntyre, Alasdair. "Regulation: A Substitute for Morality." *Hastings Center Report* 10, no. 1 (February 1980): 31–33.

Madison, James. *Writings.* Edited by Jack N. Rakove. New York: Library of America, 1999.

Marmor, Theodore R. *The Politics of Medicare.* 2nd ed. New York: Aldine Transaction, 2000.

Maxeiner, James R. "Costs of No Codes." *Mississippi College Law Review* 31 (2013): 363.

Maxeiner, James R. *Failures of American Civil Justice in International Perspective.* Cambridge: Cambridge University Press, 2011.

Maynard-Moody, Steven, and Michael C. Musheno. *Cops, Teachers, Counselors: Stories from the Front Lines of Public Service.* Ann Arbor: University of Michigan Press, 2003.

McCarthy, Eugene J. "Freedom and Political Authority." *ALA Bulletin* 47, no. 10 (November 1953): 459–66.

McGregor, Douglas. *Human Side of Enterprise.* New York: McGraw-Hill, 1960.

Mead, Walter Russell. "The Once and Future Liberalism." *American Interest*, March/April 2012.

Meares, Tracey L. "It's a Question of Connections." *Valparaiso Law Review* 31 (1997): 579–96.

Meares, Tracey L., and Dan M. Kahan, eds. *Urgent Times: Policing and Rights in Inner-City Communities.* Boston: Beacon, 1999.

Mehta, Jal. *The Allure of Order: High Hopes, Dashed Expectations, and the Troubled Quest to Remake American Schooling.* Oxford: Oxford University Press, 2013.

Melé, Domènec. "Exploring the Principle of Subsidiarity in Organisational Forms." *Journal of Business Ethics* 60, no. 3 (September 2005): 293–305.

Merton, Robert K. "Bureaucratic Structure and Personality." *Social Forces* 18, no. 4 (May 1940): 560–68.

Merton, Robert K., Ailsa P. Gray, Barbara Hockey, and Hanan C. Selvin, eds. *Reader in Bureaucracy.* Glencoe, IL: Free Press, 1952.

Mill, John Stuart. *On Liberty.* Edited by David Bromwich and George Kateb. Rethinking the Western Tradition. New Haven, CT: Yale University Press, 2003.

Moe, Terry M., and Scott A. Wilson. "Presidents and the Politics of Structure." *Law and Contemporary Problems*, Regulating Regulation: The Political Economy of Administrative Procedures and Regulatory Instruments: Part 2, 57, no. 2 (Spring 1994): 1–44.

Moulton, Lord John Fletcher. "Law and Manners." *Atlantic Monthly*, July 1924, 1–4.

Needleman, Jacob. *The American Soul: Rediscovering the Wisdom of the Founders.* New York: Tarcher, 2002.

Niebuhr, Reinhold. *The Essential Reinhold Niebuhr: Selected Essays and Addresses.* Edited by Robert McAfee Brown. New Haven, CT: Yale University Press, 1986.

Niebuhr, Reinhold. *Moral Man and Immoral Society: A Study in Ethics and Politics.* Rev. ed. New York: Scribner, 1960.

Nonet, Philippe, and Philip Selznick. *Law and Society in Transition: Toward Responsive Law.* New York: Harper & Row, 1978.

Noonan, Kathleen G., Charles F. Sabel, and William H. Simon. "Legal Accountability in the Service-Based Welfare State." *Law & Social Inquiry* 34, no. 3 (Summer 2009): 523–68.

Novak, William J. *The People's Welfare: Law and Regulation in Nineteenth-Century America.* Chapel Hill: University of North Carolina Press, 1996.

Oakeshott, Michael. "The Rule of Law." In *On History and Other Essays*, 129–78. Indianapolis, IN: Liberty Fund, 1999.

O'Neill, Onora. *A Question of Trust: The BBC Reith Lectures 2002.* Cambridge: Cambridge University Press, 2002.

O'Neill, Timothy J. "Liberal Constitutionalism and Bureaucratic Discretion." *Polity* 20, no. 3 (Spring 1988): 371–93.

OECD (Organisation for Economic Co-operation and Development). "Better Regulation in Europe: Germany." http://www.oecd.org/gov/regulatory-policy/betterregulationineuropegermany.htm.

OECD (Organisation for Economic Co-operation and Development). "Implementing Administrative Simplification in OECD Countries: Experiences and Challenges." http://www.oecd.org/mena/governance/37026688.pdf.

OECD (Organisation for Economic Co-operation and Development). "Recommendation of the Council on Regulatory Policy and Governance." 2012. http://www.oecd.org/gov/regulatory-policy/49990817.pdf.

OECD (Organisation for Economic Co-operation and Development). *Regulatory Reform in the United States.* Paris: OECD, 1999.

Osborne, David, and Gaebler, Ted. *Reinventing Government.* New York: Basic Books, 1992.

Peters, Charles. *How Washington Really Works.* New York: Basic Books, 1992.

Plato. *The Laws.* Edited by Trevor J. Saunders. London: Penguin, 2004.

Polanyi, Michael. *Personal Knowledge: Towards a Post-critical Philosophy.* Chicago: University of Chicago Press, 1958.

Polybius. *The Histories.* Edited by Robin Waterfield and B. C. McGing. Oxford World's Classics. Oxford: Oxford University Press, 2010.

Porter, Theodore M. *Trust in Numbers: The Pursuit of Objectivity in Science and Public Life.* Princeton, NJ: Princeton University Press, 1995.

Posner, Richard A. *Economic Analysis of Law.* New York: Wolters Kluwer, 2007.

Posner, Richard A. *The Problems of Jurisprudence.* Cambridge, MA: Harvard University Press, 1990.

Postema, Gerald J. "Legal Positivism: Early Foundations." UNC Legal Studies Research Paper 1975470, December 2011. http://papers.ssrn.com/sol3/papers.cfm?abstract_id=1975470.

Putnam, Robert D. *Bowling Alone: The Collapse and Revival of American Community.* New York: Simon & Schuster, 2000.

Raban, Ofer. "The Fallacy of Legal Certainty: Why Vague Legal Standards May Be Better for Capitalism and Liberalism." *Boston University Public Interest Law Journal* 19, no. 2 (Spring 2010): 175–91.

Rabkin, Jeremy. "The Secret Life of the Private Attorney General." *Law and Contemporary Problems* 61, no. 1 (Winter 1998): 179–203.

Radin, Margaret Jane. "Reconsidering the Rule of Law." *Boston University Law Review* 69 (July 1989): 1–31.

Rakove, Jack N. *Original Meanings: Politics and Ideas in the Making of the Constitution.* New York: Vintage, 1997.

Rauch, Jonathan. *Government's End: Why Washington Stopped Working.* New York: PublicAffairs, 1999.

Rawls, John. *A Theory of Justice.* Cambridge, MA: Belknap Press, 1971.

Raz, Joseph. *Ethics in the Public Domain: Essays in the Morality of Law and Politics.* Oxford: Clarendon, 1995.

Raz, Joseph. "Legal Principles and the Limits of Law." *Yale Law Journal* 81, no. 5 (April 1972): 823–54.

Rees, Joseph V. *Hostages of Each Other: The Transformation of Nuclear Safety since Three Mile Island.* Chicago: University of Chicago Press, 1994.

Reich, Charles A. "The New Property." *Yale Law Journal* 73, no. 5 (April 1964): 733–87.

Rohr, John A. "Professionalism, Legitimacy, and the Constitution." *Public Administration Quarterly* 8, no. 4 (Winter 1985): 401–18.

Romer, Paul M. "Process, Responsibility, and Myron's Law." In *In the Wake of the Crisis: Leading Economists Reassess Economic Policy,* edited by Olivier J. Blanchard, David Romer, A. Michael Spence, and Joseph E. Stiglitz, 111–23. Cambridge, MA: MIT Press, 2012.

Rose, Mike. *The Mind at Work: Valuing the Intelligence of the American Worker.* New York: Viking, 2004.

Rubin, Edward L. "Discretion and Its Discontents." *Chicago-Kent Law Review* 72 (1997): 1299–336.

Ruhl, J. B., and James Salzman. "Mozart and the Red Queen: The Problem of Regulatory Accretion in the Administrative State." *Georgetown Law Journal* 91 (2003): 757–850.

Sabel, Charles F., and William H. Simon. "Minimalism and Experimentalism in the Administrative State." *Georgetown Law Journal* 100, no. 1 (2011): 53–93.

Sahlberg, Pasi, and Andy Hargreaves. *Finnish Lessons: What Can the World Learn from Educational Change in Finland?* New York: Teachers College Press, 2011.

Sandel, Michael J. *Democracy's Discontent: America in Search of a Public Philosophy.* Cambridge, MA: Belknap Press, 1996.

Sandler, Ross, and David Schoenbrod. *Democracy by Decree: What Happens When Courts Run Government.* New Haven, CT: Yale University Press, 2003.

Schaar, John H. "Liberty/Authority/Community in the Political Thought of John Winthrop." *Political Theory* 19, no. 4 (November 1991): 493–518.

Schauer, Frederick. "Formalism." *Yale Law Journal* 97, no. 4 (March 1998): 509–48.

Schiller, Reuel E. "Enlarging the Administrative Polity: Administrative Law and the Changing Definition of Pluralism." *Vanderbilt Law Review* 53, no. 5 (October 2000): 1389–453.

Schiller, Reuel E. "The Era of Deference: Courts, Expertise, and the Emergence of New Deal Administrative Law." *Michigan Law Review* 106 (2007): 399–440.

Schiller, Reuel E. "Rulemaking's Promise: Administrative Law and Legal Culture in the 1960s and 1970s." *Administrative Law Review* 53, no. 4 (2001): 1139–88.

Schiller, Reuel E. "'Saint George and the Dragon': Courts and the Development of the Administrative State in Twentieth-Century America." *Journal of Policy History* 17, no. 1 (2005): 110–24.

Schlesinger, Arthur M., Jr. *The Disuniting of America: Reflections on a Multicultural Society*. New York: W. W. Norton, 1998.

Schlesinger, Arthur M., Jr. *The Imperial Presidency*. Boston: Houghton Mifflin, 1973.

Schudson, Michael. "The Trouble with Experts—and Why Democracies Need Them." *Theory and Society* 35, no. 5/6 (December 2006): 491–506.

Scott, James C. *Seeing Like a State: How Certain Schemes to Improve the Human Condition Have Failed*. New Haven, CT: Yale University Press, 1999.

Selznick, Philip. *The Moral Commonwealth: Social Theory and the Promise of Community*. Berkeley: University of California Press, 1994.

Shepherd, George B. "Fierce Compromise: The Administrative Procedure Act Emerges from New Deal Politics." *Northwestern University Law Review* 90 (1996): 1557–678.

Simon, William H. "Legality, Bureaucracy, and Class in the Welfare System." *Yale Law Journal* 92, no. 7 (June 1983): 1198–269.

Simon, William H. "Optimization and Its Discontents in Regulatory Design: Bank Regulation as an Example." *Regulation & Governance* 4, no. 1 (2010): 3–21.

Simon, William H. "Solving Problems vs. Claiming Rights: The Pragmatist Challenge to Legal Liberalism." *William and Mary Law Review* 46, no. 1 (2004): 127–212.

Simon, William H. "Toyota Jurisprudence: Legal Theory and Rolling Rule Regimes." Columbia Public Law Research Paper 04-79, October 2004.

Simon, Yves. *Philosophy of Democratic Government*. Notre Dame, IN: University of Notre Dame Press, 1993.

Solzhenitsyn, Aleksandr. *Solzhenitsyn at Harvard: The Address, Twelve Early Responses, and Six Later Reflections*. Edited by Ronald Berman. Washington, DC: Ethics and Public Policy Center, 1980.

Sternberg, Robert J., George B. Forsythe, Jennifer Hedlund, and Joseph A. Horvath. *Practical Intelligence in Everyday Life*. Cambridge: Cambridge University Press, 2000.

Stewart, Richard B. "Madison's Nightmare." *University of Chicago Law Review* 57, no. 2 (Spring 1990): 335–56.

Stillman, Richard J. *Public Administration: Concepts and Cases*. 9th ed. Belmont, CA: Wadsworth Cengage Learning, 2009.

Stuntz, William J. *The Collapse of American Criminal Justice*. Cambridge, MA: Belknap Press, 2011.

Sunstein, Cass R. "Problems with Rules." *California Law Review* 83, no. 4 (July 1995): 953–1026.

Sunstein, Cass R. *Simpler: The Future of Government*. New York: Simon & Schuster, 2013.

Swift, Jonathan. *Gulliver's Travels*. Edited by Albert Rivero. New York: W. W. Norton, 2002.

Tainter, Joseph A. *The Collapse of Complex Societies*. Cambridge: Cambridge University Press, 1988.

Tamanaha, Brian Z. "The Dark Side of the Relationship between the Rule of Law and Liberalism." *New York University Journal of Law & Liberty* 3, no. 3 (2008): 516–47.

Tamanaha, Brian Z. "How an Instrumental Rule of Law Corrodes the Rule of Law." *DePaul Law Review* 56 (2007): 1–51.

Tamanaha, Brian Z. *On the Rule of Law: History, Politics, Theory.* Cambridge: Cambridge University Press, 2004.

Teles, Steven M. "Kludgeocracy: The American Way of Policy." New America Foundation. December 10, 2012. http://newamerica.net/publications/policy/kludgeocracy_the_american_way_of_policy.

Thompson, Dennis F. "Moral Responsibility of Public Officials: The Problem of Many Hands." *American Political Science Review* 74, no. 4 (December 1980): 905–16.

Tocqueville, Alexis de. *Democracy in America.* Edited by Phillips Bradley. 2 vols. New York: Vintage, 1990.

Van Riper, Paul P. *History of the United States Civil Service.* Evanston, IL: Row, Peterson, 1958.

Waldron, Jeremy. "The Concept and the Rule of Law." *Georgia Law Review* 43, no. 1 (Fall 2008): 1–61.

Waldron, Jeremy. "Is the Rule of Law an Essentially Contested Concept (in Florida)?" *Law and Philosophy* 21, no. 2 (March 2002): 137–64.

Waldron, Jeremy. "The Rule of Law and the Importance of Procedure." In *Getting to the Rule of Law,* edited by James E. Fleming, 3–31. Nomos: Yearbook of the American Society for Political and Legal Philosophy 50. New York: New York University Press, 2011.

Waldron, Jeremy. "Thoughtfulness and the Rule of Law." NYU School of Law, Public Law Research Paper No. 11-13, February 10, 2011. http://papers.ssrn.com/sol3/papers.cfm?abstract_id=1759550.

Waldron, Jeremy. "Vagueness in Law and Language: Some Philosophical Issues." *California Law Review* 82, no. 3 (May 1994): 509–40.

Warren, Mark E. "Democratic Theory and Trust." In *Democracy and Trust,* edited by Mark E. Warren, 310–45. Cambridge: Cambridge University Press, 1999.

Weber, Max. *Economy and Society.* Edited by Guenther Roth and Claus Wittich. Berkeley: University of California Press, 1978.

Will, George F. *Statecraft as Soulcraft: What Government Does.* New York: Simon & Schuster, 1983.

Wood, Gordon S. *Empire of Liberty: A History of the Early Republic, 1789–1815.* Oxford: Oxford University Press, 2009.

Zimbardo, Philip G. *The Lucifer Effect: Understanding How Good People Turn Evil.* New York: Random House, 2007.

INDEX

Page numbers beginning with 189 refer to end notes.